PASSION FOR THE MOVIES

PASSION FOR THE MOVIES

Spiritual Insights from Contemporary Films

MARK STIBBE and J. JOHN

11 10 09 08 07 06 05   7 6 5 4 3 2 1

First published in 2005 by Authentic Media
9 Holdom Avenue, Bletchley, Milton Keynes,
Bucks MK1 1QR, UK
and 129 Mobilization Drive, Waynesboro, GA 30830-4575, USA
www.authenticmedia.co.uk

British Library Cataloguing in Publication Data
A catalogue record for this book is available from the British Library

ISBN 1–86024–516–1

Cover design by David Lund
Typeset by Waverley Typesetters, Galashiels
Print Management by Adare Carwin
Printed by Haynes, Sparkford, Yeovil, Somerset, UK

Contents

Introduction: Passion for the Movies

In February 2004 I was asked by the BBC to attend a special journalists' preview of a movie in preparation for a series of radio interviews a few days later. The film in question was Mel Gibson's *The Passion of The Christ*. Having now seen it a number of times I am convinced that *The Passion of The Christ* is one of the most significant cultural moments of the first decade of the twenty-first century. Not only does it highlight the new interest in Jesus in popular culture, it also points to a growing reconciliation between Christianity and film. When films first started being made at the end of the nineteenth century the story of Jesus, and particularly the Passion of Jesus, was the subject of some of the earliest movies. In fact, the Passion play at Oberammergau – with its focus on the last 24 hours of Jesus' life – provided movie-makers with some of their richest material. Now, after over a century of cinema, things have come full circle. Mel Gibson's film, focusing as it does on the last 12 hours of Jesus' life, brings us back to where we began – a passion for the movies.

There is no doubt that *The Passion of The Christ* is massively significant in terms of its genre and in terms of contemporary culture. It has compelled many people outside the church to engage in a passionate debate about

Christianity. And it has compelled many inside the church to be less dismissive of popular culture and to engage in a passionate debate about the movies. Indeed, with reference to the latter, it has been fascinating to watch evangelical believers in the USA embracing and using such a blatantly Catholic film! In this book, J. John and I want to help advance such debates, stimulate thinking and provoke reflection, encouraging people in the church to engage in a discerning interaction with modern movies, and those outside the church to consider how God might be addressing them directly or indirectly through contemporary films. For this reason, we've included 'discussion starters' at the end of each chapter. After watching one of the movies, a small group can use the appropriate discussion starter to think more deeply about what they've just watched and to prompt appropriate responses.

I have always been passionate about the movies and have sought, with my friend J. John, to help others see the spiritual and indeed Christian message of many modern films. Most of these films have been indirectly Christian, containing implied references to biblical truths, or symbolic Christ-figures. Our prayer is that this book will help all readers to engage more critically and prophetically with contemporary films.

Mark Stibbe
August 2004

1

A Life-Changing Movie
The Passion of The Christ

MARK STIBBE

ICON PRODUCTIONS, 2004

Directed by MEL GIBSON
Screenplay by BENEDICT FITZGERALD
and MEL GIBSON

JAMES CAVIEZEL as *Jesus*
MAIA MORGENSTERN as *Mary*
MONICA BELLUCCI as *Mary Magdalene*
ROSALINDA CELENTANO as *Satan*
HRISTO NAUMOV SHOPOV as *Pilate*

CLASSIFICATION: 18

Mel Gibson's *The Passion of The Christ* is one of the most talked about movies in recent times. At the time of writing, it has broken many records in the movie theatres and is now top of the DVD and video charts. As far as the cinema is concerned, the following facts alone should give us an indication of the extent of the film's impact. No other film that has opened in February has enjoyed the success that this film has. It is the sixth most successful film of all time, grossing nearly $400 million. It is the biggest ever R-rated movie (the US equivalent of an 18 certificate in the UK). It is the most successful religious film ever. It is also unique for having dipped after its opening weeks, only to make a comeback at Easter. This has never been observed before with any other film. *The Passion* was number 1 for its first three weekends in the USA, then fell back in the pack for the following three weekends, before reclaiming the number 1 spot. 'That's unprecedented. I've never seen that before. *The Passion* is just rewriting box-office history,' so said Paul Dergarabedian, President of box-office tracker Exhibitor Relations. When asked to explain why he thought this had happened, Dergarabedian replied, 'It's not just a movie. It's a religious experience for many people.'

And it is just that ... a 'religious experience'. In the weeks after the film came out in the UK (March 2004), I spent a lot of time talking about it to a number of people, both Christian and non-Christian. I based my Holy Week meditations on scenes from the movie and a colleague and I preached a whole sermon series on *The Passion* at St Andrew's Chorleywood.

In addition, I found myself as an after dinner speaker giving an address on this film, and also on another occasion having the privilege of helping four men come to faith in Christ, all of whom had been powerfully impacted as a result of seeing Gibson's graphic portrayal of Christ's love for humankind. I also gave a number of BBC radio interviews on *The Passion* on the Sunday morning before Easter. J. John pointed out that the audience for these interviews would have exceeded the number of people in church throughout the UK that Sunday.

Clearly, *The Passion of The Christ* is a movie with considerable impact, but how does it compare to the Jesus films that have gone before?

A brief history of Jesus films

Films specifically focused on Jesus Christ have appeared in just about every decade of the first hundred years of cinema.

In 1897, stage director Henry Vincent filmed *The Passion Play of Oberammergau*. The end product included magic lantern slides and a live choir.

In 1902, Ferdinand Zecca and Lucien Nouguet directed *The Life and Passion of Jesus Christ, Our Saviour*. This French film presented a series of tableaux – shots of figures posing like a Renaissance painting, with each scene separated in the 1912 US version by titles like 'The Annunciation', and so on.

In 1912, Sidney Olcott directed *From the Manger to the Cross*. This was a far more naturalistic attempt at depicting the life of Jesus and was filmed on location in Jerusalem and other settings in the Holy Land. The cast included Robert Henderson-Bland (Jesus), Gene Gauntier (Mary), Alice Hollister (Mary Magdalene), Samuel Morgan (Pilate). Scenes in the film were interspersed with Scripture passages on title cards. Most scenes were shot from a distance which means the audience never gets close enough to see what Jesus looks like. It also means that the miracles of Jesus come across with greater mystery.

In 1916, D.W. Griffith released his film *Intolerance* – a silent movie that tells four stories from different historical eras that illustrate intolerance. One of the four stories is about Jesus of Nazareth. This – the shortest of the four – is portrayed realistically and had a major impact on Cecil B. DeMille.

In 1925, Fred Niblo directed one of the first movie renditions of *Ben-Hur*, which includes the life of Christ as a sub-plot. The ending of the film shows Ben-Hur saying rather piously of the crucified Christ, 'He will live forever in the hearts of men.'

1927 saw the release of the movie *The King of Kings* directed by Cecil B. DeMille with H.B. Warner as Jesus. DeMille's production used a thematic more than a chronological approach to the gospel story. The release of this film was notable for the reaction from the Jewish community who accused DeMille of portraying Jewish characters as 'Christ killers' and of stirring up anti-Jewish sentiment. DeMille denied this but the very stereotypical depiction of Caiaphas somewhat undermined his defence.

In 1935, Julien Duvivier's film *Golgotha* was released. This French production was also known as *Ecce Homo* and covered the final week of Jesus' life. It was notable for being the first Jesus film to use sound.

In the 1950s, Jesus appeared in a number of films, *Quo Vadis* (1951), *The Robe* (1953) and *Ben-Hur* (1959). In these films Jesus is either mentioned or appears very briefly. These Roman-Christian epics explore the Christ vs. Caesar theme.

The 1960s saw a spate of movies on the life of Christ. In 1961, Nicholas Ray directed and released *King of Kings* (not a remake of Cecil B. DeMille's classic) with teen idol Jeffrey Hunter in the role of Jesus, evoking the well-known taunt, 'I was a teenage Jesus.' Shot with 70 mm film, this movie relies on huge panoramic scenes and melodramatic dialogue.

In 1962, Anthony Quinn starred in *Barabbas* (a film which portrays moments of the Passion) and in 1965 Max Von Sydow starred as Jesus in George Stevens' *The Greatest Story Ever Told* – a monotonous, ponderous retelling of the gospel story. At the time it was the most expensive Jesus film ever made though it was still a commercial failure.

The best Jesus film of the 1960s was – by common critical acclaim – Pier Paolo Pasolini's *The Gospel According to St Matthew* (*Il Vangelo Secondo Matteo,* 1964) much of which was filmed using hand-held cameras. This minimalist, low budget, black-and-white movie, with a strong political agenda, is still regarded by film critics as an Italian movie masterpiece. Here Jesus sides with the poor and opposes the corrupt imperialism of his day. Shot in a poor rustic area of southern Italy, Pasolini's fascinating film has a vivid documentary-like realism ('Cinema Verité') that many critics rightly applaud. It also has an extremely rich and varied music score, drawing on musical traditions from different cultures and continents. One of its great positives is the fact that it focuses on one Gospel rather than on a harmonisation of all four. The downside of Pasolini's presentation is his naturalistic bias; he does not include a single miracle.

The 1970s witnessed something of a change of direction in Jesus films – the one exception being the low budget *Jesus* (1979) that was extremely faithful to the Gospels and has now been watched by 5 billion people and dubbed in over 600 languages.

But this was the exception. In 1973 the musical *Jesus Christ, Superstar* hit the screens (the same year as David Greene's musical version of the Christ story, *Godspell*), with Ted Neeley playing Jesus. With music from Tim Rice and Andrew Lloyd Webber, and a screenplay by director Norman Jewison and Melvyn Bragg, this film explores the relationship between power and love. Most of the action takes place on theatre sets in Israel and focuses on a bus-load of actors with a distinctive anti-establishment ethos. There is no resurrection scene in this film and the story ends with questions rather than answers about Jesus. Like *Godspell, Jesus Christ Superstar* abandoned the naturalistic approach to the Gospels altogether.

1977 saw the release of the extremely popular made-for-TV epic *Jesus of Nazareth,* directed by Franco Zeffirelli and starring Robert Powell as Jesus. This film was presented on television in two three-hour instalments before Easter 1977. It is noticeable for its slower pace which gives much more time for characters (including Jesus) to develop. It is also noteworthy for giving serious attention to the Jewish setting of the gospel story. This attention to context gives the film a more compelling appeal and Maurice Jarre's music score is superb.

The end of the 1970s saw the release of Monty Python's *Life of Brian,* directed by Terry Jones, starring Graham Chapman as Brian. This brilliant satire of the biblical epic was criticised for being blasphemous when it came out but in reality the Python team keep a respectful distance from the person of Jesus throughout the picture. However, the final scene with crucified victims singing 'Always look on the bright side of life' borders on the absurd and drew criticism for being disrespectful towards the Passion of the Christ.

The 1980s witnessed two similarly innovative Jesus films. In 1988 Martin Scorsese directed *The Last Temptation of Christ,* starring Willem Dafoe as Jesus, based on a highly controversial novel by Nikos Kazantzakis. The movie explores the relationship between flesh and spirit in the person of Jesus and is notorious for a scene in which Jesus fantasises about a sexual relationship with Mary Magdalene.

Perhaps more interesting is *Jésus de Montréal,* a French-Canadian film in which Jesus' humanity is again explored. This Canadian film, released in 1989, stared Lothaire Bluteau as Daniel who plays Jesus in a modern Passion play. This brilliant film, directed by Denys Arcand, sees a gradual blurring of the edges between the actor and his character as a troupe of players engage in a contemporary rendition of the Passion.

Apart from the rather bland made-for-TV mini-series *Jesus* (directed by Roger Young and aired in 1999) the 1990s saw precious little new ground broken in Jesus films.

The first part of the new millennium, however, has been more significant. *The Miracle Maker* was released in 2000. Written by Murray Watts, this brilliant combination of puppet animation and cartoons made an immediate impact. The contrast between 2D and 3D animation gave the Jesus story a unique new feel and took the narrative into dimensions that previous treatments could not attain (especially in its serious representation of the supernatural and miraculous dimension to Jesus' ministry). This remains one of the best and most loved Jesus films of the last 100 years.

In 2003, *The Gospel of John* was released. The contribution of this film consists of a faithful reliance on one of our main sources for the life of Jesus (the fourth Gospel) and its inclusion of many episodes that previous Jesus films have neglected (such as the woman at the well in Jn. 4). Although it has 'made for TV' production values, Philip Saville's film, starring Henry Ian Cusick as Jesus, with Christopher Plummer as the narrator, has proven immensely popular, especially in the USA. Like *The Gospel of Matthew* (1997), *The Gospel of John* is a Visual Bible International production and uses the whole text of a Gospel.

The much-anticipated movie directed by Mel Gibson, *The Passion of The Christ,* was released in 2004. This is a distinctive and brilliant contribution to the Jesus film genre. Aesthetically, it is a monumental achievement.

On the one hand, *The Passion of The Christ* has some similarities with previous Jesus films. It is filmed in a location very close to the one used by Pasolini in *The*

Gospel According to St Matthew. Like previous Jesus films (especially DeMille's *The King of Kings*), it relies very heavily on Renaissance art. Also like some of its predecessors, *The Passion of The Christ* has evoked criticism for its portrayal of the Jews and has been accused of stirring up anti-Semitism.

On the other hand, the movie also provides some new departures. In spite of the charge that the film is anti-Semitic, *The Passion of The Christ* is the first Jesus film to give serious attention to the Jewishness of Jesus. It is also the first to present the story in the form of a foreign language film, with Jesus and his Jewish contemporaries conversing in Aramaic (subtitles with the translation are provided). Most notable of all, there is a gritty realism about the portrayal of Jesus' sufferings that is unprecedented. No holds are barred in the depiction of his agonies before and on the cross.

The Passion of The Christ is a masterpiece. It may well be a flawed masterpiece, but it is still a masterpiece. No longer do we have a blond, Scandinavian Jesus spouting 1662 prose and going to a sanitised crucifixion with a mystical, otherworldly detachment. Rather, we have a Jewish-looking, Aramaic-speaking Jesus who suffers arguably the most graphically-portrayed torture scenes ever brought to cinema. As such, *The Passion of The Christ* has both raised the bar and indeed set the tone for future Jesus films and biblical epics. It is the most passionate of all portrayals of the Passion. I want to begin looking at the film in detail by examining a segment from the opening scenes, situated in the Garden of Gethsemane.

Clip 1: The battle in the garden

[We are in the olive garden at night, illuminated by the blue-grey hues of the moon. Judas has betrayed Jesus' whereabouts and Jesus now prays as he waits for his arrest]

JESUS [*kneeling, agonising*]. Hear me, Father. Rise up. Defend me. Save me from the traps they set for me.

[Satan appears to Jesus' right, lurking in the shadow of an olive tree]

SATAN. Do you really believe that one man can bear the full burden of sin?

JESUS [*looking up*]. Shelter me, Lord. I trust in you. In you I take refuge.

SATAN. No one man can carry this burden, I tell you. It is too heavy. Saving their souls is too costly. No one. Ever. No. Never.

JESUS. Father, you can do all things. If it is possible, let this chalice pass from me. But let your will be done, not mine.

[Jesus falls prostrate to the ground]

SATAN. Who is your Father? Who are you?

[Jesus continues to pray]

[Satan releases a snake from his cloak. The snake makes its way towards Jesus who rises to his feet. He looks at Satan for the first and only time in this scene. He raises his foot, and stamps upon the snake, killing it.]

There are a number of interesting things to note about this opening scene to Mel Gibson's film – a scene charged with emotional intensity.

First, *The Passion of The Christ* begins with the moments leading up to the arrest of Jesus. In other words, it begins with the ending of the gospel story. This is a bold stroke because previous Jesus films had for the most part followed the overall gospel sequence in providing material to do with Jesus' birth, life and ministry. Mel Gibson breaks with this tradition and provides us with a starting point just before Jesus' crucifixion. In this respect he follows the tradition of the Passion play rather than conventional Jesus films.

Secondly, we should note the use of lighting in this opening scene. What we are presented with is an olive garden at night. The background is a kind of blue-grey colour, befitting the moonlight setting. It is brightly illuminated by rows of unseen lights so there is a sense of whiteness, creating the feeling of a horizon that goes on indefinitely. There is also fog on the set. This means that the olive garden has a mystical almost infinite quality to it. Incidentally, it takes a huge amount of skill to create this subtlety of lighting effect using Anamorphic lighting. Cinematographer Caleb Deschanel takes a great deal of credit here.

Thirdly, the appearance of Satan in this scene creates great dramatic tension. Satan is portrayed as an androgynous being, with the appearance of a woman but the voice of a man.

Fourthly, and perhaps most significant of all, the decision to begin the movie with Jesus in a garden confronting Satan is revealing theologically. In the Gospel records, Satan does not make a personal appearance as Jesus agonises in the Garden of Gethsemane about his impending death. Nor does a serpent make an appearance! Why does Mel Gibson choose to start his movie with such a creative reinterpretation of the Gethsemane scene?

As Mel himself said, 'Holy Scripture and accepted visions of the Passion were the only possible texts I could draw from to fashion a dramatic film.' So this means Gibson not only used the Gospels but he also relied on 'visions of the Passion', especially those of two Catholic nuns, Anne Catherine Emmerich (1774–1824) and Mary of Agreda. Emmerich's visions, recorded nine years after her death by German Romantic poet Clemens Brentano in *The Dolorous Passion of our Lord Jesus Christ*, have provided Mel Gibson with a number of ideas and scenes. One of Emmerich's visions concerns a battle between Jesus and Satan in the Garden of Gethsemane. It reads as follows:

> '[Jesus] fell on his face, overwhelmed with unspeakable sorrow, and all the sins of the world displayed themselves before him, under countless forms and in all their real deformity. He took them all upon himself, and in his prayer offered his own adorable Person to the justice of his Heavenly Father, in payment for so awful a debt. But Satan, who was enthroned amid all these horrors, and even filled with diabolical joy at the sight of them, let loose his fury against Jesus, and displayed before the eyes of his soul increasingly awful visions, at the same time addressing his adorable humanity in words such as these: "Takest thou even this sin upon thyself? Art thou willing to bear its penalty? Art thou prepared to satisfy for all these sins?"'

Gibson is evidently dependent on Emmerich here. But the main effect of portraying the agonies of Gethsemane in this particular way at the beginning of the movie is to take us right back to the beginning of the biblical story, to paradise lost as it were. In the first book of the Bible, the book of Genesis, we begin with the creation of the cosmos and of the incomparably beautiful Garden of Eden. Adam and Eve live in idyllic innocence in the garden until one day Satan, in the form of a serpent, tempts Eve and both she and Adam fall from primordial purity into guilt, shame and brokenness.

God appears in the garden and pronounces judgement first of all on the serpent, then on the woman, then finally on the man. Of all these judgements, the first is perhaps the most intriguing in the context of Mel Gibson's presentation of the opening garden scene to his film:

> 'So the Lord God said to the serpent, "Because you have done this, you will be punished. You are singled out from all the domestic and wild animals of the whole earth to be cursed. You will grovel in the dust as long as you live, crawling along on your belly. From now on, you and the woman will be enemies, and your offspring and her offspring will be enemies. He will crush your head, and you will strike his heel."'
>
> (Gen. 3:14,15, NLT)

The last two sentences of this judgement have been interpreted through the centuries as a prophecy of the eventual birth and appearance of the Messiah. The one who will crush the serpent's head has often been seen as the Messiah, who would one day come and destroy the work of the evil one. Mel Gibson obviously has this thought in mind in the opening scene of *The Passion of The Christ*. When Jesus stamps on the serpent in Gethsemane, the prophecy in Gen. 3:15 is evoked in the mind of the biblically-informed viewer. Indeed, a friend of mine, who watched the film for the first time in a movie theatre in the south of the United States, told me that the whole cinema erupted with cheers when Jesus stamped on the snake in this scene! Even at the start of the film, the victory of Jesus over the devil is indicated through symbolism.

Our second scene is the procession towards Calvary, with Jesus carrying his cross. This particular scene melted the hearts of even the most cynical film critics when the movie was first shown.

Clip 2: See, I make all things new

[Jesus has been flogged and presented by Pilate to the mob. He is now led out by the Roman guard to be crucified. He is carrying his cross. John, the beloved disciple, leads Mary

(Jesus' mother) and Mary Magdalene through the side streets to get ahead of the procession so that Mary can see her son. They find an alleyway that leads on to the road to the cross. John looks at Mary]

JOHN. Mother ...

[The soldiers whip Jesus to keep him moving. Jesus collapses. He gets to his feet. He then collapses again, this time right at the entrance to the side alley where John, Mary and Mary Magdalene are waiting. Mary is not looking. John appeals to her]

JOHN. Mother ...

[Flashback. Suddenly Mary remembers a scene from Jesus' childhood, when as a toddler he fell on a cobbled path. Breaking back into the present, she runs to him now as she ran to him then. She is gasping and weeping as she holds her arms out to her tortured son.

Flashback. Mary remembers how she picked him up as a child as he cried. She soothes him]

MARY. I'm here.

[Breaking back into the present, she helps her bleeding son, with the same words]

MARY. I'm here.

[Jesus looks straight into his grieving mother's eyes as he rises to his feet. With emotion he speaks]

JESUS. See mother, I make all things new ...

[The procession moves on, leaving Mary watching in wonder, held by the beloved disciple and Mary Magdalene]

The reader should note that Mel Gibson is very reliant in this scene on the 'Stations of the Cross'. The 14 'stations' form part of Christian worship, particularly at Easter time. The stations are 14 events from Jesus' Passion. Some of these derive from the Bible, others derive from ancient Christian tradition:

1	Jesus is condemned	Lk. 23:24
2	Jesus carries his cross	Jn. 19:17
3	Jesus falls the first time	By inference from stations 2 and 5
4	Jesus meets his mother	By inference from Jn. 19:25–27
5	Simon of Cyrene helps carry the cross	Mt. 27:32
6	Veronica wipes Jesus' face	Not recorded in Scripture
7	Jesus falls a second time	Not recorded in Scripture
8	Jesus meets the women of Jerusalem	Lk. 23:27–31
9	Jesus falls the third time	Not recorded in Scripture
10	Jesus is stripped of his garments	Jn. 19:23
11	Jesus is nailed to the cross	Mk. 15:24
12	Jesus dies on the cross	Mk. 15:37
13	Jesus' body is taken down from the cross	Lk. 23:53
14	Jesus' body is laid in the tomb	Mt. 27:60

The scene we have just looked at from the film is the ninth Station of the Cross, when Jesus falls for the third time. As you can see, this incident is not recorded in Scripture, so its origins lie in Christian worship and Christian art. Gibson brings an amazing amount of his own creative artistry to the portrayal of this 'third fall' creating a terrific sense of momentum here. Each of the three falls is fully realised yet there is no sense of things letting up. The march to Calvary is inexorable and unstoppable.

A lot of this section was shot in Matera, the town in southern Italy where much of the movie was filmed. A great deal of the procession is filmed with dolly, hand-held and Steadicam. The Steadicam work is particularly impressive because it allows the camera to get very close to Jesus and creates a sense that you are walking with him. This means that the action is not happening 'out there'.

Rather, we are pulled into the events ourselves. It also allows the camera to pick out solitary and very specific faces in the crowd.

The use of slow motion is also very powerful. The third fall is filmed partly in slow motion. This allows the pace to slow down for a moment, creating room for a flashback in which Mary remembers Jesus falling as a boy. We see her running towards her child (again in slow motion) mouthing the word 'Yeshua', Jesus' name in Aramaic. This flashback to Jesus' childhood is one of the most heart-rending moments in the entire film as the viewer really feels the intensity of Mary's agony.

This brings us to an important observation. While Jesus is the focus of the attention during the procession to Calvary, his mother Mary also features a great deal, as do other female characters. In fact, Gibson's portrayal of female characters marks something of a distinctive feature of this Jesus film. Movie critic Calvin Trager remarked:

> '*The Passion of The Christ* really belongs to the women. While Jesus endures the physical suffering, it is the women in his life that endure the emotional suffering. It is more painful and emotionally affecting to watch Mary witness her son going through the ordeal than it is to sit through the many bloody whippings. Maia Morgenstern gives the standout performance and provides the film's most powerful moments.'

Perhaps most powerful of all is Jesus' courageous statement as he rises slowly from this third fall: 'See mother, I make all things new.' At a critical moment in the film, when Jesus seems to be losing the strength to go on, his mother helps him to his feet and her son makes for me the most potent and poignant statement in the entire movie. Here the genius of Mel Gibson is seen in the striking contrast of victory proclaimed at a moment of apparent defeat. In addition, the statement itself comes from the final book of the Bible, the book of Revelation, which describes the restoration of all things – paradise regained, if you will. In Rev. 21:1–5 (the final chapter of the entire Bible), St John describes a great vision he had on the penal colony of Patmos:

> 'Then I saw a new heaven and a new earth, for the first heaven and the first earth had passed away, and there was no longer any sea. I saw the Holy City, the new Jerusalem, coming down out of heaven from God, prepared as a bride beautifully dressed for her husband. And I heard a loud voice from the throne saying, "Now the dwelling of God is with men, and he will live with them. They will be his people, and God himself will be with them and be their God. He will wipe every tear from their eyes. There will be no more death or mourning or crying or pain, for the old order of things has passed away."
>
> He who was seated on the throne said, "I am making everything new!"'
>
> (Rev. 21:1–5, NIV)

Mel Gibson cleverly inserts a great statement of faith to do with the restoration of all things into the final moments of Jesus' life. In doing so, the audience is led to a far deeper understanding of the Passion of the Christ. It is an understanding which is wholly consistent with the thrust of the Bible story as a whole – that Jesus Christ is the long awaited Messiah who reverses the curse of the fall in the Garden of Eden by dying on the cross. The cross is not the 'end' but rather 'the beginning'. It is the gateway to the regeneration of human beings and indeed the cosmos.

Our third and final clip comes from the end of the movie, when Jesus has been nailed to the cross and elevated. He is about to die.

Clip 3: It is accomplished

[We are at the top of the hill where Jesus is now on the cross. The skies are darkening. Occasional thunderclaps can be heard. The wind has picked up]

JESUS. It is accomplished.

JESUS [*he looks up to heaven*]. Father ... into your hands ... I commend ... my spirit.

[As Jesus expires, the sound of his dying, lingering breath resounds around Calvary and beyond]

[The camera switches to above the cross, looking down at the scene where Jesus has just died. A solitary teardrop falls from heaven and lands at the foot of the cross. The wind picks up. There is an earthquake]

[Cut to Pilate's palace, where Pilate sits wondering at the noise]

[Cut to the sanctuary of the temple, where the floor splits in two, leaving the Holy of Holies exposed]

[Cut to Calvary, where the guards are ordered to break the legs of the three crucified victims. The legs of the two criminals are broken, but not Jesus'. Cassius, a soldier who has looked on with pity at Jesus' sufferings, approaches Jesus to break his legs but steps back. He addresses his centurion]

CASSIUS. He is dead

ABEANOR. Make sure.

[Cassius thrusts a spear into Jesus' side. A fountain of blood followed by water pours out, and Cassius kneels in wonder, drenched by the effusion]

[Cut to the temple sanctuary, where the priests, including Caiaphas, are weeping over the destruction of their temple]

[Cut to Abeanor, kneeling, with his helmet in his hands, reverentially]

[Cut to Caiaphas weeping]

[Cut to Satan, kneeling in what looks like the same quarry in which Jesus had died. The camera is above, looking down. Satan is facing upwards, arms outstretched, veil off, screaming in agony and anger at the heavens]

[Cut to calm skies. Jesus is being lowered down from the cross. He is being carried in the arms of John, Mary and Mary Magdalene. A Jewish priest and a Roman soldier stand either side of the upright cross beam, helping them. Jesus' dead body lies in Mary's arms. She is caressing his face]

[Cut to the crown of thorns and the nails lying nearby]

[Cut to Mary caressing Jesus' face tenderly]

[Cut again to the crown of thorns and the nails lying nearby]

[Cut back to the foot of the cross. Every eye is on the dead Jesus other than Mary's. Mary looks up towards the camera, looking at us. As the camera pulls back, we see her right hand stretched out towards her son.]

There is so much that we could comment on here. For example, we should note the camera angle at the start of this sequence. It is from a Technocrane above the cross (a perspective partly inspired by Salvador Dali's painting *Christ of St John of the Cross*). This allows us to look right into Jesus' eyes as he looks up. As we look down on Jesus – from a divine perspective (the perspective of the Father to whom he is praying) – we see again the astonishing make-up effects for the wounds in Jesus' face and head. As elsewhere in the film, the visual and visceral realism pushes us to a point where we almost cannot take any more. The sound is extraordinary here, too. The volume for the sound of Jesus' final breath is greatly increased. I can still remember the sound of that last breath resounding around the auditorium from when I first saw the film in the cinema.

The tear of the Father falling from heaven is an extraordinary moment in this final sequence of events. No previous movie of the Passion has ever dared to consider how the Father responded. No previous film has lingered on how the devil must have felt either! Both of these, the agony of the Father and the fury of the devil, feature here: the first by implicit commentary, the second by direct representation.

Perhaps most noteworthy is the Pieta. The Pieta is one of the great images of Western art and it is created here at the foot of the cross, with a number of characters surrounding Jesus' corpse. In Mel Gibson's version (which is not derived from any one painting of the Pieta), the camera scene is framed with a wide shot and then pulls in for a close-up on Mary's face. Then the camera pulls out again leaving an almost static, painting-like, image of Mary cradling her dead son and her right hand outstretched, as if in reverent prayer.

One thing of note is the fact that two men stand either side of the upright pole of the cross, assisting in the process of bringing down Jesus' body. On the right (as we look at it) is a Roman soldier. On the left is a Jewish priest. Now an awful lot has been made of the portrayal of the Jewish leaders in this movie. Caiaphas and some of those who surround him are presented in a very negative light. However, this is not true of all the Jewish leaders or all the Jewish characters in *The Passion of The Christ*. It is often forgotten that Jesus himself was Jewish and that Mel Gibson has gone further than any previous producer or director (at least in Jesus films) in portraying Jesus' Jewishness – right down to the historically indisputable fact that Jesus spoke in Aramaic. But here, too, at Gibson's version of the Pieta, we see a very clear message being sent at the cross itself, a message that says 'not all of the Jewish leaders were like Caiaphas'. The presence of a sympathetic

Jewish priest at Calvary is the clearest indication that Gibson never intended any kind of anti-Semitic subtext in this film. Indeed, his fellow screenplay writer Benedict Fitzgerald has gone out of his way to denounce this suggestion. On 7 April 2004 he stated:

> 'I declare and condemn all forms of bigotry, as preached or practised by any race against any other race ... Anti-Semitism is a wretched mental disease that has resulted in terrible suffering for Jews for all recorded history ... It is in fact contrary to the spirit of Christianity ... It is neither the intent nor, I believe, the effect of *The Passion of The Christ*, to promote any such reaction.'

A movie with life-changing power

On 12 November 2004, the Christian Enquiry Agency wrote the following in a newsletter circulated to Christian leaders:

> 'We are receiving a record level of enquires about Jesus. In the first 6 months of this year over 4,000 people have contacted us – a 150% increase on the same period last year! (Total enquires last year were 2,930.) A high level of enquires continue to be received every day.'

When analysing why there had been such a huge increase in the number of UK people wanting to find out more about Christianity, the Agency made this observation:

> 'We initiated and produced "Why?" response postcards placed in cinemas showing *The Passion of The Christ* film at Easter – the result is over 2,600 enquires and more are still arriving each week. One man said, "I saw *The Passion of The Christ* film and it got me thinking. I sent off the postcard and have now just finished the book on who Jesus was. It has

touched me and I would like to learn more." This is just one of many positive responses we've received.'

The Passion of The Christ is a film with the potential to change people's lives. The reason for that is because it has to do with the death of Jesus Christ. This death is the most talked about in human history. The cross of Christ is the axis on which the whole of human history rests. When people are confronted by the love of God depicted in the tortured face of Jesus Christ, something stirs within their soul. In *The Passion of The Christ*, the potency of the events lies not just in their dramatic tension nor their aesthetic realisation but rather in their spiritual significance. These events literally change everything. They change the world and they change us. As Gibson's Jesus puts it, 'I make all things new.'

There are very few people I meet who wouldn't like to be given a second chance, who wouldn't like to have their past forgiven, and to become a brand new person. The death of Jesus leads to that possibility. The Bible teaches that by simply believing in what Jesus has achieved on the cross – the forgiveness of sins, the defeat of evil – we can be reconciled to God the Father and have a personal relationship with him that lasts for ever. The cross is critical, then. It is critical if we want to develop an eternal friendship with God. As J. John puts it, 'If you want to go to heaven, then you have to go via King's Cross.' The cross of the King of kings is accordingly more than a great movie topic. It is the hinge of history and the hope of humanity.

Perhaps the following testimony says it better than I.

'Last September, a few days before my birthday, I prayed for a perfect birthday present. I prayed that my brother-in-law, Phil (very anti-Christianity and cynical), would become a

Christian, along with his wife Cathy. We'd been praying for them for years but Phil was very hostile. Two days after my birthday, Cathy became a Christian which was amazing. Then in March, after seeing *The Passion of The Christ*, Phil couldn't sleep all night; it had affected him so much. He decided to surrender his life to Christ, and did so, with Cathy praying with him. He wrote out a testimony and mentions the fact that it was 6 months ago (last September, when I started praying) when he began wondering what his life was all about.'

Clearly, God is using *The Passion of The Christ* to change people's lives. In the rest of this book we will examine other films that God is speaking through. They may not be as overtly Christian as Mel Gibson's, but that doesn't mean that they are not in part inspired and indeed used by the Master Storyteller, Jesus Christ.

DISCUSSION STARTERS

(You will need some potting compost, flower seeds, small plastic pots and a trowel.)

Personal reflection: This is one of the most powerful films you are ever likely to see. Take a little while to compose your thoughts about what you have witnessed. How did you respond, emotionally, intuitively? Which were the film's most powerful moments, for you, and why? What have you learned about Jesus that you didn't know before?

Discuss: The film is likely to have affected different people in your group in different ways. Discuss the relationship between how the film makes you *feel*, and what it makes you *think*. Where does the power come from, in this film? How does it differ from other powerful films you may have seen before?

Read: Jn. 12:24. What do you think this passage means?

Act: In your group, each of you should take a seed (or seeds) and plant it in a pot. As you bury the seed in the compost, consider Jesus' words again – 'Unless a seed falls to the ground . . .' Seeds need darkness to grow. And they take patience – they don't appear straight away.

You will need to take your pot away and water it. Every time you do so, try to remember the tears which fell from heaven in the film, when Jesus died. And thank God for the pain he suffered, as a father, when he lost his child.

Depending on what kind of seed you have planted and when, you may need to wait several months to see anything happen. But when it does, it will remind you of the death and resurrection of Jesus.

Once you've planted your seed, take a few moments of quiet to contemplate the darkness of solitude of Jesus' death. Hold your pot and thank God for new life that comes from death.

Discuss: In what Mark describes as the most moving moment in the film, Jesus looks at his mother as he picks himself – and the cross – from the floor, and says, 'See mother, I make all things new.' That includes you. Tell each other what you would look forward to in being made new. What can you no longer do, that you used to love? What parts of you do you feel need refreshing, revitalising? You can think about this from both a physical and spiritual perspective. In what ways, do you think, will your soul or inner self be made new? In what ways does it *need* to be made new?

Personal reflection: Think, for a few moments in the stillness, about a caterpillar that becomes a chrysalis and then turns into an amazing butterfly. Have you stopped recently to consider what an amazing transformation that is? The caterpillar and butterfly is a scintillating metaphor for our own personal transformation into the likeness of Jesus, as we become 'born again' into his life, death and resurrection. It's not only a new start, but one that let's us spread our wings, show off our amazing colours, and fly!

Pray: 'Lord Jesus Christ. You became a man, lived among us, loved us like a brother, and led us by serving us. Thank you for the terrifying death you suffered in our place. Help us to believe in you, and follow you, so that in your death, we might now begin to live. Amen.'

2

The Hand that Pulls the Strings *The Godfather* Trilogy

J. JOHN

PARAMOUNT PICTURES, 1972

Directed by FRANCIS FORD COPPOLA
Screenplay by MARIO PUZO
and FRANCIS FORD COPPOLA

MARLON BRANDO as *Don Vito Corleone*
AL PACINO as *Don Michael Corleone*
ROBERT DE NIRO as *Young Don Vito Corleone*

CLASSIFICATION: 18

In 1972, a movie was released based on Mario Puzo's novel, *The Godfather*. Over 30 years on, Francis Ford Coppola's film maintains its position as one of the most popular and critically acclaimed in cinematic history. It won three Oscars: for best picture, best screenplay and best actor (although Marlon Brando refused to accept the award). *The Godfather*, along with its two sequels, *The Godfather: Part II* (1974) and *The Godfather: Part III* (1990), form the famous trilogy depicting the life of the Corleone family. It has become such a cultural icon that in the 1998 film *You've*

Got Mail, Tom Hanks even suggests that the answers to all life's questions can be found in *The Godfather*.

A family within 'the Family'

The Corleones are not just any old family: they are deeply enmeshed in the underworld of organised crime. *The Godfather* is about Mafia don, Vito Corleone, and the passing of the 'family business' to one of his sons, Michael. This is an insightful study of violence, power and corruption, honour and obligation, justice and crime. In the opening scene of the film, the camera pulls back very slowly from the face of a man in Vito Corleone's office, where he is regally and ruthlessly carrying on his business during his daughter's wedding reception (being held in the compound of his home). In the low-lit office, Corleone sits behind his desk, while he lovingly and gently strokes the head of a cat perched on his lap. Although he moves stiffly, Corleone wields enormous, lethal power as he dispenses his own terrifying form of justice, determining who will be punished and who will be favoured.

The Godfather is also a film about family. It begins at a wedding, and *Part I* ends at a baptism. *Part III* ends with the family going to the opera. In between, the action is interspersed with scenes of weddings, funerals, pregnancies, illnesses, family dinners and family feuds.

This is the great paradox of *The Godfather*: on the one hand, it portrays the common life of a family, while on the other it shows the bizarre, sensational, violent life of 'the Family' (i.e. the Mafia).

Clip 1: The baptism scene

Michael Corleone, Vito's son, has agreed to become godfather to his new nephew. The baptism scene that follows is one of the most memorable in cinematic history. In a beautiful Italian church, Michael and his wife Kay stand holding baby Michael, who is dressed in an ornate Christening gown. As the priest prepares the baby for baptism, he asks Michael Corleone a number of questions.

'Do you believe in the Father, the Son and the Holy Ghost? Do you renounce evil?'

'Yes,' Michael replies to each in turn, without batting an eyelid. There is no hint in his face as to what is happening elsewhere. But as the questions are being asked, we cut one by one to the brutal killing of six men, gunned down in cold blood on Michael Corleone's orders. The organ reaches its dramatic crescendo in the church as elsewhere guns fire and blood is spilled. The priest concludes the service with: 'Go in peace, and may the Lord be with you.'

Religion and reality

It is never enough simply to mouth Christian platitudes. It is not enough to be baptised, married and buried in the church. The Christian faith is all about transformed lives. *The Godfather* presents us with extreme examples of hypocrisy, but these all started in small ways somewhere earlier. It should make us ask whether we are riding along the same tracks of hypocrisy that led, ultimately, to the spectacular examples we see in the film.

The easiest person for you to deceive is yourself. There is always a danger that we separate what we say from what we do, which enables us to pretend to be something or someone we are not. So, mouthing religious platitudes does not guarantee us acceptance by Christ, his approval or a ticket to heaven. You might tell the hospital receptionist, for instance, that your religion is 'C of E', but have you ever been along to your local church?

I once asked a man why he didn't go to church and he replied that he sent his wife along instead to 'keep up the insurance policy'. I pointed out to him the fact that God doesn't issue joint policies. You need to believe in him for yourself.

Being religious does not in itself guarantee a relationship with God. Instead, friendship with God involves humility and honesty. After all, you don't become a saint just by putting on Marks & Spencer underwear.

Who's pulling your strings?

The title scene of the film uses the same image that appears on the original cover of the novel. It depicts an arm reaching downwards, with its hand clasping a wooden crosspiece, to which strings are attached. This symbol points to the central theme of both the novel and the film.

In the book, Don Corleone proclaims to the other dons, 'We are all men, who have refused to be fools, who have refused to be puppets dancing on a string, pulled by the men on high.' But what controls *us*? Don't we *all*, to some degree or other, have strings attached?

Take the past, for example. We can't seem to escape it, and it affects us all. It is no good pretending otherwise. Then there is the issue of genetics: at a biological level, we are all complex chains of DNA, which seem in some way to determine who we are and who we are to become. Of course, it's becoming ever easier to blame our behaviour on our genetic make-up. It's tempting to abdicate responsibility for our actions, suggesting instead that it's the fault of our genes.

You also often hear people blaming their present behaviour on the way their parents have brought them up. 'I had a lousy background,' they say. 'I only do what I saw my parents doing. It's too late to change.'

The present also comes with strings attached. In today's environment of global capitalism and market forces, there is enormous pressure to have everything, and to want more. Peer pressure also affects us. Have you ever done something wrong, only to say, 'My mates made me do it'? Force of habit is another good excuse: 'I have always done it; I can't get out of it; I can't break the bonds.' And, of course, there's the small matter of fate, destiny, bad luck or even a curse …

Freedom from the ties that bind

The strings of both the past and the present can only be broken by Jesus Christ. In the Bible, Ps. 129:4 (NLT) states that 'the Lord is good; he has cut the cords used by the ungodly to bind me'. Elsewhere, God tells the prophet Hosea: 'I led them [the people of Israel] with cords of human kindness, with ties of love; I lifted the yoke from their neck and bent down to feed them' (Hos. 11:4, NIV).

Can we ever escape our strings? In one sense, no. After all, a puppet without strings is a pile of wood. But we need oversight and guidance, not control.

At the beginning of time, Adam and Eve were tempted to break free from God, and disastrous consequences followed. They put themselves, and us, under the control of someone else, who pulls our strings and makes us dance towards destruction.

God holds the strings to salvation, but he never pulls them for us. He won't force us into anything. He offers us the free gift of salvation through what Jesus has done on the cross. But he will never compel us to accept that gift. We must choose of our own free will, and we must express that choice by honestly admitting our need of forgiveness.

Clip 2: Confession in the garden

In another very powerful scene from *The Godfather: Part III*, Michael Corleone is speaking to an old priest outside a beautiful church building bordered with flowers. The priest picks a stone from a fountain and asks Corleone to look at it. He smashes it open, and shows him that even though it's been in water, the stone is bone dry inside. This, he says, is exactly the same as the people of Europe. They have been surrounded by the Christian faith, and yet Jesus does not live within them.

The priest offers to hear Michael's confession.

'But it's been too long,' protests Corleone. How can he repent after 30 years? He's convinced that he's beyond redemption.

The priest urges him to seize the moment: after all, what has Corleone got to lose? So he starts confessing.

He has betrayed his wife, he confesses.

The priest encourages him to continue.

A bell tolls.

He has betrayed himself, too – by killing a man.

'Go on,' says the priest once more.

Corleone hesitates. There is more: he ordered the killing of his own brother.

He then begins to cry.

'Your sins are terrible,' acknowledges the priest.

He speaks words of absolution in Latin, and once again, a bell tolls. This time, it's louder. Corleone is broken.

We can all change

For the past few years, *ER* has ranked among the most popular television series. In one episode, a white man was brought into the emergency room. The camera revealed a tattoo on his shoulder that read 'KKK' – standing for Ku

Klux Klan. It so happened that a black nurse was standing over the patient. The man looked up into the face of the woman and asked to be seen by a white nurse. His reason for doing so, however, was different from what we might first assume.

The white man explained to the black nurse, 'I didn't want you to look at the symbols that represent the animosity and hatred of my past. I'm saved now. I am a follower of Jesus Christ.'

The nurse was silent.

The man asked her, 'Do you think a person can truly change?'

She quietly replied, 'Yes, I do.'

It is worth asking three simple questions.

First, do you think a person can truly change? Is it really possible?

Second, do you need to change? Is there a habit that has you in its grip and from which you need to break free? Is there an attitude that you have been carrying that you need to let go of? Is there an activity that you have been involved in, that you need to quit?

Third, if you think people can change, and if you think you need to change, then how are you *going* to change? What will it take? Can you change by the sheer determination of your will? Can you change by keeping a positive mental attitude? Do you simply need a good example to follow? What will it take for you to really change?

People *can* change, and there isn't a single person who doesn't need to change in some way. But it will take more than the force of our own wills, more than a positive attitude and more than a good example to follow. For us to truly change, we need to recognise the extraordinary act of love that God has demonstrated in the death of his son. We must see the great lengths that God the Father has gone to in order that we might be reconciled to him and be a part of his family for ever.

Mary Ann Bird told of a childhood experience that changed her life.

> '"I grew up knowing I was different and I hated it," she said. "I was born with a cleft palate, and when I started school, my classmates made it clear to me how I looked. When I was asked, 'What happened to your lip?' I'd tell them that I had fallen and cut it on a piece of glass. Somehow, it seemed more acceptable to have suffered an accident, than to have been born different.
>
> "I was convinced that no one outside my family could love me.
>
> "There was, however, a teacher in the second grade that we all adored – Mrs Leonard. Annually, we had a hearing test. Mrs Leonard gave the test to everyone in the class, and finally it was my turn. I knew, from past years, that as we stood against the door and covered one ear, the teacher sitting at her desk would whisper something and we would repeat it back. She'd whisper things like, 'The sky is blue' or 'Do you have new shoes?'
>
> "I waited for those words, those seven words that changed my life. Mrs Leonard said, in her whisper, 'I wish you were my little girl.'"'

Cords of heavenly love

Every one of us has been deformed, ever since our strings were severed from God. But God desires each one of us to be his daughter or his son. His love is sufficient to begin to change our lives. God loves us with a love that will not let us go, even though everyone else may choose to give up on us. This is good news!

However, we also need to ask ourselves how we avoid just turning into fake Christians. After all, that's not real change. As we said, it's not enough to go through the motions, or to mouth religious platitudes.

So, first, we need to be inwardly changed by Christ, not just externally conformed to his teaching or to the culture of the church. Then, we need to allow the presence of God, through his Holy Spirit, to work in us and produce good 'fruit'. We need to be honest with ourselves, honest with each other and we need to be honest with God. The whole process begins by 'repenting', which means turning away from everything we know is wrong and turning to Jesus.

Nobel's legacy

The Nobel Peace Prize is the supreme award given to those who have made an exceptional contribution to improving the world. Other Nobel Prizes are given to those who have made outstanding contributions in the arts and sciences.

Alfred Nobel was a Swedish chemist, who made his fortune by inventing powerful explosives and licensing the formula to governments to make weapons.

One day, Nobel's brother died, and a newspaper, in error, printed an obituary notice for Alfred, instead of his deceased brother. It 'remembered' Alfred as the inventor of dynamite: a man who made his fortune by enabling armies to achieve new levels of mass destruction.

Alfred had a unique opportunity to read his own obituary and to see how he would be remembered. He was shocked to think that he would ultimately be recorded in history as a merchant of death and destruction. So, he used his fortune to establish the awards, for accomplishments, which we know today and which contribute to the furtherance of life, not death. Nobel is remembered for his contribution to peace and human achievement – not, as he originally feared, as the man who pedalled death and destruction to the masses.

Nobel had spent much of his life being 'successful' in the business world, only to realise that he had made a huge mistake. Like Scrooge in Charles Dickens' *A Christmas Carol,* he got a glimpse of the future, and he didn't like what he saw.

If people who know you could write your obituary, what would they write? If you were incredibly honest, how would you write your own? Why don't you try? It could change the way you see your life – for good.

Will you let Christ hold the strings of your life? Will you let Christ heal your broken threads? Although most of us are nowhere near as bad as Don Corleone and his family, we all engage in little acts of wrongdoing that are the first link in a chain of destruction. All of us feel the need to repent, and many of us struggle with the idea that anyone could forgive us.

The good news is that God, through his son Jesus, is able to forgive everything we have done, no matter how bad. And in doing so, he welcomes us into the ultimate family – the family of God.

DISCUSSION STARTERS

(You will need pieces of string and scissors.)

Personal reflection: In the film *You've Got Mail,* Tom Hanks suggests that the answers to all life's questions can be found in *The Godfather* trilogy. Which questions do *you* think it helps to answer? Stop, for a moment, to think about the questions you have. Which are the most important to you? Which have you struggled to answer?

Discuss: What are those questions? Offer them to the group – not so that everyone else can answer them, but so that they can hear the kind of questions we all have. Then discuss whether the film helps to address these questions, and if so, how.

Read: The film portrays the Mafia family as being close knit – until, that is, someone steps out of line. We are members of God's family – the Bible says that we are his children – and this family is just as tightly knit as the Corleones, but it lives according to different values (see Rom. 12:4–13).

Act: *The Godfather: Part III* shows a beautiful christening scene that is full of hypocrisy. J. John says that sometimes 'the easiest person for you to deceive is yourself'. It's easy to become a religious hypocrite – going to church and mouthing platitudes but not really living according to the words of Christ. Write down three words which you have heard at church – and used – which you might try harder to put into practice (e.g. 'love', 'grace', 'forgiveness' …). Beside each of the words, write yourself one sentence about how you can speak these words into being through your life.

Discuss: J. John suggests that we are all 'puppets on a string' to one degree or other with strings attached. We can choose to be tied with 'cords of love' to God – or controlled by unhelpful forces. Who, or what, controls us? What do we blame when things go wrong?

Personal reflection: In a few quiet moments, take a piece of string. Give it a name, privately – the name of something you feel controls you unhelpfully. Pray that God will help you to break the cords that bind you – and cut the string with scissors. Keep the two pieces of string in your pocket to remind you that you have cut the cords …

Act: J. John asks three questions: 'First, do you think a person can truly change? Second, do you need to change? Third, if you think people can change, and if you think you need to change, then how are you *going* to change? What will it take?'

It's time to write your own obituary. With these questions in mind, consider two things: how you'd be remembered – honestly – and how you'd like to be remembered if you could change.

Alternatively, you might prefer to think of your epitaph, written on a gravestone. One simple phrase or sentence that helps to sum up who you are / were to passers-by.

If you feel confident enough, read them to the rest of the group. You might appreciate a time of feedback, when you can all comment on each others words.

Read: Eph. 4:25–32

Act: 'Do not let the sun go down while you are still angry …' (Eph. 4:26). Together, you might pray that God will help you to change. And in a few moments of quiet at the end of your time together, try to think whether there is anyone that you are angry with, or who is angry with you. If there is, resolve to put this right as soon as possible – tonight, even – through a phone call or a visit. Try to break with convention by being the first to apologise – even if you feel you are in the right!

3

The Ship of Dreams
Titanic

J. JOHN

20TH CENTURY FOX, 1997
Directed by JAMES CAMERON
Screenplay by JAMES CAMERON
LEONARDO DICAPRIO as *Jack Dawson*
KATE WINSLET as *Rose DeWitt Bukater*
CLASSIFICATION: 12

I wasn't very keen to see *Titanic* when it first came out. A few particularly bad experiences of sea-sickness in small boats, miles from land, coupled with thoughts of how terrifying it would have been to sink into the icy waters of the North Atlantic that fateful night in 1912, meant that I was not looking forward to watching the inevitable unfolding of a tragedy in which nearly 1,500 people died.

However, I was both surprised and moved by a film that turned out to be the most expensive to date, costing $200 million to make. The ill-fated voyage of the opulent ocean liner was represented on screen in all its glorious excess, thanks to the writing, directing and editing of James Cameron, together with a haunting soundtrack from James Horner. The film went on to receive 15 Academy awards and was the top grossing film of all time, taking over $1.8 billion at the box office – double the amount of the previous record holder, *Jurassic Park*. It crossed the lines of age, gender and race in a way that few films seem to manage.

Titanic presents the fictional love story between Rose (Kate Winslet) and Jack (Leonardo DiCaprio) which takes place aboard the historical setting of the famously 'unsinkable' ship. It is a story that perhaps we can all, in some ways, relate to. Although, stereotypically, we think that young women are looking for romance from films, while men crave for adventure, in fact all of us, if we are honest, long for both.

This is a film of contrast and comparison. Cameron gives us both intimate details of the voyage and the grand spectacle of it all. He is able to contrast all that is arrogant and selfish in humanity with the sacrifice and dignity that we can, at our best, embody so nobly. Commenting on the film, he said, '*Titanic* is not just a cautionary tale – a myth, a parable, a metaphor for the ills of humankind. It is also a story of faith, courage, sacrifice and above all else, love.'

A story of towering pride

Titanic really aspires to be not just a 'parable, a metaphor for the ills of humankind', but a 'story of faith and love', so it is certainly worth stopping to ask how such a movie compares with the Bible – the greatest story of faith and love, sacrifice and redemption. After all, Christians believe that the Bible is not only a 'story of faith', but *the* story. It may well pay to compare the story of the *Titanic* with the 'original script' – the Bible.

Perhaps among the Bible's many narratives, the one that compares most closely to *Titanic* is the story of the Tower of Babel, which is found in its opening book, Genesis. With the same ambition as the *Titanic*'s shipbuilders, the people of Babel decided to build a tremendous tower 'with its top in the heavens'. The moral of the biblical story is that humanity had decided, with new-found technology, to try to usurp God's power. Seeing what was happening, God decided that such pride and arrogance could not go unpunished. The tower fell into ruin, and the proud people who tried to build it were 'scattered all over the face of the earth'.

I remember seeing a book illustration that helped the reader visualise the size of an ocean liner by standing it on end and comparing it to one of the world's tallest buildings.

The *Titanic* was a skyscraper at sea. It expressed both the technological prowess of its day and the pride and optimism of the people who built her. The owner, J. Bruce Ismay, is portrayed in the film as saying that he selected the name '*Titanic*' to 'convey sheer size ... and size means stability, luxury, and above all strength.'

The word 'titanic' is derived from the word 'Titan', and the Titans were gigantic gods in Greek mythology. They were the twelve children of Uranus and Gaia – heaven and earth.

The *Titanic* was acclaimed for its great size and its seeming invincibility, and proclaimed to be the 'ship of dreams'.

Clip 1: Setting sail

It is the present day, and an elderly woman is talking directly to camera. She is reminiscing about the *Titanic*, the 'ship of dreams'. 'And it was. It really was,' she says, wistfully. The picture fades, and we see the bow end of the old boat, resting, rusting in its murky, blue watery grave. And the picture again fades to replace the underwater image with a gleaming, pristine boat, sitting in Southampton docks on a sunny day.

The harbour is a frenzy of busyness and excitement, as passengers get ready to board, and friends and family crowd to watch them. A shiny, red Model-T Ford is winched onto the ship, as below, a line of cars draws up. From one of them steps a beautiful and clearly wealthy girl, together with her fiancé and her mother. It is Rose. She appears quite unmoved by the amazing sight that towers before her, observing sniffily that the *Titanic* doesn't even look as big as the *Mauritania*. 'Oh it is,' replies her fiancé, smugly – 'in fact, it's a hundred feet longer, and much more luxurious.'

Rose's mother surveys the scene with something approaching scepticism. 'So this is it,' she says. 'This is the ship they say is unsinkable.' To which the man replies, proudly: 'God himself could not sink this ship.'

Flying in the face of God

A survivor of the real *Titanic*, Eva Hart, recalled that her mother refused to go to sleep while aboard the maiden voyage, 'because she had this premonition, solely based on the fact that she said to declare a vessel unsinkable was flying in the face of God'. Of course, in the biblical story of the Tower of Babel, it is God who brings the prideful building project to ruin. But for the people on board the *Titanic*, it's an encounter with an iceberg which brings disaster upon them.

Premonitions and suspicions aside, the real enemies of the *Titanic* that fateful day were within. The decision was made by the ship's owners and captain to press on, at full speed, across the cold, dark waters of the North Atlantic, despite the fact that icebergs presented a very real danger. They were too preoccupied with the pride and prestige of achieving the fastest ever transatlantic crossing to worry that the ship might hit an iceberg and sink. After all, they had told the world that it was unsinkable, and unsinkable they believed it to be.

Although it's an iceberg that brings down the *Titanic*, God does have a role in the film – at least, he gets a mention. First, there is the music that is played just before the ship sinks. The band famously played on as the liner went down. Such hymns as 'Eternal Father, Strong to Save' and 'Nearer My God to Thee', became the soundtrack to an unimaginable disaster. God features, too, in the prayers and comments of those who turn in desperation to him for help. As the terrified passengers race to the highest point of the ship to escape the rising water, one reads from the Bible: 'Yea, though I walk through the valley of the shadow of death, I will fear no evil.' It's a comment that provokes Jack to ask sarcastically, 'You want to walk a little faster through that valley?' Yet, the God implied by these appeals for mercy is one who does not intervene.

Clip 2: The sinking

A seaman stands on deck, keeping watch through the night. He surveys the darkness before him through binoculars. Suddenly, he looks scared. There is a huge iceberg ahead, and it's too close for comfort – far too close. The *Titanic* has been set on 'full speed ahead' to break the transatlantic crossing record, despite the possibility of danger from icebergs. The seaman sends the message to the bridge: 'Iceberg! Iceberg!' It's passed frantically on, and the officers send an order to the engine room.

The ship's huge iron engine shafts grind to a halt, and then crank the propeller into reverse. But it's too late, of course. The ship cannot turn in time and hits the ice. Water cascades through the gash in the liner's side, while bodies cascade out. The ship's captain is woken and enters the bridge. 'What was that?' he asks his colleague, Mr Murdoch. 'Iceberg,' comes the reply. The captain knows from Murdoch's expression that this is a fatal blow.

Elsewhere, as people begin to get the measure of what's happening, the lower class passengers are locked downstairs on their deck, so that those in first class can get to the lifeboats. The violinist in a string quintet starts playing 'Nearer My God to Thee', and his colleagues, who were leaving, return, and join in. And as the music plays, the panic sets in around them.

The captain stands at the bridge, waiting, as the water rises. We see the designer of the *Titanic,* the man who dreamed this unsinkable vessel into being, standing in his luxurious quarters, realising that this ship is indeed sinkable after all. He checks his watch and sets a clock on his mantelpiece. He knows that there is nothing he can do. Everywhere, people are scrambling, shouting, running, looking for lifeboats, as the water sweeps onto the upper deck. We see the captain for one last time, as the water pressure smashes the windows on the bridge and the sea consumes him.

Outside, the water surrounds one of the glorious red funnels that were the hallmark of the liner. Its weight sends the huge tower crashing like a tree being felled, and it crushes all in its path as it falls. Meanwhile, in the mayhem, Jack has found Rose on deck. They have to stay on board for as long as possible, he says. The water is freezing, and it is filling up the lower decks, cascading through the ballroom and the opulent corridors of first class. It is tearing through the cages of the lower decks, where hundreds of men, women and children are trapped.

On the upper deck, a clergyman recites verses from the Bible: 'There will be no more sorrow or pain,' he says. 'The old world has passed away.' Terrified passengers cling to his words – and to his hands. Suddenly, all the lights go out. And the whole scene is cast into an eerie, dark silence for a matter of seconds. It is the calm before the storm. Suddenly, the ship rips in two, or almost in two, as the first half sinks down head first. Bodies are flying everywhere, as the second half – still joined to the first at its bottom – is hoisted vertically by the downward force.

Jack and Rose have clambered to the bow of the liner, and cling on as it rises higher in the air, until it sits vertically, a colossal skyscraper in the sea that is about to descend into the depths for ever. They hang on to the bars for dear life, as, like a rollercoaster ride, the second half of the ship begins to plummet. Jack shouts to Rose to take a deep, deep breath on his command, then to kick towards the surface, and keep kicking and to hold on to his hand and never let go. 'This is it. Here we go!' The ship is disappearing into the water, and they are the last people to take the plunge. Jack screams to Rose: 'We're gonna make it, Rose. Trust me!' And at that, the waters close on the bow, for ever – at the very spot where Rose and Jack had fallen in love.

The folly of human arrogance

The question that this film raises in my mind is whether we, in the twenty-first century, have fallen into the same dreaming innocence as the passengers of that ill-fated ocean liner, who were dancing and dining while the 'ship of dreams' sailed towards destruction. They did not contemplate the fate that awaited them, either from the iceberg or from the terrible and tragic events that were threatening to unfold across Europe and the world after 1912. Confident in their wealth and technological prowess, and convinced that, should earthly treasures fail, a loving God would step in to rescue them, the ship carried on regardless.

Like them, we tend to forget about the past all too easily, and frequently ignore what the future seems to hold. Could our own ignorance carry us towards a similar fate today? Perhaps this hugely popular film will help to remind us of the folly of human arrogance, and sound a warning shot across our bows.

In 1898, 14 years before the *Titanic* sank, the author Morgan Robertson wrote a novel, *Futility*, which told the story of a British ship called the *Titan*. It, like the *Titanic*, was on its maiden voyage from Britain to New York in the month of April with 2,000 people on board. While it was attempting to cross the Atlantic in record time, it, too, struck an iceberg and sank. Most on board also died because, as with the *Titanic*, there were not enough lifeboats. Could this have been an amazing coincidence, or a prophetic parable?

The twentieth century was characterised as the age of ideology, the time of the 'isms': communism, socialism, Nazism, liberalism, humanism, scientism, and so on. Everywhere, such ideologies nurtured the idea that we humans could progress towards a better world without the help of God; they made us believe that we could bring about the ideal society, whether by revolution, racial genocide or scientific technology. Such an attitude is betrayed in *Titanic*, of course, when Rose's fiancé proudly boasts that 'even God himself could not sink her'.

But she did sink. And other idols have sunk, too. Nazism, of course, was for ever disgraced by the horrors of its concentration camps and gas chambers. The Soviet

Union and its dream of communism seemed to crumble, at least in the West, along with the Berlin Wall. Around the globe, socialist nations are ever more eager to establish 'free' economies. Even science, which for so long has been hailed as a saviour, threatens to behave like Frankenstein's monster, which turned on its own creators. Most new discoveries and technologies can be used for good, but frequently they also threaten destruction.

Our anchor in the storms of life

When we look at the past, all our major ideological constructions seem to have failed and been tossed onto the scrap heap of history. Only one compelling claim to the truth remains convincing. We still have one secure hope, one way of seeing and understanding our place in the world: Christianity. The church has lived through two millennia because its founder, Jesus Christ, remains the same – yesterday, today and for ever.

On the fateful night of the *Titanic*'s downfall, passengers who somehow still believed the hype, even refused to get into the lifeboats, despite being told that the ship was going down. They clung to their belief that the ship was unsinkable – and were actually offended when officers told them to evacuate, when they had paid such enormous sums of money for luxury accommodation. Other passengers were unable to get a place on the lifeboats because of the privileged few, who felt no concern for anyone but themselves. As a result, many of the boats, which were built to hold up to 60 people, left the *Titanic* with only 15 aboard.

Through this film, the *Titanic* has been 'raised' for another generation of people to feel the impact of its tragic demise. It is an important warning against selfishness and arrogance, as well as a wonderfully positive affirmation of love, which transcends all lines of class, wealth and status.

Jesus Christ demonstrated the supreme act of love in human history by dying on our behalf and being raised from the dead. If, as a race, we are sinking like the *Titanic*, then he has provided a lifeboat and we must all climb aboard. To miss it is to sink and die. Too many of us today continue to believe that the world is secure and safe, and that we're fine to press on, full speed ahead into the darkness. But we need Jesus – and there is more than enough room for everyone at the cross.

DISCUSSION STARTERS

(You'll need as many stones as people in your group, and a bucket of water.)

Personal reflection: You'll almost certainly have placed yourself in the shoes of the victims, the survivors, the rich and the poor passengers on board *Titanic*. How has the film made you feel? What issues has it raised for you, in particular?

Discuss: Discuss these issues with each other. The film may have prompted negative feelings about death and destruction, or positive ones about the power of love. What will you take away as the 'essence' of *Titanic*?

Act: We take much for granted in our everyday lives – the safety of a car or plane, for example, our health or the permanence of our relationships. Think of times when you, or someone you know, might have had a 'near miss' – escaping an accident unscathed, perhaps, or missing your train, only to find that it's crashed … (If you haven't had a near miss, try to imagine what it would be like.)

Think about how you or your friend felt. How did you re-evaluate your life in the light of the narrow escape? Have you – in the time that has now passed – grown complacent once more, about the fragility of life, or the fallibility of human technology?

Act: Now, write yourself a note – as if it were from your 'dead' self, the 'you' that didn't make it because you *did* board the train that fateful day. What would you say to yourself about the way you are living, and the things in life that you are taking for granted?

Discuss: J. John writes, '[the director] Cameron is able to contrast all that is arrogant and selfish in humanity with the sacrifice and dignity that we can, at our best, embody so nobly.'

It's an amazing thing that even amid tragedy and negligence, there is always great human dignity to be seen. Why is this? To what extent do you sense a similar thing happening within your self – a battle between good and bad? How can we help the good to triumph?

Read: Gen. 11:1–9.

Discuss: J. John suggests that the *Titanic* was 'a skyscraper at sea'. What contemporary forms of the *Titanic* can we see around us in the world today? Is history doomed to repeat itself for ever? Jesus might be able to save our individual souls, but how can he save the entire human race from itself?

Act: In a final act of worship, take a stone and hold on to it. Think about one thing you would like to do to change, for good. See the stone as a symbol of that thing you'd like Jesus to take from you – and then drop it into the bucket. As it sinks, thank God that Jesus died so that we might find a way off the sinking ship.

4

How Far Will You Go?

Fargo

MARK STIBBE

MGM, 1996

Directed by JOEL and ETHAN COEN
Screenplay by JOEL and ETHAN COEN

FRANCES MCDORMAND as *Marge Gunderson*
WILLIAM H. MACY as *Jerry Lundegaard*
STEVE BUSCEMI as *Carl Showalter*

CLASSIFICATION: 18

Temptation is an experience common to every human being so we should not be surprised to find that it's a frequent and popular theme in the movies and television. Many films and programmes explore the destructive results of giving in to temptation. In fact, there is even a television show that's entirely devoted to this subject, called *Temptation Island*.

The film *Fargo* was written, produced and directed by the Coen brothers, Joel and Ethan, whose cinematic work is offbeat and outstanding. *Fargo* is essentially a study in temptation. The Coen brothers claim that it's based on a true story of a kidnapping in Minnesota in 1987, though no one has been able to confirm that. It is violent, but the violence serves a moral purpose, to highlight the appalling consequences of giving way to temptation.

The main character is Jerry Lundegaard (acted by William H. Macy). Jerry is a car salesman in Minneapolis. Desperately insecure, he works for his rich, successful father-in-law, Wade Gustafson, who clearly dislikes him. He is married to a neurotic wife called Jean and has one son, called Scottie.

Jerry hires two incompetent criminals to kidnap his wife. His plan is to put up a ransom of $1,000,000 and to use the kidnappers to get the money from his father-in-law. In addition, he will rescue his wife, be a hero in her eyes, and pay off all his debts. He will pretend to the kidnappers that the ransom is only $80,000 and give half to them. This is his plan.

Where temptation starts

The Bible talks a lot about the phenomenon of temptation. In the book of James we read: 'When tempted, no-one should say, "God is tempting me." For God cannot be tempted by evil, nor does he tempt anyone; but each one is tempted when, by his own evil desire, he is dragged away and enticed. Then, after desire has conceived, it gives birth to sin; and sin, when it is full-grown, gives birth to death' (Jas. 1:13–15, NIV). Here James describes temptation as a process involving three stages: (1) the desire for something destructive leads to (2) sinful or selfish actions, and these in turn lead to (3) self-death, the death of relationships, and so on.

Jerry Lundegaard is a man who succumbs to temptation. Driven by a need to succeed, he believes that success will earn him the respect and admiration of his wife and father. In order to fulfil his false dream, Jerry falls for the commonest desire of all, the love of money, which the Bible says is the root of all evil (1 Tim. 6:10, KJV).

Clip 1: The plot is hatched

In the opening scene of the film, Jerry drives into a small town in mid-winter. The snow is falling. He enters the bar. In contrast to the classic Western saloon scene, no one even turns to look at Jerry as he enters. The music goes on playing and the people continue to talk. Jerry sits down with two men who turn out to be the villains of the film, Carl Showalter (Steve Buscemi) and Gaear Grimsrud (Peter Stormare). In the dialogue that follows, Jerry enlists the help of these two foul-mouthed characters to initiate the plan to kidnap his wife, though even these two criminals express surprise at the depravity of his plan.

CARL. You want your own wife kidnapped?

JERRY. The thing is, my wife, she's wealthy. Her dad, he's real well off. Now, I'm in a bit of trouble …

CARL. What kind of trouble you in, Jerry?

JERRY. Well … that's … I'm not going to get into that … See … I need the money. See, her dad, he's real well off.

CARL. So why don't you ask *him* for the money?

JERRY. Well … they don't know I need it. See, OK, there's that. And even if they did, I wouldn't get it. So there's that …

In spite of the insane and irrational nature of the plan, the two crooks agree to take on what they call the 'mission' and a catastrophic chain of events is begun. Desire has been conceived. Sin is about to be born.

Rita Mae Brown once said: 'Lead me not into temptation, I can find the way myself.' That is exactly what Jerry does. He finds the way himself. He runs into temptation with the relentless, irrational drive of a lemming. He is totally enticed by the thought of something forbidden. Roman poet and historian Tacitus said that 'Things forbidden have a secret charm.' Jerry discovers that early on in the movie. He is enchanted by the very thing that will bring about his ruin. This is always where temptation starts. It starts with 'the fascination of the forbidden'. It begins with desiring that which will ultimately destroy who we are and what we value. Many films express this perverse, illogical self-destructive tendency in our human nature. *Fargo* is perhaps the most disturbing and yet the most interesting of all recent movies on this theme.

Where temptation leads

Let's go back to our passage from the book of James. James says that 'each one is tempted when, by his own evil desire, he is dragged away and enticed. Then, after desire has conceived, it gives birth to sin; and sin, when it is full-grown, gives birth to death.' Remember, the Bible is a very practical book. It deals with real-life issues. Here James tells us exactly what every human being can expect if they embark on the process of giving way to temptation. They can expect entanglement to follow enticement, and entrapment to follow entanglement. The end of the road, says James, is death.

This is the exact story of Jerry Lundegaard. The actions initiated by Jerry's desire are truly terrifying. The two goons kidnap Jerry's wife, but they are stopped on a remote road for driving a car without number plates. They shoot the State trooper who pulls them over, as well as a young couple who just happen to be driving by.

They end up killing Jerry's father-in-law, and a car park attendant, before finally killing Jerry's wife. Then, one of the kidnappers – Gaear – turns on his accomplice and kills him. He is finally arrested, and so is Jerry, who is hiding out in a dingy motel room.

Clip 2: Assessing the mayhem

The effects of Jerry saying 'yes' to temptation are vividly and brutally presented in the film. We have a chance to reflect on the carnage when two police officers are at the scene of the first killings. They are drinking coffee and chatting about everyday life. A car lies on its back in the snow beside the state freeway. A young couple lie hidden from our view inside. Both of them have been shot dead. A state trooper lies about 50 yards away, his blood starkly contrasts with the whiteness of the snow. The chief of police approaches the state trooper's body and examines it, perfectly reconstructing the trail of destruction through the footprints and other clues. She correctly realises that this is 'an execution type deal' and says of the state trooper, 'Looks like a nice guy. It's a real shame.' She then gets into her police car with Lou, the other officer, and returns to town discussing number plates.

The portrayal of the actual killing of these three people, not to mention this subsequent examination of the crime scene, is graphic. The viewer should be warned. But the Coen brothers are not being gratuitous in their depiction of the chaos that emerges from Jerry's plan. The graphic violence serves to underline the base and bestial depravity that human beings will sink to when temptation overpowers just one person. Ordinary people with 'decent' lives can self-destruct with spectacular pathos under the alluring and seductive power of temptation. In a movie called *Fargo*, the Coen brothers have come up with a story that vividly and despairingly illustrates how far we will go when tempted. Temptation leads towards a dark horizon, just like the freeways in *Fargo*.

Where temptation ends

Back to James 1:15, 'After desire has conceived, it gives birth to sin; and sin, when it is full-grown, gives birth to death.' Temptation ends in death. This is the case for Jerry Lundegaard. His sinful deeds lead to the death of many people and indeed to his own self-death. He loses absolutely everything, even his dignity. Indeed, when he is finally captured, he is arrested in his underpants; screaming and whining like a trapped animal. This final glimpse of Jerry, supercharged with pathos, serves to act as a reminder to everyone that temptation involves a road to self-destruction. It involves everything being stripped away. The moral message is 'do not succumb to temptation'. Do not allow sinful desires to lead you astray. Terminate them at conception. Otherwise, it will all end in tears.

One of the ways in which this point is highlighted is through the Coen brothers' brilliant creation of the character, Marge Gunderson (acted by Oscar winner, Frances McDormand – Joel Coen's wife). Marge is the female police chief who follows the trail of destruction in the movie. She is heavily pregnant and cannot stop eating. We first see her asleep in bed with her devoted husband Norm (i.e. 'Normal') who seems to spend the entire film either cooking or eating. During his first words in the film he says 'I'll fix you some eggs' three times! Their marriage is portrayed as decent, simple and orderly, befitting the Scandinavian ancestry their surname suggests. While Marge is depicted as a moral being, Jerry is depicted as immoral. While Marge represents the triumph of decency,

Jerry represents the tragedy of indecency. The contrast between them is as black and white as the landscapes they inhabit.

Clip 3: The dinner with Mike

Marge also experiences temptation in the film, when an old school friend called Mike rings her. Marge accepts an invitation to a meal, dresses in a flowery dress, dons an unusual amount of make-up, and enters the restaurant.

Marge sits opposite him and they exchange pleasantries. She asks Mike about his marriage and, before he answers, he moves over to the other side of the table sitting very close to Marge. As he sits he asks, 'Do you mind if I sit over here?' Marge looks away and without hesitation says emphatically, 'No, why don't you sit over there? I prefer that.' Mike moves back saying, 'OK, sorry.' He then invents a pathetic story about his wife Linda's death (which turns out in fact to be a lie). 'I've been so lonely,' he sobs.

The difference between Marge and Jerry is superbly highlighted throughout this scene. On the one hand, Jerry falls for temptation. A sinful desire is conceived in his heart and, at a restaurant table, he initiates a disastrous sequence of events. Marge, on the other hand, terminates temptation at conception. Her very definite act of resistance (also at a restaurant table) offers the clearest contrast to Jerry's lack of moral will. These two characters show that there are really two places temptation can end. Either we succumb to temptation and have it all end in destruction (Jerry). Or we can end the whole ugly process before it is even born (Marge).

> 'All the water in the world, however hard it tries
> Can never sink the smallest ship unless it gets inside

And all the evil in the world, the blackest kind of sin
Can never hurt you in the least unless you let it in.'

(Author unknown)

Asking God for help

A much-loved man who attended our church, Dave Harding, died in 1998. Shortly before he died, Dave gave an amazing testimony about how God had miraculously set him free from alcohol addiction. The following is a transcript taken from the tape.

'Before 1997 my life was a real shambles, totally unmanageable and totally dominated by alcohol – supplemented, when possible, with drugs. It is difficult to explain how all-pervasive it was. Doctors would ask me what time of the day I started drinking. That was a completely ridiculous question. If I woke at three in the morning, I would start. If I woke at three in the afternoon, I would start. It just dominated all my actions and all my thoughts.

Since the age of 20 – I am 50 now – I have tried various means of stopping. I have been in and out of hospitals, clinics, treatment centres, and various types of therapy and counselling. I was frequently warned that my liver was going bad.

In the end, something happened on Boxing Day 1997. I had my last drink on 26 December. I then started experiencing DTs [dehydrated tremors] and it was absolutely dreadful. I honestly thought I was going to die that night, but in that place of despair, I prayed. I think for the first time in my life I was utterly defeated. I knew no power on earth could help me and there was only one possible way out. That was to pray to the Lord to help me through that night and to take away the desire I had for alcohol. That's where it all starts, with desire.

A sort of peace came over me and I had this hope that life did not have to be as it had been. I was completely alone except for the Lord, and I asked him in to my life and he came and he answered my prayer.

I used to pray in a rather insincere fashion. I'd pray in the morning with a drink in my hand asking that I might not drink too much that day. But when I prayed for myself on 26 December, this time I was sincere. That night, Jesus came in to my heart.

Strange as it sounds, since Boxing Day 1997, I have not had a single desire to drink and that is a miracle. The consultant I was under said it was very unusual in his experience for someone of my age and history of drinking to manage to stop just like that. I told him it came from the Lord, and he suggested I should stick with that.'

Not long after that, Dave Harding died. But when J. John and I visited him on the evening of his death, we met a man who had conquered his addiction and was at peace with God. Dave Harding was a man who had known the destructive power of temptation. When he asked Jesus into his heart, he experienced a miracle. God took away the desire for alcohol. God can do that with our temptations, too. He can take the desire, if we ask.

A movie with a message

Fargo is like a postmodern morality tale. It is a very stark reminder of the dangers of giving in to any temptation, but particularly the temptation of money. Just before the movie finishes, Marge sits in a police car with the surviving villain in the back, behind a cage. She speaks to him as she looks at his reflection in the mirror. The man remains silent.

'And for what?' she asks. 'For a little bit of money. There's more to life than a little money, you know. Don't you know that? And here you are. And it's a beautiful day. Well, I just don't understand.'

At this point, the haunting music score by Carter Burwell kicks in and the scene moves to the motel of Jerry's arrest.

Marge's lament at the end of this film is so poignant. There really is more to life than money, yet so many people's lives are destroyed by the temptation of financial greed. Other people, like Dave Harding, experience different kinds of temptation. However, it is probably right to say that the most common is the love of money. As the Apostle Paul wrote, in his first letter to Timothy, 'People who want to get rich fall into temptation and a trap and into many foolish and harmful desires that plunge men into ruin and destruction. For the love of money is a root of all kinds of evil' (1 Tim. 6:9,10, NIV). It is so sad that many of us fail to heed the warning.

I conclude with a true and tragic example of how – in the process of temptation – desire leads to sinful actions, and sinful actions end in death.

In November 2001, a 28-year-old Japanese woman called Takako Konishi was found wandering around at a landfill and truck stop in Bismarck, North Dakota. A man found her and took her to the police station where she showed officers a crude map of a tree next to a highway. She believed that this was the place where Carl Showalter had buried the kidnapper's ransom in the movie *Fargo*, and she was trying to find it.

The police tried to persuade her that *Fargo* was just a movie (though there really is a place called Fargo in North Dakota), but the woman insisted that the film had been based on a true story, therefore the treasure must be buried somewhere. The Bismarck police tried in vain to convince her that the movie was fictional, not factual, but to no avail. Miss Konishi left the police station, boarded a bus, and went to Fargo.

A few days later, a hunter stumbled across her body in a grove of pine trees in Detroit Lakes. She had taken some sedatives, but the cause of death was put down as exposure. Her death was eventually ruled a suicide when it was discovered that she had sent a letter to her family in Japan expressing her intention to take her own life.

She came to Fargo having succumbed to a foolish and irrational temptation – to seek out money that never existed.

DISCUSSION STARTERS

(Prepare some blank slips of coloured paper which are the size of £5 notes. You'll also either need a metal bucket (if possible) and / or a cross.)

Personal reflection: Fargo may well have raised issues within you that are painful, embarrassing or shameful. Instead of running from these, or sweeping them under the carpet, try to be honest with yourself about the times when you have succumbed to temptation. Think about the way it has affected you, and those around you.

Read: Jas. 1:13–15.

Discuss: Mark says that '(1) the desire for something destructive leads to (2) sinful or selfish actions, and these in turn lead to (3) self-death, the death of relationships, and so on.'

Do you think James (in the reading above), and Mark, are exaggerating when they say that succumbing to temptation leads to a form of 'self death'? Try to think of an example in which you have begun to 'die' a little, inside, because you have given in to temptation. Be honest if you can, but don't feel pressured.

Personal reflection: The Bible says that ' ... the love of money is a root of all kinds of evil'. It's the greatest form of temptation going. Stop to think whether you have ever succumbed to temptation of a financial nature. Have you compromised a relationship because of cash? Have you cheated a friend out of money they were due? Have you neglected to give to the poor or those in need, when you have plenty?

Read: Lk. 19:1–10 (the story of Zacchaeus).

Act: Resolve, tonight, to make amends. If you have cheated someone, decide to ask for their forgiveness, and pay them back. If you have neglected to give to the poor, resolve to do so ... On the back of a bank note it says, 'I promise to pay the bearer ...' Write yourself a 'bank note' tonight on a slip of paper, which promises to put something financial right. Place this 'bank note' in your wallet or purse, as a reminder of what you have decided.

Discuss: What is success? Jerry's temptation began because he saw himself as unsuccessful, in the eyes of a watching world. But what is 'success'? How do we tend to measure it? And how might we measure it differently? How do you think Jesus would qualify the term 'success'?

Act: On a coloured piece of paper, write down one temptation that you must make sure you resist – then fold the paper so that no one else can read it. While a piece of music is played quietly, place your piece of paper at the foot of the cross, or in the bucket provided. Spend some time looking at it, sitting there among all the others. We are all tempted – and it's no sin. It's what we do with the temptation that counts. Hand it over, in your heart, to

Jesus, and ask for his strength to overcome it. If you can burn the slips of paper symbolically in the metal bucket, then do so. If you can't do that safely, dispose of them in an appropriate way.

Pray: One of you could then pray a short prayer of thanks: 'Jesus, you resisted temptation in this life, so that we might not die but know life to the full. Help us to start to live more fully, by making the right choices each day. Amen.'

5

Time and Eternity
Cast Away

J. JOHN

DREAMWORKS SKG, 2000

Directed by ROBERT ZEMECKIS
Screenplay by WILLIAM BROYLES JR

TOM HANKS as *Chuck Noland*
HELEN HUNT as *Kelly Frears*

CLASSIFICATION: 12

I remember daydreaming in a boring lecture at theological college one day, when the lecturer stopped and asked, 'Mr John, will you tell me why you keep looking at your watch?' I had to think quickly. 'Yes, sir,' I said. 'I was concerned that you might not have time to finish your interesting lecture.'

Someone who perhaps paid a little more attention in their classes, Albert Einstein, once said, 'When a man sits with a pretty girl for an hour, it seems like a minute. But let him sit on a hot stove for a minute and it's longer than any hour. That's relativity.' Time plays a significant role in our lives, and we can't ever seem to shake it off.

In *Cast Away*, Tom Hanks plays Chuck Noland, a manic Federal Express troubleshooter who travels the world at a moment's notice. Both his professional and personal life are ruled by the clock, and the words, 'time', 'watch' and 'pager' are spoken of twenty-four times in the film's first 15 minutes. Early on in the film, Noland, a man seemingly in control of everything, gives a speech on the theme of time to a group of Russian Federal Express employees.

Clip 1: The speaking clock

A boy runs over a bridge, clutching a parcel with Federal Express labels on it. It's snowy and cold. He keeps running. We cut to the scene inside what looks like a warehouse, where Chuck Noland is lecturing Russian Federal Express employees on the virtues of timekeeping. It's all a battle against the relentless march of time, he argues passionately. Clocks tick away as his visual aid to people of another country, another culture, for whom this idea seems a little foreign. A Russian translator keeps up with his increasingly frenetic exhortations to 'keep time'.

Suddenly, he notices that the boy with the parcel is before him, panting. He grabs it, and opens it. 'What could it be?' he asks, patronisingly. His tone prompts sarcasm from the translator, who says something he can't understand.

Pulling out the contents, it's ... another clock, a stop-watch, in fact, that he sent to himself by Federal Express and which he started the moment he left Memphis for Russia. It has taken 87 hours, 22 minutes and 17 seconds for the package to arrive.

Too long! It's just not good enough! What if the parcel had been something really important?

Noland then turns to the job in hand: the Russians have a pile of packages that must be gathered and loaded onto a truck in under 15 minutes to be sent to the airport. 'It's crunch time,' he declares. 'Let's go!'

If only there was enough time

I'm sure you'd agree that the pace of life is hectic. We talk of the 'peak' or 'rush' hour. We are always telling our children to 'hurry up, get a move on!' It is because our days are too full and because they move too fast that we never seem to catch up with ourselves. Our work and the demands upon us seem to expand to fit all the time that we have. Time is increasingly in short supply. And we spend a good deal of our time complaining about it.

How often have you heard yourself, or others say, 'If only I had the time'? Or, 'There's never enough time.' 'I don't know where the time goes.' 'But how do you find the time?' 'I'm hard pressed for time at present.' 'I'll try to find time.' 'Is that the time already?' 'My, how time flies!' 'Could you fit in time?' 'I'm short of time.' 'Mustn't waste time, must we?' 'I just ran out of time.' 'I don't even get time to think.'

We have a wide range of other expressions as well: 'I haven't got a moment to spare.' 'There are never enough hours in the day.' 'We always seem to be on the go.' 'There's always so much to do.' 'I never seem to stop.' 'We're flat out at the moment.' 'I've just got to rush.' 'The week's simply flown.' 'Back to the treadmill.' 'No rest for the wicked.' Then, there's the revealing invitation: 'You must come around some time ...'

The pace of many people's lives is literally killing them. We have bought into the crazy idea that the busier we are, the more important our life is. We live in a society in which the expression 'time is money' has come to refer to the value of time. The only problem with this is that money cannot buy more time. We forget that money can be replaced, but time can never be replaced. We would be far richer as individuals and as a society if we were to say that 'time is priceless'. Then we might treat it with more respect.

Our modern hustle and bustle places us in the grip of what the psychologist Paul Tournier calls 'universal fatigue'. People are constantly complaining about how tired they feel. We even feel tired when we wake up in the morning. Diane Fassel wrote in her book *Working Ourselves to Death* that 'work is god for the compulsive worker, and nothing gets in the way of this god.' Work becomes an end in itself, a way to escape from family, from the inner life, from the world.

When time stands still

Following his speech in Russia, Chuck flies back to Memphis to see his long-time girlfriend Kelly (played by Helen Hunt), the girl he's about to propose to. But Chuck lives in such bondage to time that he can't even schedule time for a dental appointment. During a Christmas dinner, his pager goes off. He is called immediately to South East Asia to deal with another Federal Express problem. He and Kelly hurriedly open their Christmas gifts to each other in the car, on the way to the airport. Chuck gives Kelly a journal and a pager in order to record her life in the world of time. She gives him a pocket watch – a family heirloom, in fact – with her picture inside.

He says, 'I will keep it on Memphis time – Kelly time.' He then hands her a ring box with the parting words, 'I'll be right back.'

Halfway over the Pacific Ocean, his plane is brought down by a terrible storm. Chuck is the only survivor. Somehow, he reaches the shore of a small deserted island. The first thing Chuck removes is his pager, which is filled with water, and then his pocket watch, which has stopped.

Time as he knew it had ended. The clock is no longer a pulsating, relentless taskmaster. Having lived his life by the second hand, Chuck realises that time is not under his control any more than the circumstances of his existence. This awareness forces him to face the self-imposed limitations of his life. Chuck tried to measure everything with time, but didn't know how to use it. He abused and ignored people. He now gets pushed outside time – cast away. The maddening thing for him is that while his own clock may have stopped, the world's time marches on.

So, we have a man obsessed with time who is trapped in a purgatory that he cannot regulate. He goes from clocking seconds digitally to tracking the seasons by the movement of the sun. He no longer controls time – it controls him. In a touching scene he looks at the ID of one of the dead crewmen who was washed ashore, just before burying him – and realises that he didn't even know his real name. It is a moving testimony to the tyranny of the urgent and how busyness can distract us from relating to the people who are close to us at a deeper level.

We then see how Chuck figures out the four basic elements for human survival: food, water, shelter and fire. But there is a fifth element he needs badly – companionship. Federal Express packages from the plane crash begin to wash ashore – packages he can't deliver. Chuck finds novel uses for their contents, but decides not to open one particular parcel that is adorned with angel wings. The wings become a symbol of hope for him, one that far outweighs any physical use he could have found for what was inside.

In one of the boxes, he finds a volleyball. Having cut his hand, and then grabbing the volleyball, his bloodstain leaves an image of a strangely compelling face. With slight modifications of his own, Chuck uses his own blood not only to create, but also to bond with his new companion. 'Wilson' becomes the 'friend' who keeps Chuck sane while he's on the edge.

Only after four years does Chuck make a daring – and successful – escape from the island. He returns to civilisation a profoundly changed human being, but realises that he can't pick up where he left off. On the plane flying home, his friend Stan tells Chuck they held a funeral for him. They put in his coffin a phone, beeper and Elvis CDs – which they had decided were the things that best represented his life.

Clip 2: All the time in the world

Chuck is sat in a house, in semi-darkness, talking to his friend. He has a drink in his hand, and is reflective. He tells of how he talked to Kelly when he was on the island; that even though he was totally alone, she was with him. He knew, or thought he knew, that he would get ill, or injured, and die. Everything had been out of his control ... apart from one thing: his own death. The only choice he had, the one thing he could determine, was how and when and where it would happen. So, he'd made a rope and climbed a hill to hang himself. He tested the rope first, to see if it would bear his weight, but the log he used snapped the branch on which the rope hung. He realised that he didn't have power over anything. He couldn't even kill himself properly! But all of a sudden, he said, a feeling came over him – like a warm blanket. He knew, somehow, that he had to stay alive, keep breathing – even though there was no reason to hope, and even though he didn't believe that he would ever see this room again – so that's what he did. And the tide came in and washed up a sail ... and here he is, talking to his friend, in Memphis.

But after all that, after everything, after his hope in the face of despair, he'd lost Kelly again. And he's desperately sad about it. But, in the face of that sadness, he can remain happy that she was somehow with him on the island. And now? He's got to keep breathing, once more. Tomorrow, he says, the sun will rise. And who knows what that could bring?

The absence of God

Cast Away, to use a quote from the Berlioz requiem, is 'haunted by the absence of God'. In contrast, Daniel Defoe's seventeenth-century novel *Robinson Crusoe* is filled with God's presence. Crusoe is a man who rebels against his parents to become a sailor. He joins up with a ship to set out for the seven seas in search of adventure.

He becomes the sole survivor of a shipwreck, condemned to live out his days on a desert island. Though Chuck Noland and Robinson Crusoe experience similar circumstances – both being stranded on a desert island – Crusoe, in direct contrast, begins to contemplate time and eternity.

The book *Robinson Crusoe* is full of his thoughtful, probing encounters with God – his weaknesses, fears, temptations. It explores how Crusoe learns to love God and the world. He is someone who runs from God and who cries out to God. And this is what's disappointing about *Cast Away*. In the end, the film only offers a picture of the person that seems far away from the reality of human experience. Crusoe's pilgrimage rings true in a way that *Cast Away* simply does not.

At the beginning of the film, Chuck Noland stresses three points in his speech in Russia. First, he states that time rules over us without mercy. Christians might disagree and argue that it is God who rules with mercy. Second, he says that we live and die by the clock – rather than by the grace of a sovereign God. Third, he says, never turn your back on the clock or commit the sin of losing track of time – it is a pulsating, relentless taskmaster. But he has no concept of a loving, compassionate God.

The psalmist writes:

> 'Our days on earth are like grass; like wildflowers, we bloom and die. The wind blows, and we are gone – as though we had never been here. But the love of the Lord remains forever with those who fear him. His salvation extends to the children's children of those who are faithful to his covenant, of those who obey his commandments!'
>
> (Ps. 103:15–18, NLT)

The writer of Ecclesiastes states beautifully that 'God has placed eternity in our hearts'. And because God has placed 'eternity in our hearts', we know that nothing of 'time' will permanently satisfy us.

One thing we can observe from films like *Cast Away* is the utter emptiness of life without God. Life derives its true meaning not from self-fulfilment or success, but from a personal relationship with our creator. As C.S. Lewis once said, 'If I find in myself a desire which no experience in this world can satisfy, the most probable explanation is that I was made for another world.'

When God intervenes

There is a story from Jesus' life recorded in the book of John that is worth us looking at:

> 'Inside the city, near the Sheep Gate, was the pool of Bethesda, with five covered porches. Crowds of sick people

> – blind, lame or paralysed – lay on the porches. One of the men lying there had been sick for thirty-eight years. When Jesus saw him and knew how long he had been ill, he asked him, "Would you like to get well?"
>
> '"I can't, sir," the sick man said, "for I have no one to help me into the pool when the water is stirred up. While I am trying to get there, someone else always gets in ahead of me."
>
> Jesus told him, "Stand up, pick up your sleeping mat, and walk!"
>
> Instantly, the man was healed! He rolled up the mat and began walking!'
>
> (Jn. 5:2–9, NLT)

The man had been lying there for 38 years, his eyes staring at the water; his gaze fixed on his only hope of something better. The very cause of his need prevented him from having that need met. Suddenly, his world is interrupted by a voice asking him if he wants to be made well. What a strange question! Surely, the answer is obvious? But his answer is revealing: it's not 'Yes, that's what I've been longing for', but a statement of the problem as he sees it – he has no one to help him into the pool.

Originally, all he wanted was to be healed, to walk and run as others could. Now, all he wants is someone to help him into the water. The pool has become the object of his longing, and he cannot see any other solution to his problem. Sometimes, the search, however wearying and unfulfilled, becomes everything for us.

In fact, all he needed was a word from Jesus and, in an instant, the pool which had been his hope and his despair for 38 years, seemed unimportant.

No matter how hard we try, we cannot pull ourselves out of the quicksand of time. That is why we need someone to change the way we see things, to lift our eyes, so that we can peer beyond time and be led towards eternity.

That someone is Jesus. Our search for eternity brings us to him. Jesus said, 'I am the way and the truth and the life.' Life with Christ is an endless hope; without him, it is a hopeless end.

At the crossroads of life

In the movie *The Last Emperor*, the young child anointed as the last Emperor of China lives a life of luxury with 1,000 servants at his command. 'What happens when you do wrong?' his brother asks. 'When I do wrong, someone else is punished,' the boy replies. To demonstrate, he breaks a jar, and one of his servants is beaten.

In Christianity, Jesus reversed that ancient pattern: when the servants erred, the King was punished. Grace was free only because the giver himself bore the cost.

At the end of *Cast Away*, we see Chuck Noland standing at a crossroads. He is in the middle of the road, able to go in any one of four different directions.

Clip 3: At the crossroads

Chuck Noland parks at a sweeping crossroads, in the middle of, well, seemingly nowhere. One road seems white, sandy, yet the others are dark. It's a hot day, and the sky is blue. The landscape is flat and yields no clues about direction. He gets out of his car and unfolds a map. Another car swings by and stops. A woman, happy, smiling, helpful, tells him he looks lost. 'Where you headed?' she asks. That was what he was trying to figure out, he replies. She tells him exactly where each road leads, which directions he can choose. And with that, briefly, she wishes him luck, and drives off, up the white path – her dog peering at him from the back of her pickup. Chuck stands there, watching her drive into the distance. He looks round at every path, slowly. And stares once more along the woman's path.

The road Noland was standing on was in the light, but the other three were in the dark. The movie's final scene ends with Chuck seeing the wings on the woman's truck.

Making time for what really matters

In St Paul's Cathedral in London hangs Holman Hunt's painting, *The Light of the World*. It is a picture of a cottage that is run down, and bushes and briars have grown around it. The path is covered by weeds and grass. Standing at the door, Jesus is holding a lantern in one hand that gives off light to every part of the picture, and he is knocking with the other hand. After Hunt completed the picture, one discerning critic said to him, 'Mr Hunt, you made a mistake. There is no handle on the door.' The artist replied, 'No, I did not make a mistake, for there is a handle. The handle is on the inside.'

Once, a little girl and her father were standing in the cathedral. They were mesmerised as they looked at the painting. Then the girl asked, 'Daddy, did they ever let him in?'

A few years ago, I had a dialogue with an atheist professor. He spent a good deal of time mocking both Christ and my experience of him. In front of me was a fruit bowl, and I ate a tangerine. After I had finished, I asked the professor, 'Was the tangerine sweet or sour?' He said, 'How can I know whether it was sweet or sour when I never tasted it?' And I replied, 'And how can you know anything about Christ if you have not tried him?'

God our Father is the maker of everything that exists. He is the author of the world of nature, and the creator of both space and time. Without God, there would be no past, present or future: no summer or winter, spring or autumn, seedtime or harvest. There would be no morning or evening, or months or years. Because God gives us the gift of time, we have the opportunity to think and to act; to plan and to pray; to give and to receive; to create and to relate; to work and to rest; to strive and to play; to love and to worship. Too often, we forget this, and we fail to appreciate God's generosity. We take time for granted and fail to thank God for it. We view it as a commodity and ruthlessly exploit it. We cram it too full, waste it, learn too little from the past, or mortgage it off in advance.

In doing so, we also refuse to give priority to those people and things which should have chief claim upon our time. We need God's help to view time as he sees it, and to use it more as he intends. It is crucial to try to distinguish between what is central and what is peripheral; between what is really pressing, and what can wait; between what is our responsibility and what can be left to others; and between what is appropriate now and what will be more relevant later.

We need God to help us guard against attempting too much because of our false senses of indispensability, ambition, rivalry, guilt and inferiority.

We also need God to help us not to mistake our responsibilities, underestimate ourselves, or overlook our weaknesses and to understand our proper limits. We need to realise that, important though this life is, it is not *all* that there is. So, we should view everything we do in the light of eternity, not just our limited horizons. It is a matter of true perspective.

God is not so much timeless, as time-full. He does not live above time so much as holds all times together. Despite its inadequacies, the film *Cast Away* is, above all, a timely reminder.

DISCUSSION STARTERS

Act: For five minutes at the start of this session, sit in silence together. You might even like to lie down, or make yourself comfortable. Practise the art of slowing down. Breathe deeply. Listen to the silence. (If a clock is ticking try to ignore it.) And try not to think of anything. (You'll probably be surprised at how long five minutes of silence seems.)

Personal reflection: At the end of five minutes (someone can keep an eye on the time), spend another few moments reflecting personally about the film. *Cast Away* has probably got you thinking. But how? Spend a short while quietly contemplating your own life, in the light of the film. What have you got to learn?

Discuss: How did the film make you think? Could you identify with Chuck Noland? Are you ruled by the clock? Do you enjoy living a breathless life? Do you feel more important, the busier you are? How did the film make you feel, and what did you think about its conclusions?

Act: Most of us complain about how little time we have. But perhaps there are ways of creating a little more space for ourselves within the busy schedules.

Stop to think of how you might free up some more time for yourself – even an hour a week is a start, if you use it wisely. Do you waste time watching too much TV? Do you work 'smartly' enough, so that you can leave work promptly at night?

Write down one idea on a post-it note and stick it to the wall, along with everyone else, so that you can see each other's ideas.

Discuss: What ideas do you have for 'slowing down' a little? (There's an organisation called the 'Slow Food

Movement' – www.slowfood.com – which advocates the opposite of the 'fast food' lifestyle. Cooking slowly, with local ingredients, and savouring meals together is symbolic of so much more in life.) What else might you try, positively, to reclaim your time, and relationships?

Read: Ps. 103:15–18.

Act: What's most important to you? What helps to sum you up? Stan tells Chuck they held a funeral for him. They put in his coffin a phone, beeper and Elvis CDs – which they had decided were the things that best represented his life. What best represents your life? Be honest! Draw on a plain sheet of paper a selection of no more than three items that might be placed in your coffin. Go round the group and tell each other what they are, and say whether you'd be pleased or not to find them in there.

Act: To finish with, hold a minute's silence in memory of your former self. In that time, think about how you can change, in order to be remembered more positively as someone who had time for God and other people – instead of just for work and 'busyness'.

6

The Value of a Single Life
Saving Private Ryan

MARK STIBBE

PARAMOUNT PICTURES, 1998

Directed by STEVEN SPIELBERG
Screenplay by ROBERT RODAT

TOM HANKS as *Captain Miller*
TOM SIZEMORE as *Sergeant Horvath*

CLASSIFICATION: 15

Erich Fromm once said, 'People are born equal but they are also born different.' In other words, every person is a unique individual, infinitely precious in the sight of God. In an age when the group was superseding the individual in terms of rights, Thomas Fuller said it this way: 'A whole bushel of wheat is made up of individual grains.'Community is critical to the future of humanity, yes, but not at the expense of individuality. Few if any have put it better than Mother Teresa: 'To us what matters is an individual ... I believe in person to person. Every person is Christ for me, and since there is only one Jesus, that person is the only person in the world for me at that moment.'

Leaving ninety-nine to search for one

Jesus taught and demonstrated the value of a single life. For him, every individual was of inestimable value. Every individual, however ordinary and sinful, was worth saving. As he said, 'the Son of Man' [referring to himself] 'came to seek and to save what was lost'.

To underline the point, Jesus told a story about a sheep that wandered off from its flock:

> 'What do you think? If a man owns a hundred sheep, and one of them wanders away, will he not leave the ninety-nine on the hills and go to look for the one that wandered off? And if he finds it, I tell you the truth, he is happier about that one sheep than about the ninety-nine that did not wander off. In the same way your Father in heaven is not willing that any of these little ones should be lost.'
>
> (Mt. 18:12–14, NIV)

A parable is really an earthly story illustrating a heavenly truth. Here the heavenly truth being illustrated is the value of a single life. Jesus tells of a shepherd who leaves ninety-nine sheep in order to find one sheep that has got lost. The shepherd leaves ninety-nine on the hills on their own, vulnerable and without protection, in order to find just one. He does not leave the ninety-nine safe in a sheepfold or a barn. He leaves them on the hills where robbers, wolves and bears had every chance of finding them. How foolish can you get!

J. John has a great way of making Bible truths very relevant and fresh. When he speaks on this passage, he explains it like this: imagine you have £500 in £5 notes. You have them all together and you hold them close to your chest. You are so happy with these bank notes you won't let them out of your sight. You take them to bed with you. You take them everywhere with you. You are extremely attached to them. One day, you go out for a long walk in the hills. You sit down for a rest on a bench and in an idle moment, you start counting them. Unfortunately, the wind gets up and one of the £5 notes blows away. You decide you can't bear to live without the one that's lost, so you leave all the other ninety-nine £5 notes on the bench and you wander off to find the one lost. At last, you find it and return to the other ninety-nine notes, reuniting them. You laugh and dance and shout for joy. This is not because you found the ninety-nine still on the bench where you left them, but because you found the one that had blown away!

Put like this, you can see the humour and the surprise in the parable. You can see the reckless love of our Father in heaven, who rejoices over just one lost person being found and rescued.

The value of the individual

Steven Spielberg is one of the most famous and successful film directors of all time. It has been said that the most beautiful words you can read on a film screen are, 'A film by Steven Spielberg'.

Spielberg has for a long time been interested in the value of a single life. Think of his movie about the Holocaust, *Schindler's List*. This film tells the true story of Oscar Schindler, a non-Jewish businessman who rescues many Jews from the Nazi concentration camps. At the end of the movie, some of his rescuers present Schindler with a gold ring. Inside the ring is inscribed in Hebrew, 'He who saves a single life saves the world entire.' Clearly, the value of a single life is a key theme in *Schindler's List*.

To prove the point, remember that the movie is filmed in black and white. Yet, from time to time, a young girl appears wearing a red coat. The coat itself is in colour while the rest of the picture is not. The reason for this recurring image is critical. This singling out of a solitary child through the use of colour brings into the foreground Spielberg's preoccupation with the value of a single life. It is the camera's way of saying, 'Look, she's important.'

Saving Private Ryan is another World War II movie that explores the same theme. This film earned Spielberg an Oscar for Best Director, and was also awarded four other Academy Awards. It is commonly regarded as the most graphic war film ever made.

The film tells the story of Captain John Miller, who is sent on a mission after the D-Day landings in June 1944. Having successfully landed on Omaha beach, Miller is sent with a small squad of soldiers to locate a Private James Ryan. Ryan's three other brothers have been killed in action and so it is decided that James Ryan must be rescued. It is simply inconceivable that a mother should lose all four sons. So Miller takes his squad on a journey of suffering, all in search of just one solitary life. Not a general, not a spy, or a politician – just a private!

Here again, we see Spielberg's fascination with the idea of the value of the individual. In the great chaos of war, where human beings fight each other en masse, where names are often forgotten, where individuality becomes increasingly irrelevant, Spielberg chooses to remind us that every person counts. Each gravestone, each cross, each memorial has marked on it an individual's name, representing a unique life history with unrepeatable memories. Every 'dog tag' is a symbol of a life, a soul, a person that will never again visit the stage of human history. This means that individuals count. They are worth rescuing. Or, to use the favoured metaphor of the film title, they are worth 'saving'. As the words on the theatrical trailer read, 'In the last great invasion of the last Great War, the greatest danger facing eight men was saving ... *one.*'

Clip 1: The decision to save one man

After a harrowing re-enactment of the Omaha landings, the scene switches to the War Department back in the United States. The authorities discover that three Ryan brothers have been killed and so they speak to their commanding officer, General Marshall.

GENERAL MARSHALL. Ah, damn it.

COLONEL 1. All four of them were in the same company in the 29th Division but we split them up after the Sullivan brothers died on the *Juno*.

GENERAL MARSHALL. Any contact with the fourth son, James?

COLONEL 1. No, sir. He was dropped about 15 miles inland near Neuville. But that's still deep behind enemy lines.

COLONEL 2. There's no way you can know where in the hell he was dropped. General, first reports are that the 101st is scattered all to hell and gone. There are mis-drops all over Normandy. Now assuming that Private Ryan even survived the jump, he could be anywhere. In fact, he's probably KIA [killed in action]. And frankly, sir, we go sending some sort of rescue mission, flat-heading throughout swarms of German reinforcements all along our axis of advance, they're going to be KIA, too.

GENERAL MARSHALL [*pauses, walks to his desk, picks out an old book, and extracts a letter from it*]. I have a letter here, written a long time ago to a Mrs Bixby in Boston. So bear with me.

[reads]

'Dear Madam,

I have been shown in the files of the War Department by the Adjutant General of Massachusetts that you are the mother of five sons who have died gloriously on the field of battle.

I feel how weak and fruitless must be any words of mine that would attempt to beguile you from the grief of a loss so overwhelming. But I cannot refrain from tendering to you the consolation that maybe found in the thanks of the republic they died to save.

I pray that our Heavenly Father may assuage the anguish of your bereavement and leave you only the cherished memories of the loved and lost, the solemn pride that must be yours to have made so costly a sacrifice upon the altar of freedom.

Yours very sincerely and respectfully

Abraham Lincoln'

[pauses]

If the boy's alive, we are going to send somebody to find him. And we are going to get him the hell out of there.

It is with this scene that the plan to rescue Ryan is put into action. Everything depends upon the audience being persuaded, not only by the moving pictures of mother Ryan's obvious shock (played out just before this scene), but also General Marshall's trump card of the Lincoln letter. In a sense, the comments made by the second Colonel are apposite. It is a foolhardy and irrational idea to rescue Private James Ryan. The rescuers would stand little chance, and in any case, Ryan might well be dead already. The mission is set up here as fraught with problems. Yet, the ageing General Marshall takes a fatherly and compassionate perspective. Ryan is in a hell of a predicament (notice how the word 'hell' permeates the dialogue above) and he *must* be saved. Marshall does not want Mrs Ryan to lose *all* her sons. So he reads the letter written by Abraham Lincoln and the camera then zooms round the three other US officers, showing their obvious tacit agreement to the mission. Then he concludes with something of a rousing call to arms, 'We're going to get him the *hell* [this word is given emphasis] out of there.'

The headquarters of heaven

The Bible tells a story of salvation, too. The name Jesus (Yeshua in the original language) literally means 'salvation'. God sent Jesus into the world to save us from our sins and to rescue us from the *hell* of a godless eternity. As the Gospel of John puts it, 'For God so loved the world that he gave his only Son, so that everyone who believes in him will not perish but have eternal life' (Jn. 3:16, NLT). The initiative for sending Jesus into the world to be our Saviour was God's. Our Heavenly Father made the decision. In the headquarters of heaven, God the Father came up with the rescue plan that brought us life.

A vicar was about to start his sermon during an evening service when he briefly introduced a visiting minister in the congregation. He said that the visitor was one of his dearest childhood friends and, accordingly, asked him to say a few words. With that, the elderly man walked to the pulpit and told a story:

> 'A father, his son and a friend of his son were sailing off the Pacific coast when a fierce storm hit them and the three were swept into the sea as the boat capsized. Grabbing a rescue line, the father had to make the most painful decision of his life. Who was he to throw the lifeline to? The father knew his own son was a Christian and that the son's friend was not. The father yelled, 'I love you,' to his boy and threw the line to the boy's friend, pulling him to safety, while his son disappeared for ever beneath the waves. The father knew his son would

step into eternity with Jesus, but couldn't bear the thought of the friend stepping into an eternity without Jesus. Therefore, he sacrificed his son to save the son's friend.'

Concluding, the visitor said, 'How great is God's love for us that he gave his only Son that we should be rescued. So take hold of the lifeline that the Father is throwing you in this service tonight.'

With that, the old man finished and the vicar took his place in the pulpit, and preached his message.

At the end of the meeting, some teenagers came up to the visitor. They had been looking very sceptical throughout the old man's story and had not responded to the appeal. 'That wasn't a very realistic story,' they said mockingly. 'No dad would do that.'

'You've got a point,' said the visitor. 'But I'm standing here tonight to tell you that this story gives me personally a great glimpse into the Father's love for us. You see, I was that father, and your vicar here is my son's friend.'

The film *Saving Private Ryan* offers us a striking parable of the biblical drama of salvation. The avuncular and compassionate figure of General Marshall is like God the Father – beyond the battlefield, and yet deeply moved by the suffering of the people in his care. His role reminds us that God devised a rescue plan for us, too. Our Heavenly Father could not live with the agony of seeing us torn apart by sin and death. So he asked his one and only Son to come as our Saviour. Not crossing an ocean and landing on a beach in France, but crossing from heaven to earth and touching down in Bethlehem. This was the Father's plan – to send his Son to invade enemy occupied territory. To fight against the evil one and to rescue us from sin with the gospel of love. This is what God is really like. He is a Father whose heart bleeds with compassionate love for his children. He is the perfect Father who loves with deeds not just with words.

The saviour of Private Ryan

In *Saving Private Ryan,* it is General Marshall who has the plan, but it is Captain Miller, acted by Tom Hanks, who fulfils the mission. He chooses a team of eight men to find Private James Ryan. Hanks' portrayal of Captain Miller is nothing short of a masterpiece of acting. He manages to convey with commanding realism the way in which war throws ordinary people into extraordinary contexts, evoking extraordinary character traits. Hanks – now considered Hollywood's leading male actor – communicates in the most poignant way the role of the reluctant hero. It is hard to imagine anyone not being drawn into empathising with this married schoolteacher who becomes a brilliant, yet broken, leader of men.

When one of his rescue squad, Caparzo, has been killed by a sniper, Miller starts to reminisce with his sergeant about Caparzo and about another soldier called Veccio, lost in a previous mission. The scene takes place in a church where the squad is billeted for the night. Captain Miller is 'confessing' to his sergeant the agony he feels over losing just one man. In the process of his confession, Miller offers his own rationale for the death of his soldiers and considers whether Private Ryan is worth the mission.

Clip 2: Confession in church

CAPTAIN MILLER. Veccio, yeah. Caparzo. You see, when you end up killing one of your men, you tell yourself it happened so you could save the lives of two or three or ten others. Maybe a hundred others. But you know how many men I've lost under my command?

SERGEANT HORVATH. How many?

CAPTAIN MILLER. Ninety-four. But that means I've saved the lives of ten times that many. Doesn't it? Maybe even twenty. Right? Twenty times as many? And that's how simple it is. That's how you ... how you rationalise making the choice between the mission and the man.

SERGEANT HORVATH. Except that this time the mission is a man.

CAPTAIN MILLER. This Ryan'd better be worth it. He'd better go home, cure some disease, or invent the longer lasting light bulb, or something. The truth is I wouldn't trade ten Ryans for one Veccio or one Carpazo.

SERGEANT HORVATH. Amen.

In this scene, Miller gives voice to Spielberg's overriding theme, the value of a single life. For Miller, it is important to remember the names and the idiosyncrasies of each of his men. The death of an individual soldier is a heartfelt event for Miller. It calls for an explanation. So, Miller reasons that one man dies to save others from dying – even up to as many as twenty others. The problem with the mission Miller is engaged in is that Ryan is not regarded in the same light. Ryan is an unknown quantity. 'He'd better be worth it,' Miller states. 'He'd better go home, cure some disease, or invent the longer lasting light bulb, or something. The truth is I wouldn't trade ten Ryans for one Veccio or one Carpazo.'

Jesus' parable of the lost sheep illustrates beyond doubt that he considers individuals as uniquely precious and infinitely worth saving. The shepherd left ninety-nine sheep to rescue just one. Even though we were sinners in rebellion against God, wandering like sheep, Jesus pursued us out of love. We may be ordinary people like

Private James Ryan, but Jesus Christ still came to rescue us, and he came willingly (not reluctantly) unlike Miller. He came for us as individuals.

Clip 3: The supreme sacrifice

In the end, Miller makes the supreme sacrifice for Ryan, as do most of his squad. The final scenes of the film are fraught with emotion. Miller has located Ryan behind enemy lines but Ryan has chosen to stay with his own men to defend a bridge. Miller and the remains of his squad stay with Ryan and together they hold the bridge at great cost.

Miller sits dying on the bridge, shot by a German soldier whom he had, ironically, set free earlier in the film when others had wanted to execute him. Miller says something under his breath and Ryan leans over to hear.

'James, earn this. Earn it.' These are Miller's last words.

The camera eventually focuses on the young Ryan's face as he stands over the body of his saviour. The voice of General Marshall is heard again reading the words of Abraham Lincoln's letter, quoted at the start of the film (the end returning to the beginning, as it were). Then the face of the young Ryan turns into the face of the elderly Ryan, 50 years later, standing at a cross with Captain John Miller's name on it in a war cemetery. Ryan is wracked with grief and guilt. He kneels and speaks to his dead rescuer:

> 'My family is with me today. They wanted to come with me. To be honest with you, I wasn't sure how I would feel coming back here. Every day I think about what you said to me that day on the bridge. I've tried to live my life the best I could. I hope that was enough. I hope that at least in your eyes I've earned what all of you have done for me.'

Ryan stands and his wife joins him. Ryan turns to her and asks, 'Tell me I've led a good life … Tell me I'm a good man.'

The film ends with Ryan saluting. The camera lingers on the white cross that gives the briefest hint of the value of Miller's unique life.

JOHN H. MILLER
CAPT. 2 RANGERS BN
PENNSYLVANIA JUNE 13 1944

The final shot is of an American flag fluttering in the wind.

Salvation is a free gift

When I first saw this film in the cinema, I remember feeling uneasy as the dying Miller told Ryan to 'earn this'. As a Christian I believe without equivocation that our salvation is something freely given by God, not something earned through good works on our part. This is what the Apostle Paul wrote in his letter to the Ephesians:

> 'Once you were dead, doomed forever because of your many sins. You used to live just like the rest of the world, full of sin, obeying Satan, the mighty prince of the power of the air. He is the spirit at work in the hearts of those who refuse to obey God. All of us used to live that way, following the passions and desires of our evil nature. We were born with an evil nature, and we were under God's anger just like everyone else.'
>
> (Eph. 2:1–3, NLT)

This is the bad news. But the good news is that Jesus came into the world to save us. We could not save ourselves, so Jesus did it for us on the cross. And so Paul goes on to say:

> 'God saved you by his special favour when you believed. And you can't take credit for this; it is a gift from God. Salvation is not a reward for the good things we have done, so none of us can boast about it.'
>
> (Eph. 2:8,9, NLT)

Here we see the great difference between *Saving Private Ryan* and the New Testament. In *Saving Private Ryan,* salvation has to be earned. Miller insists that Ryan must earn what he has done for him, thereby condemning Ryan to 50 years tormented by guilt. 'Have I been good enough?' Ryan asks. All this as the camera ironically focuses on the cross – symbol and reminder of God's grace and that God has freely given us the gift of salvation. We cannot earn this salvation by works. We can only receive it by faith.

Saving Private Ryan has many parallels with the Christian message. Both the movie and Christianity are about the death of sons. Both explore the theme of sacrifice. Yet in the final analysis, Spielberg's theology is one in which salvation has to be earned. In the New Testament, the opposite is true. When the crucified Jesus cries, 'It is finished,' he is declaring that everything necessary for our salvation has been achieved. Nothing else is required. The price has been paid. All I need to do is say, 'I admit my need of salvation, I believe that Jesus has done everything necessary for me to be rescued, I choose to receive the free gift of forgiveness won for me when Jesus died. I decide now to ask Jesus into my life to be my Saviour, Lord and very best friend. I choose to follow him for the rest of my days.'

DISCUSSION STARTERS

(You'll need an ink-pad and a large sheet of paper.)

Personal reflection: You may have had parents or grandparents who fought and even died in battle. You may know of others who did. At the start, take a few moments to reflect quietly on the sacrifice they made for us.

Act: You might even wish to speak out their names, to remind us that they were all, like us, individual human beings who are remembered today. And following this period of meditation, if any of you have any war stories to tell, from your grandparents or parents, take the time to tell them, in remembrance, so that their stories come to life again.

Discuss: How did the film leave you feeling? What effect did the 'realism' of the cinematography have upon the message of the film? How would you feel if you were ordered to take part in this particular mission – to save one man? Do you think it would be worth it? How tempted would you be to make sure he knows the price you paid?

Read: Mt. 18:12–14.

Discuss: How do you interpret this story in the light of the film? What does it show you about God that you might not have thought about before? (If you are familiar – or over-familiar – with the parable, try to see it through the eyes of a child, for the first time.)

Act: Think about snow falling, for a moment. Every flake is different – not one is the same. And yet the flakes together can create vast landscapes of beauty. Now think about yourself. Each one of us is unique. For a start, feel your pulse. And try to relax, so that your pulse slows a little. Thank God for the simplicity, yet the rich complexity, of our individual – and collective – human life.

Act: Now, each person should take the ink-pad in turn and make their thumbprint on the sheet of paper. When you've finished, you've created a symbol of the uniqueness of each individual, yet your connectedness within the group.

Alternatively, you might all like to create a page of thumbprints so that each of you can take one home to stick on your fridge as a reminder of your relationships throughout the week.

Read: Jn. 15:12–14. 'Greater love has no-one than this, that one lay down his life for his friends.'

Discuss: How do you think Private Ryan must have felt to be told by Miller to 'earn this' at the end of the film? *Can* you earn such a thing? Does *Saving Private Ryan* help you to understand something more about the story of Jesus who freely laid down his life? If so, how should we respond?

Pray: If it's appropriate, pray this short prayer to end: 'Dear God, thank you for going through hell and back to save me. I don't know what you really went through. And I'm aware that every day I don't live up to the price you paid for my life. But I want to try to make it worthwhile by loving you – and loving others – more deeply. Please help me this week to live a grateful, humble and passionate life for you. Amen.'

7

The Truth Shall Set You Free!

The Matrix

MARK STIBBE

WARNER BROS. STUDIOS, 1999

Directed by ANDY and LARRY WACHOWSKI
Screenplay by ANDY and LARRY WACHOWSKI

KEANU REEVES as *Neo*
LAURENCE FISHBURNE as *Morpheus*
CARRIE-ANNE MOSS as *Trinity*

CLASSIFICATION: 15

The Matrix is one of the most exciting as well as thought-provoking science fiction pictures ever made. There are few films more stylish, insightful and groundbreaking in terms of special effects (e.g. the invention of 'bullet time'). Written and directed by the Wachowski brothers, produced by Joel Silver, and starring Keanu Reeves, *The Matrix* quite simply redefines the word 'cool'.

The Matrix is the story of Neo Anderson, who discovers that the world he lives in is, in reality, a computer-generated world designed to deceive and enslave humanity. Only a few know the truth: a man called Morpheus and a woman called Trinity, plus their small band of rebels. Their spaceship, the *Nebuchadnezzar*, travels from the one remaining city on earth that has not been enslaved – a city called Zion, near the earth's core. They search for the chosen one who will rescue humanity from their slavery and they find Anderson, believing that he's the one.

If ever there was a film that invited a spiritual interpretation, it's this one. In fact, you could approach it from the viewpoint of a number of faiths. You could examine it from a Buddhist perspective (the world as illusion). You could study it from a Jewish perspective (Neo as a liberator like Moses, a deliverer of people from bondage). There are many different ways you can look at this film, but perhaps the most obvious is a Christian one. The name of the spaceship, the *Nebuchadnezzar*, is the name of an Old Testament Babylonian king. The name of the city, Zion, is one that you can find in both the Old and the New Testaments of the Bible. The name 'Trinity' is overtly Christian: it is the technical term describing the Christian's unique understanding of God as three in one.

Then of course, there is Neo himself. There are very strong parallels between Neo and the Messiah of the Bible. Neo means 'new' in Greek. 'Ander' means 'man', so 'Anderson' could be transliterated as 'son of man', making 'Neo Anderson' 'new son of man'. When you consider that 'Son of Man' was Jesus' preferred way of describing himself in the Gospels, this is obviously significant. Neo Anderson, who dies and is resurrected in the movie, is an obvious Christ figure in modern cinema.

As in the Gospels, the central theme of the film really comprises bad news and good news. The bad news is the truth that we are slaves and that we don't realise it. The good news is that freedom has been made possible through sacrifice. This is the central theme of *The Matrix* and it's the central theme of the New Testament. The New Testament story tells of a world enslaved by the devil, with every human being unwittingly born into slavery to sin. But Jesus came in to this enslaved world to awaken us to our true situation. He came to die a sacrificial death in order that we might be set free from sin.

As Jesus said to those who would follow him: 'you will know the truth, and the truth will set you free' (John 8:32, NIV).

How much do you know?

The Matrix is a great parable of our spiritual condition, as described in the Bible. This film encourages us to look very carefully at ourselves and to ask three basic questions about our lives. First: how much do we know? Second: what is the truth? Third: how can we be set free? In what follows, let's look at how the Bible answers these questions, and how *The Matrix* answers them, too.

So, first of all, how much do you really know? Dee Hock, the visionary leader of VISA, said this:

> 'The problem is never how to get new, imaginative thoughts into your mind, but how to get the old ones out. Every mind is a room packed with archaic furniture. You must get the old furniture of what you know, think and believe, out before anything new can get in. Make an empty space in any corner of your mind and creativity will instantly fill it.'

The clear message of the Bible is this: our minds are basically full of darkness. Until we have experienced the illumination of God's Spirit, we are portrayed in the New Testament as ignorant, blind and asleep. Our thinking is described as futile and our understanding as darkened. We do not live God-centred, but self-centred lives. Consequently, our minds are full of confusion and deception, not clarity and truth. As the Apostle Paul put it, 'The god of this age has blinded the minds of unbelievers, so that they cannot see the light of the gospel of the glory of Christ, who is the image of God' (2 Cor. 4:4, NIV).

You couldn't get a clearer or more damning diagnosis than that. We are not enlightened, according to the Bible. We may be knowledgeable scientifically, but we are not knowledgeable spiritually. We are slaves to sin, and our minds are therefore asleep. The only answer according to the Bible is to choose to turn from an old way of thinking to a new way of thinking, to empty our minds of the old furniture of what we know, and to make space for the light of God's truth. The Bible calls this repentance: making a U-turn from a sinful to a godly life. This kind of repentance is a human choice. It is the most vital decision we make.

Clip 1: Making the right choice

About half an hour into the movie, Neo Anderson is beginning to realise that something is badly wrong with the world. He meets up with a woman called Trinity who takes him to see Morpheus. She takes him to a door and says, 'This is it. Let me give you one piece of advice. Be honest: he knows more than you can imagine.'

Neo enters and sits opposite Morpheus. The room is dark, the clothing is black, but the armchairs are red. 'You have the look of a man who accepts what he sees because he is expecting to wake up,' Morpheus says. Ironically, this is not far from the truth.

Morpheus continues to explain why Neo has come to see him. 'You are here because you know something. What you know you can't explain but you feel it. You've felt it your entire life, that there's something wrong with the world. You don't know what it is, but it's there, like a splinter in your mind.'

Morpheus challenges Neo, 'Do you know what I'm talking about?'

Neo answers correctly, 'The Matrix.'

Morpheus asks, 'Do you want to know what it is?'

Neo nods and Morpheus explains that the Matrix is all around them. It is the world of illusion that has been designed to blind people from the truth.

When Neo asks, 'What truth?', Morpheus replies, 'The truth that you are a slave, Neo. Like everyone else you were born into bondage ... into a prison for your mind.'

Morpheus concludes that no one can be told about the Matrix. They have to see it for themselves. He then offers Neo a last chance to make a decision.

Morpheus gives Neo a choice between a blue pill, which will enable Neo to forget the conversation and to wake up in his bed oblivious to everything, and a red pill, the path to seeing the truth. 'Remember,' he says, 'all I'm offering is the truth. Nothing more.'

As Neo takes the red pill, Morpheus says, 'Follow me.' Neo then begins his journey of enlightenment.

What a picture this is of our spiritual condition without God. We know deep down that this life is not all there is to human existence. We sense that there must be more. As Morpheus puts it, you can feel it when you go out to work, or go to church. You just know that there's more to know than you know. It's like an itch in your soul.

Benjamin Disraeli once said, 'To be conscious that you are ignorant is a great step to knowledge.'

Jesus said, 'you will know the truth'. So how much do you know?

What is the truth?

We are told in society today that there is no absolute truth. All truth is relative; it is subjective; you construct your own reality.

Recently, I was speaking to someone whose husband is receiving counselling. Their marriage is suffering and it's looking as though they are going to end up getting divorced. One reason why there is no reconciliation in this situation is because the counsellor is encouraging the husband to construct his own reality. He is being told, 'If that's what you perceive happened, then that's what happened.'

Personally, I think this is incredibly dangerous advice. It does not help people to face reality. It does not help people to change with any degree of depth and integrity. True transformation only comes when you see the truth, when you move from subjective perception to objective reality. It's only when you see things as they really are that you can be free.

Let me give you a personal example. Shortly after our birth, my twin sister and I were placed by our mother in an orphanage in Hackney, North London. For much of my life my perception of my birth mother has been, accordingly, very negative. This affected my relationship with my adoptive mother and my relationship with women generally.

However, I was watching a production in a theatre in London. A friend of mine, Brian Doerksen, wrote a musical called *The Father's House*, a theatrical parable about our relationship with God as our father. He had asked a few of his friends to see a preview and comment on it before it went on general release. I duly went, not expecting anything other than a time of constructively critiquing Brian's work.

However, there was a scene in this musical when a young mother was agonising about giving up her child for adoption. This single mother was weeping over the prospect. She wasn't doing it callously. To express her pain, she sang a poignant, heart-rending song. Suddenly, I found myself crying. All those years thinking that my birth mother had been uncaring melted away. I began to understand the pain that she, as a single mother, must have gone through. I began to see her from a more truthful perspective.

A few months later my adoptive mother sent me a letter that she had received from my birth mother after I had been adopted. The letter is the only thing I have from my biological mother and it expresses how she felt when she gave my sister and I up for adoption. There were a couple of lines in it which gave the clearest indication that she had agonised over the decision and found it very hard to let us go. She hadn't cruelly abandoned us, as I had assumed, but had given us up only as the last resort. As I reflected on this, I saw that my perception of reality and reality itself were two different things. I had perceived my mother to be heartless, and all my life I'd had this very negative impression of mothers. Now I saw things very differently. I saw the truth, and the truth set me free from years of bitterness and unforgiveness.

Clip 2: The desert of the real

Jesus said, 'you will know the truth, and the truth will set you free'. He was not talking about our perception of the truth, but the truth itself. It's only when you see things as they really are that you can be free.

This is in fact what Neo discovers in *The Matrix*. There is reality and there's your perception of reality. Neo takes the red pill and boards the *Nebuchadnezzar*. Morpheus introduces him to his crew.

Morpheus now shows Neo what the world really looks like, without the illusion created by the Matrix.

Morpheus shows Neo the world that he knows, the world of the late twentieth century – an urban landscape of skyscrapers and busy people. Morpheus explains that this is a computer simulation, a dream world.

He then shows Neo what the world truly looks like, not what is presented to Neo's senses by the Matrix. An American city lies devastated under a sea of ash. There is literally nothing left. Morpheus calls it 'the desert of the real'.

He then relates how all this came about. Mankind, in the early twenty-first century, was united in celebration, marvelling at the magnificent achievement of giving birth to AI (artificial intelligence). A singular consciousness spawned an entire race of machines. War broke out between the machines and humans. The machines won, and started to use the bio-electric energy of human bodies. Today, Morpheus continues, there are endless fields of human bodies (no longer born, but grown) being harvested for their energy. People live in pods, unconscious that their bodies are being abused in this way, living in a dream world, unaware that they are not free. 'The Matrix,' says Morpheus, 'is a computer-generated dream world built to keep us under control in order to change a human being into this.' Morpheus shows Neo a battery. Neo resists. Morpheus concludes, 'I didn't say it would be easy, Neo. I only said it would be the truth.'

What is the truth?

According to the Bible, in the beginning God created the heavens and the earth. Human beings lived in perfect harmony with God and each other. Then the devil entered the garden, tempted Adam and Eve to disobey God, and since that day, the cosmos has been under the dominion of evil. Human beings have not been free. Rather, they have become slaves to sin. We live in denial about this. We choose to live in a dream world of consumerism. But this never satisfies the deep longings of the soul. We long for the truth. We long for liberation. The cry of freedom rises up from within our hearts.

Clip 3: Death and resurrection

Back to *The Matrix*. Morpheus and his crew have been searching for the one who will set them free from the tyranny of the Matrix. They believe Neo is the person who will do this. Neo is the Messiah figure in *The Matrix*.

How then does freedom come to the slaves of the Matrix?

Two hours into the film, Neo is trying to exit the Matrix and return to his real body on board the *Nebuchadnezzar*. He is running towards a ringing telephone – the means by which he and his crew re-enter the ship. But three Matrix agents are on to him and what's worse, the *Nebuchadnezzar* is under attack, too.

Neo finds his way to the ringing phone only to find Agent Smith waiting there. The agent points his pistol at Neo's chest and fires. Neo falls to the ground. The agent empties his cartridge into Neo's body as the phone continues to ring. Back on board the ship, Morpheus and Trinity are dumbstruck as Neo's vital signs register his death. 'It can't be,' Morpheus declares.

Back at Neo's corpse the agents realise, he's gone. Agent Smith bids him farewell. Then we are back on board the ship again. Trinity is leaning over Neo's body. She tells him that she loves him and kisses him on the lips. 'You can't be dead, because I love you. You hear me? I love you.'

In a neat reversal of *Sleeping Beauty,* Neo awakens as he is kissed. Back in the Matrix, he stands up. The agents fire at him, but Neo manages to freeze the bullets in mid flight and they fall to the ground. As the music builds to a crescendo, Morpheus says, 'He is the one.'

Agent Smith charges at Neo, but he is no match for the reborn Neo and he is killed, light pouring out of his body after Neo has dived through him. The other agents run in terror. Neo returns to the *Nebuchadnezzar*. The attack lifts and he embraces Trinity once again.

The film ends with 'system failure' registered on the central computer program of the Matrix.

The offer of freedom

In *The Matrix,* freedom becomes a possibility through the death and resurrection of Neo Anderson. But *The Matrix* is fiction, not fact. What happened to Jesus of Nazareth is fact, not fiction. Jesus died on a cross outside the walls of Jerusalem in about AD 30. He himself said that he was the 'Son of Man' and that he was going to give his life 'as a ransom for many'. The blood that he shed at Calvary was the price paid that we might be redeemed, set free from our slavery to sin.

However, the events of Good Friday were not the end of the story. On the following Sunday, in the early hours of the morning, God raised Jesus from death. The resurrection of Jesus is the most critical moment in human history. Hundreds of people met the resurrected Jesus in the 50 days between his resurrection and his return to his Father beyond space-time. Jesus had conquered the powers of darkness through his sacrificial death and his supernatural resurrection. Through these momentous events, the devil's hold over the earth has been destroyed. Human beings can be freed from sin to know God and live life in all its fullness – we can experience the kiss of the Trinity.

The saddest scene in the movie involves a man called Cypher, the Judas figure in the film. He is the one who betrays Morpheus and his band. During the scene in question, Cypher re-enters the Matrix (without his friends' knowledge) and has a meal with Agent Smith. Cypher is eating steak and drinking red wine. He knows they are not real, but he would rather live as a slave than as a free person. As he puts it, 'After 9 years, you know what I realise? Ignorance is bliss.' So, he asks that once he has betrayed his friends he would be re-introduced to the Matrix as a wealthy person so that he can live in a dream world rather than the real world. 'I want to remember nothing,' he says.

If you want it, the truth will set you free – it's your decision. As someone has said, 'You are free to choose, but the choices you make today will determine what you will have, be, and do in the tomorrows of your life.'

I feel a little like Morpheus (though not as well dressed!). I am holding out a red pill and a blue pill. It's your choice. As Morpheus says to Neo, 'I can only show you the door. *You* have to walk through it ...'

DISCUSSION STARTERS

(You'll need red and blue sweets – Smarties or M&Ms.)

Personal reflection: *The Matrix* is a contemporary parable with deeply spiritual and Christian overtones. But what did it make you think about the world in which you live? Could you identify with its themes? What, for you, was the most important message of the film?

Read: Jn. 8:32.

Discuss: How much *do* we know? And how might we think again about the world around us? The brands we buy, the adverts we see, the way things are ... How are we *not* free? What can we do to un-learn the way of the world, and to make room for something different?

Act: Blindfold one member of the group and ask them to try to identify three of four other people by touching their faces.

We get so used to the way we see the world, but when we are forced to 'look' differently at it, things can change. Ask the blindfolded person how their blindness might change the way they 'see' other people – their perceptions of beauty, for example, or age ...

Discuss: Talk about this together. How do we 'see' the world? As Christians? Consumers? Capitalists? Men? Women? In terms of race, or class, or background? And can we learn to see things more through the eyes of Christ?

Read: Jn. 18:36–38.

Discuss: What is 'truth'? Is it a set of written propositions about the world? Or is it more than this? How come Pilate couldn't see the 'truth' when it was staring him in the face? What difference would it make if the 'truth' we believed in was more about a relationship with someone, than ticking the boxes of all the right things to believe?

Act: You should each take a red and blue sweet from the bowl. The blue one means you can keep on going as before – as Cypher said, 'Ignorance is bliss.' Or, you can take the red one – meaning that you will go after the truth and have to face the consequences in your own life. As you take one of the sweets, symbolically, say a quiet prayer to the God who said he was 'the way, the truth and the life'.

Prayer: If it's appropriate, pray a short prayer: 'Dear God, we're glad that things aren't always what they seem. Please help us to see the world – and each other – through your eyes. Help us not to judge by the world's standards, but by yours. And help us to fight with courage for the kingdom that is to come. Amen.'

8

Overcoming the Darkness

The Lord of the Rings: The Fellowship of the Ring

MARK STIBBE

NEW LINE CINEMA/WINGNUT FILMS, 2001

Directed by PETER JACKSON
Novel by J.R.R. TOLKIEN
Screenplay by FRANCES WALSH, PHILIPPA BOYENS and PETER JACKSON

ELIJAH WOOD as *Frodo*
IAN McKELLEN as *Gandalf*
CATE BLANCHETT as *Galadriel*
JOHN RHYS DAVIES as *Gimli*
SEAN ASTIN as *Sam*
ORLANDO BLOOM as *Legolas*
HUGO WEAVING as *Elrond*
SEAN BEAN as *Boromir*
IAN HOLM as *Bilbo*

CLASSIFICATION: PG

Someone once said that you can't tell a book by its movie. That is generally true, except in the case of Peter Jackson's film version of J.R.R. Tolkien's *The Lord of the Rings: The*

Fellowship of the Ring. For those of us who were brought up on Tolkien's epic tale of the hobbit Frodo, Jackson's film does not in any way disappoint. It is simply a five star rendition of the most popular book written in the twentieth century. Sitting in the cinema with my family watching the awe-inspiring landscapes of New Zealand, the valiant and heroic goodness of the little people of the Shire, the spectacular special effects and the great acting from an all-star cast, was – to be honest – one of life's great moments. This film has inspired my children to read like no other film has, and it has also generated a great deal of healthy debate about the reality of the spiritual war going on in our world between good and evil, light and darkness.

And that really is the great theme of *The Lord of the Rings*, which is why I have given this chapter the title, 'Overcoming the darkness'. For those of you who are not familiar with it, the story of Tolkien's trilogy goes something like this.

The Lord of the Rings describes in amazing depth and detail a mythical world known as Middle Earth. This is a pagan world that has not yet been enlightened by the good news about Jesus. So even though Tolkien himself was a committed Christian, *The Lord of the Rings* is not a Christian allegory like, say, C.S. Lewis' *The Lion, the Witch and the Wardrobe*. There are echoes of the Bible in *The Lord of the Rings*, but the story itself depicts a world before Christ.

Around 3,000 years before the story proper begins, a ring with supernatural power was fashioned by the dark lord Sauron. Using this ring, Sauron sought to rule the whole of Middle Earth but he was defeated in battle and the ring was captured by Isildor. Instead of throwing the ring back into the fires of Mount Doom in Mordor (the only place where it could be destroyed), Isildor kept the ring for himself. He was then killed and the ring was lost for many centuries, until, that is, it was discovered by a hobbit known as Bilbo Baggins.

Bilbo keeps the ring secretly and through its power his life is prolonged. However, the spirit of the dark lord Sauron has started to stir again. Sauron knows that the ring has been found and seeks to be reunited with it so that his domination of Middle Earth will be complete. Bilbo knows that he must give up the ring and it therefore passes to a hobbit called Frodo Baggins, played superbly in the movie by Elijah Wood. The first book, *The Fellowship of the Ring*, is about Frodo's acceptance of the challenge to face the darkness spreading like a cloud over Middle Earth. His quest is to take the ring back to the very heart of Sauron's kingdom, to Mount Doom, where the fires of Mordor still burn. There he will be called upon to throw the ring into the flames so that Sauron's plans will be ended and peace restored to Middle Earth.

Clip 1: I cannot do this alone

This brings me to the first clip from the movie that I find so powerful. The story has been unfolding for a while and Frodo is now well aware of his great responsibility. He is speaking with Galadriel, the Queen of Lorien (played by Cate Blanchett). Frodo has been struggling to stay on the side of the light. He knows that he must not give in to the darkness but Sauron's seductive power is so strong and the temptation to misuse the ring is great, too. As he speaks with Galadriel he opens his heart.

FRODO. I cannot do this alone.

GALADRIEL. You are a ring-bearer, Frodo. To bear a ring of power is to be alone. This task was appointed to you and if you do not find a way, no-one will.

FRODO. Then I know what I must do. It's just I'm afraid to do it.

GALADRIEL [*Galadriel bends down towards Frodo*]. Even the smallest person can change the course of the future.

[Scene skips to the evil army of Lord Sauron preparing to advance, and then to Frodo and the fellowship leaving Lorien by boat. Galadriel, dressed in white, is standing on the riverbank bathed in light. She raises her hand to bless Frodo and the fellowship]

GALADRIEL. Farewell Frodo Baggins. I give you the light of Eärendil, our most beloved star. May it be a light for you in dark places when all other lights go out.

Choosing the light

This is one of the most powerful scenes in the movie for me. I remember sitting next to my four children in the cinema – Philip, Hannah, Johnathan and Sam. At the time they were all under 13 years of age. When Galadriel stooped towards Frodo and said, 'Even the smallest person can change the course of the future', I looked at my children. Even little people can make a big difference. I found it intensely moving.

But for little people to make a big difference in an evil world – a world where the forces of darkness are plainly at work and indeed increasing in power – those little people have to choose the light. They have to make a decision to stand against the darkness and to stand for the light.

According to the Bible we are all of us presented with this choice during our lifetime here on the earth. The Bible says that God is light, and that Jesus Christ his one and only son is the Light of the World. To the little ones (as Jesus calls his followers), the Bible gives a vision of being 'lights to the world'. This is the destiny of all those who follow the Lord Jesus Christ: to be a people who change the course of the future from death to life by being God's light bearers.

To fulfil that destiny we must make a choice. In a letter in the New Testament, John the Apostle declares, 'This is the message he has given us to announce to you: God is light and there is no darkness in him at all' (1 Jn. 1:5, NLT). To become a people that overcome the darkness we must, like Frodo, choose the light. Even though the temptation to give in to the alluring power of darkness may be very great, we must choose in this life to be children of the light. Even though the odds may be stacked against the light bearers of this world, the Bible declares about Jesus that 'The light shines through the darkness, and the darkness can never extinguish it' (Jn. 1:5, NLT). Indeed, the Bible as a whole reveals that the darkness will never overcome the light; that even though darkness may spread more and more over the earth, in the final analysis the light will conquer the darkness and the cosmos will be purified.

All the more important then to make right choices while we have time! We need to make a choice now. Our destiny flows out of our decision. Neutrality is impossible. As William James, the philosopher of religion once said, 'When you have to make a choice and don't make it, that in itself is a choice.' C.S. Lewis put it in these very challenging words:

> 'When the author walks onto the stage, the play is over. God is going to invade, all right; but what is the good of saying you are on His side then? ... It will be too late then to choose your side. That will not be the time for choosing; it will be the time when we discover which side we really have chosen, whether we realised it before or not. Now, today, this moment, is our chance to choose the right side.'

Resisting the darkness

Once we have made the choice to be a person of the light, the key from that moment on is to resist the temptation to go back to the darkness from which God has rescued us. Resisting temptation is of course difficult. Temptation would not be a problem if it did not have such a pull upon our hearts. In fact, most of us are very weak when it comes to temptation. We don't fall into temptation. We jump into it. Consider the following conversation.

'Son,' ordered a father, 'Don't swim in that canal.'

'OK, Dad,' he answered.

But he came home carrying a wet bathing suit that evening.

'Where have you been?' demanded the father.

'Swimming in the canal,' answered the boy.

'Didn't I tell you not to swim there?' asked the father.

'Yes, Sir,' answered the boy.

'Why did you?' he asked.

'Well, Dad,' he explained, 'I had my bathing suit with me and I couldn't resist the temptation.'

'Why did you take your bathing suit with you?' he questioned.

'So I'd be prepared to swim, in case I was tempted,' he replied.

Throughout the story of *The Fellowship of the Ring,* Frodo faces one temptation after another. Throughout his journey to Mount Doom, he is tempted to use the power of the ring but he resists its allure. In this respect, the hobbits are stronger than human beings.

In the next clip, Gandalf is talking to Elrond, Lord of the Elves. The scene is in Rivendell and Elrond is bemoaning the way in which this present darkness has come upon Middle Earth. If only human beings had resisted temptation in the beginning.

Clip 2: No strength in the world of men

ELROND. Gandalf! The ring cannot stay here. This peril belongs to all Middle Earth. They must decide now how to end it. The time of the Elves is over; my people are leaving these shores. Who will you look to when we are gone? The Dwarfs? They hide in the mountains seeking riches; they care nothing for the troubles of others.

GANDALF. It is in men that we must place our hope.

ELROND. Men! Men are weak. The race of men is failing, the blood of Numenor is all but spent, its pride and dignity forgotten. It is because of men the ring survives. I was there, Gandalf, I was there 3,000 years ago when Isildor took the ring. I was there the day the strength of men failed. I led Isildor into the heart of Mount Doom, where the ring was forged – the one place it could be destroyed.

[Flashback to Mount Doom where Elrond is speaking to Isildor, who holds the ring]

ELROND. Cast it in to the fire! Destroy it!

ISILDOR. No!

ELROND. 'Isildor!'

[Back to Gandalf and Elrond in the present]

ELROND. It should have ended that day, but evil was allowed to endure. Isildor kept the ring, the line of kings is broken. There is no strength left in the world of men.

If the darkness is to be overcome in our world, we must choose to stay in the light. This means being strong in the face of temptation. As we read in 1 Jn. 2:

> 'Stop loving this evil world and all that it offers you, for when you love the world, you show that you do not have the love of the Father in you. For the world offers only the lust for physical pleasure, the lust for everything we see, and pride in our possessions. These are not from the Father. They are from this evil world.'
>
> (1 Jn. 2:15,16, NLT)

Those who follow Jesus Christ are called to resist the lust for pleasure, the lust for power and the lust for possessions. The ring in Tolkien's trilogy represents all these things – 'one ring to rule them all and one ring to bind them'. The darkness has a great power to entice and then to entrap people. Isildor refused to resist the enticing power of the ring and was entrapped by it. This is always the final destination of a consistent failure to resist temptation. What looks so alluring has the power eventually not only to bind people but to destroy them.

In the Australian bush country grows a little plant called the 'sundew'. It has a slender stem and tiny, round leaves fringed with hairs that glisten with bright drops of liquid as delicate as fine dew. Woe to the insect, however, that dares to dance on it. Although its attractive clusters of red, white and pink blossoms are harmless, the leaves are deadly. The shiny moisture on each leaf is sticky and will imprison any bug that touches it. As an insect struggles to free itself, the vibration causes the leaves to close tightly around it. This innocent-looking plant then feeds on its victim.

Working with others

Overcoming the darkness depends not only on choosing the light. It also depends upon resisting the darkness.

Beyond that it depends upon pulling together with others. It depends in other words on working in community not in isolation.

I wonder if you've ever watched wild geese in flight? It is fascinating to read what has been discovered about their flight pattern and their in-flight habits. Four come to mind.

Those in front rotate their leadership. When one lead goose gets tired, it changes places with one in the wing of the V-formation and another flies point.

By flying as they do, the members of the flock create an upward air current for one another. Each flap of the wings literally creates an uplift for the bird immediately following. One author states that by flying in a V-formation, the whole flock gets 71 per cent greater flying range than if each goose flew on its own.

When one goose gets sick or wounded, two fall out of formation with it and follow it down to help and protect it. They stay with the struggler until it's able to fly again.

The geese in the rear of the formation are the ones who do the honking; it's their way of announcing that they're following and that all is well.

One lesson stands out above all others: it is the natural instinct of geese to work together. Whether it's rotating, flapping, helping, or simply honking, the flock is in it together ... which enables them to accomplish what they set out to do.

The Lord of the Rings is a great celebration of the power of friendship and camaraderie. Frodo Baggins does not take the quest on by himself, though ultimately it is his own individual destiny to be the bearer of the ring. Around him eight others form into what is called the Fellowship of the Ring. These nine together pledge to work as one to defeat the dark lord Sauron's powers and to restore peace to the whole of Middle Earth.

Clip 3: Establishing the fellowship

One of the finest scenes in the movie is when the fellowship is formed at Rivendell. As the visitors to Rivendell start arguing about who can possibly take the ring to Mount Doom, Frodo rises to the challenge:

FRODO. I'll take it, I will take it. I will take the ring to Mordor, though I do not know the way.

GANDALF [*smiling affectionately at the hobbit*]. I will help you bear this burden Frodo Baggins, as long as it is yours to bear.

ARAGORN. If by my life or death I can protect you I will. *[Aragorn walks over to Frodo]* You have my sword.

LEGOLAS. And you have my bow.

[Legolas walks over to join Frodo]

GIMLI. And my axe.

[Gimli walks over to Frodo and the others]

BOROMIR. You carry the fate of us all little one. If this is indeed the will of the council then Gondor will see it done.

[From behind a bush Sam appears and rushes to stand beside Frodo]

SAM. Mr Frodo's not going anywhere without me.

ELROND. No, indeed it is hardly possible to separate you even when he is summoned to a secret council and you are not.

[Merry and Pippin appear from behind a column]

MERRY. Wait, we are coming too.

[They run to join Frodo]

MERRY. You'll have to send us home tied up in a sack to stop us.

PIPPIN. Anyway you need people of intelligence on this sort of mission, quest, thing.

MERRY. Well that rules you out, Pip.

ELROND. Nine companions! So be it. You shall be the Fellowship of the Ring!

PIPPIN. Great! Where are we going?

What a wonderful picture of teamwork!

When Jesus Christ brought the light of God into this dark world, he chose just twelve people to accompany him. Through this team of twelve disciples, Jesus has caused the light of his kingdom to permeate throughout the entire world. In doing this, community has been the key. This is why the church is so vital. Together, in community, we can combine into a fellowship of the light. As long as we keep the darkness at bay, together we can enjoy a fellowship that makes us strong. As we read in 1 Jn. 1:7 (NLT): 'if we are living in the light of God's presence, just as Christ is, then we have fellowship with each other'.

So the lesson of *The Lord of the Rings* is first, choose the light; second, resist the darkness; third PULL TOGETHER! No one person has got it all together. But altogether we've got it.

The call to sacrifice

There is also a fourth and final lesson, and this must never be forgotten. Overcoming the darkness requires that we give our all. In other words, it requires sacrifice. The eradication of evil in the end usually boils down to a few making supreme sacrifices on behalf of the many. It involves vicarious suffering. This was true in World War II of the Royal Air Force, about whom Winston Churchill said, 'Never in the field of human conflict has so much been owed by so many to so few.' A few brave men and women held the forces of darkness at bay, and at huge cost.

In the final scene I want to mention from *The Lord of the Rings*, the fellowship is beginning to break up. Boromir has died trying to protect Merry and Pippin but they have been captured by the Uruk-Hai. Frodo now stands weeping, resolving to go ahead to Mount Doom without his friends.

Frodo is standing alone at the edge of the river about to leave the remaining companions in the fellowship. His closest friend, Sam, is running through the words calling out to him. Frodo is weeping and holding the ring in his open hand.

Clip 4: The power of friendship

FRODO [*says to himself*]. I wish the ring had never come to me. I wish none of this had happened.

GANDALF [*Frodo hears Gandalf's voice*]. So do all who live to see such times, but that is not for them to decide. All you have to decide is what you do with the time that is given to you.

[Frodo closes his hand over the ring and climbs in to a boat off the shore. We see Sam running through the trees to the river only to see Frodo rowing away]

SAM. Frodo! No! Frodo!

FRODO [*turns to his friend*]. No Sam.

[Sam begins to run into the water after Frodo]

FRODO. Go back Sam; I'm going to Mordor alone.

SAM. Of course you are, and I'm coming with you.

FRODO. You can't swim.

[Sam begins to struggle and you see him go under the water]

FRODO. Sam!

[The camera focuses on Sam drowning under the water. Just as it looks as if Sam is lost, Frodo's arm appears out of the light at the surface and grabs hold of Sam by the hand, pulling him out of the water into the boat]

SAM. I made a promise Mr. Frodo. 'Don't you leave him, Sam Wise-Gangey.' And I don't mean to, I don't mean to.

FRODO. Oh, Sam.

[Frodo and Sam hug]

FRODO. Come on then.

A magazine once offered a prize for the best definition of a friend. Among the thousands of answers received were the following:

> 'One who multiplies joys, divides grief, and whose honesty is inviolable'
>
> 'One who understands our silence'
>
> 'A volume of sympathy bound in cloth'
>
> 'A watch that beats true for all time and never runs down'.

The winning definition read:

> 'A friend is the one who comes in when the whole world has gone out.'

Sam is that kind of friend – one who comes in when the whole world has gone out. He is a friend who is prepared to give his all, even to lay down his life for the one that he loves. Jeremy Taylor put it this way: 'By friendship you mean the greatest love, the greatest usefulness, the most open communication, the noblest sufferings, the severest truth, the heartiest counsel, and the greatest union of minds of which brave men and women are capable.'

In 1 Jn. 3:16 (NLT), the apostle John – a true friend to Jesus, known as the 'beloved disciple' – speaks about the real meaning of love. He writes: 'We know what real love is because Christ gave up his life for us. And so we also ought to give up our lives for our Christian brothers and sisters.'

One of the abidingly attractive qualities of *The Lord of the Rings* is the extraordinarily Christ-like love of some of its noblest characters. In the scene above, Sam is prepared to lay down his life for his friend. Earlier in the film, at the Bridge of Kazuk Dum, Gandalf lays down his life for his friends. In that scene, Peter Jackson shows Gandalf falling backwards into the abyss, with his arms outstretched, in the perfect shape of a crucified man. This is in fact one of a number of places where the director gives an explicitly Christian resonance to scenes and dialogue that in Tolkien's original script are either barely visible or absent. Jackson has cleverly – and without ever being either crass or preachy – evoked some of the definitively Christian values of Tolkien's work. Nowhere is this more evident than in those scenes where sacrificial love is the dominant motif. Here, true love, manifested supremely in the Calvary event, is poignantly and often beautifully represented. As the apostle John says:

> 'God showed how much he loved us by sending his only Son into the world so that we might have eternal life through him. This is real love. It is not that we loved God, but that he loved us and sent his Son as a sacrifice to take away our sins.'
>
> (1 Jn. 4:9,10, NLT)

Overcoming the darkness

The movie version of *The Lord of the Rings: The Fellowship of the Ring* is a triumphant expression of what it means to overcome the darkness. The world in which we live is becoming increasingly beset by many evils. A dark cloud is spreading not only over the shires of Great Britain but over the whole globe. This cloud is made up of many things but behind it all lurks a sinister presence, a coordinating intelligence, a depraved and power-hungry personality, much like what we find in *The Lord of the Rings*. Who will combat this present darkness? Only those who choose the light, who resist the darkness, who pull together and who give their all.

Now of course the second of the three movies has hit the screens: *The Lord of the Rings: The Two Towers*. Who can have failed to spot the sinister connotations of the words 'the two towers'? Since the terrifying attack on the Twin Towers in Manhattan the world has grown less stable and secure. In the words of Tolkien (from *The Two Towers*), 'the world changes, and all that once was strong now proves unsure. How shall any tower withstand such numbers and such reckless hate?'

Tolkien's epic is truly a work for our times and for all times. It speaks to us powerfully and it stimulates hope that good will prevail after all. It is not a story like some that promotes an unhealthy interest in the occult. The quest of *The Lord of the Rings* is to get rid of occult power (represented by the ring) not to use it. *The Lord of the Rings* is composed by a Christian with a very real and very clear moral compass. It is truly a bright light in our dark days.

In the final analysis, however, Tolkien's other writings (particularly his classic essay on fairy stories) suggest to me that he would not be content with us saying that his work contains fragments of light. For Tolkien, the true light was Jesus Christ, and the great story to which all stories ultimately point – at least in some measure – is the story of the Gospels. This story is not fiction but fact and guides us towards a vision of the world where there can truly be a happy ending.

Jesus Christ once said, 'I am the light of the world.' To alter the words of Galadriel ever so slightly, 'May He be a light for you in dark places, when all other lights go out.'

DISCUSSION STARTERS

(You will need pens or pencils, paper and a waste paper bin.)

Personal reflection: Galadriel said to Frodo that, 'Even the smallest person can change the course of the future.' But do we really believe that? Don't we leave it up to the celebrities, the pastors, the worship leaders, the politicians ... The big people? What is our attitude to the people who don't usually get noticed, who seem weak in the eyes of this world? Have you stopped to think?

Read: Mt. 13:31,32.

Discuss: The kingdom of God can appear to be small, weak and vulnerable. What other biblical pictures or analogies can you think of relating to the idea that big is not, necessarily, always best?

Act: What about you? Do you ever use your size, shape or apparent lack of talent as an excuse not to do things? In your group, stick a blank piece of paper onto everyone's back. Then, invite everyone to stand up and write the things that they appreciate most about each different person on their back. Afterwards, spend some time reflecting (on your own, or silently, within the group) on what people have said about you.

Discuss: We often forget or politely ignore children. 'But Jesus called the children to him and said, "Let the little children come to me, and do not hinder them, for the kingdom of God belongs to such as these"' (Lk. 18:16, NIV). When was the last time you looked at something as if through the eyes of a child? What might you learn – or re-learn – about the nature of God's kingdom from a child's perspective?

Personal reflection: Mark writes: Those who follow Jesus Christ are called to resist the lust for pleasure, the lust for power and the lust for possessions. The ring in Tolkien's trilogy represents all these things – 'one ring to rule them all and one ring to bind them'.

Many things in life have symbolic value, as the ring does in the film and the book. For a few minutes try to think about what might best symbolise your weaker side – and your stronger side. It might be an object, or a picture, or anything 'symbolic'.

Act: Draw or model the symbols. Place a waste paper bin in the centre of the room, and ask people to drop their negative symbols into the bin. You might pray a short prayer at the end to ask God for greater strength. Then, for a few minutes, share with each other what you feel symbolises your strength. Exchange symbols with someone else, and take theirs home. Each time you see it, remember to pray that God will develop their strengths, and help them overcome their weaknesses.

Discuss: Why is the ring such a potent symbol within the book and the film? What is it, in particular, that is symbolic about a ring? If you are wearing a ring, there is often a story behind it. Share your stories together as a group. You might like to take your ring off and place it where everyone can see it as you tell them about it.

Pray: If it's appropriate, pray a short prayer to end: 'Lord, you are the author of the greatest story ever told. Thank you for the part you've given us to play in this amazing adventure of life. Help us to resist temptation and to encourage each other to keep our mission in mind – to defeat evil, and follow you. Amen.'

9

There Can be Miracles
The Green Mile

MARK STIBBE

CASTLE ROCK ENTERTAINMENT, 1999

Directed by FRANK DARABONT
Screenplay by FRANK DARABONT

TOM HANKS as *Paul Edgecomb*
DAVID MORSE as *Brutus 'Brutal' Howell*
MICHAEL CLARKE DUNCAN as *John Coffey*

CLASSIFICATION: 18

The Green Mile is one of those films that takes you by surprise. Hearing that it is based on a Stephen King novel, I suspected that it was going to be a gruesome horror film. Although there are several scenes that are horrific (especially one unnecessarily graphic botched execution), the overall tale is actually extremely moving and indeed spiritual. Like *The Shawshank Redemption* – a film likewise directed by Frank Darabont, likewise filmed in a prison, and likewise based on a Stephen King story – *The Green Mile* is a really stirring story of how human and indeed divine goodness can arise in even the most desperate and bleak circumstances. *The Green Mile* is a film I keep revisiting and a novel I keep rereading. It has become one of my top ten favourite movies.

So what's the story? *The Green Mile* refers to the green floor of death row in a 1930s Louisiana prison. It is both a stretch of floor leading to 'Old Sparky' (the electric chair) as well as a metaphor for the road that we must all take to our own deaths.

It is on this Green Mile that the action of most of the film takes place. The story revolves around a prison guard called Paul Edgecomb (played by Tom Hanks) who supervises the executions at the Cold Mountain Penitentiary during the years of the Great Depression. Even though Edgecomb does his job professionally, you also feel from his performance that it is something he does reluctantly. Maybe the Depression has forced him into this line of work. In any event, he performs his duties with humanity and compassion. Indeed, the power of this film lies not in great scenes of action but in the wonderfully realised relationships between Edgecomb and the prisoners on death row.

Onto death row comes an extraordinary prisoner, a giant of a black man called John Coffey (played by Michael Clarke Duncan). Coffey is a huge man with a childlike heart. He can barely spell. He is afraid of the dark. Yet he is a man who physically exudes great strength. Coffey is on the mile because he has been sentenced for the murder of two little girls. Later on in the film we learn that he is innocent of these charges. The immorality of racism and the questionable morality of capital punishment become major themes in the story as a result. But at the start of the film we don't know this and we are, like Edgecomb, drawn into the enigma of John Coffey.

Here is their first dialogue.

Clip 1: Scared of the dark

[The scene opens with Paul Edgecomb standing in front of John Coffey in a cell. Edgecomb's fellow prison warders are standing with him. Dean, 'Brutal' and Harry]

EDGECOMB [*referring to the handcuffs*]. If I let Harry take those off you, you going to be nice?

[Coffey nods his head in agreement]

[Harry steps forward and unlocks the handcuffs]

EDGECOMB. Your name is John Coffey?

COFFEY. Yes sir, boss. Like the drink, only not spelt the same.

MARSHALL. Oh you can spell, can you?

COFFEY. Just my name boss.

EDGECOMB. My name is Paul Edgecomb. If I'm not here you can ask for these three gentlemen right there.

[Camera pans to the three wardens standing outside the cell]

EDGECOMB. Questions?

COFFEY. Do you leave the light on after bedtime? 'Cos I get a little scared in the dark sometimes. If it's a strange place.

EDGECOMB. It stays pretty bright around here all night long; we always keep a few lights burning out there in the corridor.

COFFEY. Corridor?

EDGECOMB. Right out there.

[Coffey turns and looks out from his cell then turns back and stretches out his hand to Edgecomb to shake it. The guards get nervous. Edgecomb pauses and then stretches out his arm and Edgecomb and Coffey shake hands]

[Edgecomb turns and leaves the cell]

EDGECOMB. You can sit.

[Coffey turns and sits on the bed and the cell is locked]
[The camera focuses on Edgecomb's face through the bars and then on Coffey's face. Edgecomb looks surprised and perplexed by the new inmate on the Green Mile.]

Miracles are funny things

From this point on the film focuses on Edgecomb's relationship first with several other condemned prisoners and then with Coffey himself. Of all the prisoners, it is Coffey who becomes the focal character. As the plot unfolds it becomes clear that he is a really good man, a gentle giant, full of exceptional kindness. He is extremely sensitive to the beauty as well as the ugliness of humanity. Even the prison guards come to respect and perhaps love John Coffey.

Not only that, Coffey is able to perform miracles. Edgecomb, suffering from an appalling bladder infection, is healed miraculously when Coffey lays his hands on him through the prison bars. A mouse called Mr Jingles – beloved by one of the other prisoners – is cruelly killed by one of the prison guards, Percy Whetmore, a loathsome individual. Coffey takes the mouse in his hands, breathes on the creature, and Mr Jingles is resuscitated supernaturally. Coffey is certainly no ordinary inmate. He is a man who performs miracles in the darkest place. As Edgecomb narrates in the trailer:

> 'Miracles are funny things. You never know when they're going to happen. And when they happen in a place like this, that's the most incredible miracle of all. This is the story of a miracle that happened where I work – on the Green Mile.'

Later on in the film we learn that the governor of the prison, Hal Moore, is suffering emotional agony because his wife Melinda is dying of a brain tumour. Hal and Melinda are close friends of Edgecomb and his wife Jan. One night, lying in bed, Edgecomb conceives a plan to take Coffey to Melinda, even if it means risking going to prison himself. He figures that if Coffey can heal a bladder infection, maybe he can heal Melinda's tumour. If the plan is to succeed, however, Edgecomb must first persuade his colleagues on the Green Mile to help him. So he and his wife Jan invite them to a picnic lunch in their garden.

Clip 2: A 'praise Jesus' miracle

HARRY. You sure do know how to cook chicken.

JAN. Well, thank you.

DEAN. This is one delicious treat, ma'am.

JAN. Well I'm glad you are enjoying it.

DEAN. Hey Brutal, you going to hog all those potatoes?

BRUTAL. Yes I am.

EDGECOMB [*changing the subject, and referring to Jon Coffey bringing Mr Jingles*]. You all saw what he did to the mouse.

BRUTAL. I could have gone the rest of the day without you bringing that up.

DEAN. I could have gone the rest of the year.

EDGECOMB. He did the same thing to me. He put his hands on me; he took my bladder infection away.

JAN. It's true. He came home that day and he was ... [*pauses and smiles*] all better.

DEAN. Oh now wait, you're talking about an authentic healing, a praise Jesus miracle?

EDGECOMB. I am.

JAN. Oh yeah.

BRUTAL. Oh, well if you say it I accept it. What's it got to do with us?

JAN [*referring to the Prison Warden's wife*]. You're thinking about Melinda.

BRUTAL. Melinda? Melinda Moore?

JAN. Yes, oh Paul, do you really think you can help her?

EDGECOMB. Well, it's not a bladder infection or even a busted mouse. I think there might be a chance.

HARRY. Hold on there, you're talking about our jobs. Sneaking a sick woman into a cellblock.

EDGECOMB. Oh no. Hal would never stand for that. You know him, he wouldn't believe anything even if it fell on him.

HARRY. So you're talking about taking John Coffey to her.

EDGECOMB. Yes.

HARRY. That's more than just our jobs, Paul. That's prison time if we get caught.

DEAN. You're damn right it is.

EDGECOMB. No, not for you, Dean. You see the way I figure it you stay back on the mile. That way you can deny everything.

BRUTAL. I'm sure she's a fine woman.

JAN. The finest

EDGECOMB. What is happening to her is an offence, Brutal. To the eye, the ear and the heart.

BRUTAL. I have no doubt, but we don't know her like you and Jan do, do we?

HARRY. And let's not forget, John Coffey is a murderer. What if he escapes? I would hate to lose my job and go to prison, but I'd hate worse to have a dead child on my conscience.

EDGECOMB. I don't think that's going to happen. In fact I don't think he did it at all. I do not see God putting a gift like that in the hands of a man who would kill a child.

HARRY. Well that's a very tender notion but the man is on death row for the crime and plus he's huge. If he tried to get away it would take a lot of bullets to stop him.

BRUTAL. No, we'd all have shotguns and I'd issue the side arms. I would insist on that. If he tried anything, anything at all we would have to take him down. You understand. So tell us what you had in mind.

Pressing in for healing

It is truly remarkable to see such an open discussion of spiritual healing in a modern movie. 'You're talking about an authentic healing?' asks Dean. He qualifies this by adding, 'Praise Jesus miracle'. Edgecomb readily confesses that he is, and Brutal (played with customary grace by David Morse) replies, 'well, if you say it, I accept it.' No further proof required!

In addition to identifying Coffey's extraordinary gift, Edgecomb expresses for the first time his belief that Coffey is totally innocent of the charges brought against him. 'I do not see God putting a gift like that in the hands of a man who would kill a child,' he says. Edgecomb has already done some research on Coffey outside the prison. He has visited the lawyer who defended him, who informs Edgecomb that no one knew where Coffey had come from. It was like he just 'dropped out of heaven'. Now, around the table in his own garden, Edgecomb finally confesses what his instincts have been telling him right from the start: Coffey is an innocent man about to die for another's sins.

So the story continues. The guards agree to help their boss, Paul Edgecomb. Dean stays behind to hold the fort whole Edgecomb, Brutal and Harry take Coffey in a truck late at night to the house of Hal and Melinda Moore. Coffey goes to the front door, pushes past the perplexed and frightened Hal, and goes up the stairs to the bedroom where Melinda is lying. Her face is disfigured by suffering. The tumour has caused her mind to lose its clarity and confusion and anger pours out of her mouth. John Coffey sits down on the bed next to Melinda as Hal and the others enter the room and watch. Even though Hal wants to intervene, Edgecomb stops him, asking his friend to trust him and to watch what is about to unfold.

Clip 3: By his wounds ...

MELINDA. Why do you have so many scars? Who hurt you so badly?

COFFEY. I don't hardly remember, ma'am.

MELINDA. What's your name?

COFFEY. John Coffey, ma'am, like the drink, only not spelt the same.

COFFEY [*Coffey leans over Melinda*]. Ma'am?

MELINDA. Yes, John Coffey.

COFFEY [*referring to her tumour*]. I see it.

[Melinda begins to cry]

MELINDA. What's happening?

COFFEY. Shhh, you be still now, you be so quiet and so still.

[John Coffey leans right over her and inhales the illness from her. The house rocks. Lights brighten as Coffey takes Melinda's sickness into his own body]

[As Coffey moves back away from Melinda we see her completely healed, her face is young and beautiful – no longer disfigured. Hal sits on the bed and takes his wife by the hand]

MELINDA. How did I get here? We were going to the hospital remember?

HAL. Shhh it doesn't matter. It doesn't matter anymore.

MELINDA. Did I have the X-ray? Did I?

EDGECOMB. Yes, yes, it was clear. There was no tumour.

[Hal leans forward and embraces his wife, sobbing uncontrollably with relief at the miraculous transformation of his wife.]

A modern day Christ figure

Notice the first thing Melinda says to Coffey here, 'Why do you have so many scars?' Perhaps at this point we should come clean about the very obvious parallels between John Coffey and Jesus Christ. John, like Jesus, drops out of heaven. John, like Jesus, is an innocent man full of purity. John, like Jesus, is a man of extraordinary love and compassion. John, like Jesus, is a man who is wrongly accused of a crime and executed for it. John, like Jesus, is a man who performs miracles, particularly miracles of healing. John, like Jesus, is a man of scars who takes into his own body the sicknesses and sins of others. John Coffey, in short, is one of the most powerful and obvious Christ figures in contemporary cinema. Indeed, I have to pinch myself to remember that this is a Stephen King story!

In his introduction to the novel *The Green Mile,* Stephen King reveals that the parallels between John and Jesus are indeed intentional, and therefore not the imposition of an overzealous Christian reading. Indeed, he informs us that even John Coffey's initials (J.C.) were created to bring about a greater alignment to the person of Jesus Christ. Originally, John had been Luke Coffey. As King confesses, 'Luke Coffey became John Coffey (with a tip of the chapeau to William Faulkner, whose Christ-figure is Joe Christmas)...'

Six hundred years before the birth of Jesus Christ, a prophet called Isaiah had a vision of the death of Jesus on the cross:

> '... There was nothing beautiful or majestic about his appearance, nothing to attract us to him. He was despised and rejected – a man of sorrows, acquainted with bitterest grief. We turned our backs on him and looked the other way when he went by. He was despised, and we did not care.
>
> Yet it was our weaknesses he carried; it was our sorrows that weighed him down. And we thought his troubles were a punishment from God for his own sins! But he was wounded and crushed for our sins. He was beaten that we might have peace. He was whipped, and we were healed! All of us have strayed away like sheep. We have left God's paths to follow our own. Yet the Lord laid on him the guilt and sins of us all.
>
> He was oppressed and treated harshly, yet he never said a word. He was led as a lamb to the slaughter. And as a sheep is silent before the shearers, he did not open his mouth. From prison and trial they led him away to his death. But who among the people realised that he was dying for their sins – that he was suffering their punishment? He had done no wrong, and he never deceived anyone. But he was buried like a criminal; he was put in a rich man's grave.'
>
> (Isaiah 53:2–9, NLT)

John Coffey, like Jesus, exhibits many of the characteristics of this Suffering Servant of the Lord. More than anything else, John Coffey is someone who dies a cruel and terrible death for the sins of others. He is truly led like a lamb to the slaughter with quiet resignation. From prison and trial he is led away to his death. What could be more poignant than that?

In the last scene I want to reference, Edgecomb comes with Brutal to Coffey in his prison cell a few days before Coffey's execution. Edgecomb is tormented by guilt and grief at the prospect of killing an innocent man and wants somehow to get out of the predicament. Indeed, some have likened Paul Edgecomb to Pilate in this respect. Whatever the truth of that, the scene that follows is full of spiritual and specifically Christian resonances.

Clip 4: The Last Supper

COFFEY. Hello boss.

EDGECOMB. Hello John, I guess you know we are coming down to it now. Another couple of days.

[Edgecomb walks into the cell and sits opposite Coffey]

EDGECOMB. Is there anything special you want to eat for dinner that night? We can rustle you up almost anything.

COFFEY. Meatloaf would be nice, mash potatoes, gravy, okra, maybe some of that fine corn bread your missus make. If she don't mind.

EDGECOMB. Well what about a preacher, someone to say a little prayer or whatever?

COFFEY. Don't want no preacher. You can say a prayer if you like.

EDGECOMB. Me? Suppose I could if it came to that.

EDGECOMB. John, I have to ask you something very important now.

COFFEY. I know what you are going to say and you don't have to say it.

EDGECOMB. No I do, I do have to say it. John, tell me what you want me to do. Do you want me to take you out of here? Just let you run away? See how far you can get?

COFFEY. Why would you do such a foolish thing?

EDGECOMB. On the day of my judgement, when I stand before God and he asks me why did I kill one of his true miracles what am I going to say? That it was my job … my job?

COFFEY. You tell God the Father, it was a kindness you done.

[Coffey places his hands over Edgecomb's hands]

COFFEY. I know you're hurting, I can feel it on you. But you ought not to quit on it now. I want it to be over and done with. I do. I'm tired boss, tired of being on the road, lonely as a sparrow in the rain, and I'm tired of never having me a buddy to be with me to tell me where we're going to, coming from and why. Mostly I'm tired of people being ugly to each other. I'm tired of all the pain I feel here in the world every day; there's too much of it, it's like pieces of glass in my head all the time. Can you understand?

EDGECOMB. Yes John, yes I can.

BRUTAL. Well, there must be something we can do for you, John? There must be something that you want?

[Coffey thinks for a moment then smiles]

COFFEY. I ain't never seen me a flick show.

[The scene shifts to a hall in which a black and white film is playing on an old projector system. Coffey is the only one besides Edgecomb watching the film. It is a movie of Fred Astaire and Ginger Rogers dancing to the song, 'I'm in Heaven' – a tune that Coffey will sing to himself as he sits in the electric chair a few days later.]

Faithful to the end

As Edgecomb prepares Coffey for his last supper, the full angst of his predicament comes to the surface. Edgecomb simply cannot come to terms with the awful realisation that he is killing one of God's miracles. He offers Coffey a way out but Coffey will not let the cup pass. He stays the course. The execution scene that follows is one of the most harrowing in modern cinema. The room is laid out like a church, with chairs in rows facing not an altar but Old Sparky. The people who have come look like they are in their Sunday best clothes. As the execution is prepared even the guards weep. Edgecomb, who has had his hand shaken by Coffey at the start of the film, now steps forward to shake Coffey's hand at the end. John dies with extraordinary courage and dignity.

The Green Mile is a great story and a great film. It is also a film that invites a Christian interpretation. In Stephen King's novel, Coffey is very clearly portrayed as a Christian. His prayer goes as follows: 'Baby Jesus, meek and mild, pray for me, an orphan child. Be my strength, be my friend, be with me until the end.' In the novel, Paul Edgecomb is clearly depicted as a man with a Christian sensibility. After the death of one of his prisoners, Eduard Delacroix, he muses as follows:

> 'Only God could forgive sins, could and did, washing them away in the agonal blood of His crucified Son, but that did not change the responsibility of His children to atone for those sins (and even their simple errors of judgement) whenever possible. Atonement was powerful; it was the lock on the door you closed against the past.'

The Green Mile, like other stories by King (such as *Desperation, The Stand, The Girl who Loved Tom Gordon,*

Storm of the Century and *The Shawshank Redemption*) is a story filled with Christian themes. Indeed, in *The Green Mile*, the world's leading horror writer reveals that he is also one of our most spiritually-attuned novelists. In this respect, King is very like his creation John Coffey, a person full of paradoxes!

There can be miracles

In the final analysis, however, the power of *The Green Mile* lies in its portrayal of the miraculous. Miracles of healing have not been commonplace or seriously treated in twentieth-century cinema, not least because of the anti-supernatural worldview of the Enlightenment period. But the days we are living in now are not Enlightenment but post-Enlightenment. This does not mean rejecting reason and science. It does, however, mean developing a more postmodern perspective in which the material and the spiritual can be integrated. As postmodernity progresses, films are becoming noticeably more serious about treating the spiritual dimensions of life, including the Christian dimension. Frank Darabont's faithful rendition of Stephen King's novel brings this dimension to the surface in a way that modern filmgoers can find accessible and non-preachy. It is a filmic answer to the great question posed by George Bernard Shaw's St Joan: 'Must a Christ die in every generation for those who have no imagination?'

I do not know what your perspective is on what Dean in *The Green Mile* calls 'Praise Jesus miracles'. All I can say is that since becoming a Christian I have seen many events that I regard as miraculous. I have seen clear evidence of the supernatural and life-giving power that flows into people's lives when we pray in the name of Jesus. Though I have seen some not healed, I have seen many who have. If you have a great need today, ask Jesus to reveal himself to you. Come to the one who died on the cross that you might be saved, healed and delivered.

To encourage you I would like to end with the testimony of a person who wrote to me recently. She is a member of our church (St Andrew's) and this is the story of what happened to her earlier this year (2003).

Dear Mark

Firstly, I want to thank you so much for St Andrew's. If it weren't for St Andrew's, I would still have a very despairing daughter, who came to the Alpha course almost two years ago and was changed into a happy, calm, contented and lovely human being, when life had treated her so badly. Through no fault of her own, it had made her bitter and helplessly lost. We are now very close and I feel St Andrew's has introduced her to Jesus and he has given me back my loving daughter.

My daughter then encouraged me to go to Alpha, so I went to see what 'wonderful' thing had managed to change her so much. I too changed. Although always a believer, as J. John says in one of his videos, the Lord was in the boot of my car, safely locked away! Not any more! I went to the Beta Group after the Alpha course and became involved on sitting in on the next Alpha course. From then I have been involved in serving people who do not come to church through Lunch Break – a meeting for busy mums.

A lot has happened to me in the past 15 months and I have met so many lovely Christian people. I myself was given the privilege of encouraging someone else to attend the Alpha course who was in a desperate state, and she has found God's love and is a changed person. That encouraged me so much, I can't tell you ...

Finally, when Marc Dupont came to do those healing meetings about eight weeks ago, I was helping with the team on Saturday, when Marc called anyone with digestive problems (I have a hiatus hernia) and several of us where prayed for.

On Wednesday evening I had a very strong feeling that I must go to Marc's last healing meeting. I got there late and someone kindly found me a seat as the church was bursting at the seams.

Within minutes Marc asked all the people with back problems to stand; I stood, having had a bad back since the age of 14 (not something that had come along with 'old age' as I am now 61!). Marc encouraged us to go to the front of the church to be prayed for. In my heart, I thought I couldn't be healed but I said to Jesus, 'If you need to give me more pain to be able to heal me, then please do it now.' He did ... Great pressure on the base of my spine and lots of movement inside.

Someone was praying over me from the front and back, it was a lovely feeling and very spiritual. I went home and heard a loud 'click' in my spine, but I was still in some pain as always!

I went to bed and in the night I was woken by another loud 'click' and a muscle movement in my spine. In the morning I stepped out of bed normally, not slowly, stiffly and painfully as usual ... I couldn't believe it ... I still can't! It has improved daily, every day since (I've had two operations in the last six years!). My bonus is that now I can stretch my hamstrings (couldn't before). I can lie on my back or front in comfort. I can sit normally in a chair without being surrounded by cushions ... And much, much more.

An added bonus: when I visited my daughter in Australia, where she now lives, we actually went horse riding together – something I haven't been able to do since I was 14 years old. Although we rode bare back in the sea and my large horse sat down and dumped me in the water, it was brilliant, and I had no aches at all the next day even though on three occasions I jumped down from my steed as there was no one to help. I'm 5 ft nothing and it was a very long way down! Did I lay the fleece?

Guess what? I had an Indian meal and my digestion is just fine!

I thank God every day for what he has done for my family and me. I even had the opportunity to speak at our ladies club last week and instead of a talk I had prepared I felt very strongly that all this had been given to me so I had the opportunity to spread the word. I told them about my 'miracle'. They asked me to close with a prayer and I, although very nervous, did that, too.

I hope this letter encourages you.

DISCUSSION STARTERS

(You will need coloured paper cut into strips, pens and a small branch or twig from a tree.)

Personal reflection: *The Green Mile* explores several big themes of life and death, of punishment and forgiveness, of illness and healing. What part of the film made you think – or moved you – the most? Why did it? Can a film such as *The Green Mile* actually change you in any way? If so, how?

Act: Write down what moved you the most. And think about one thing in particular that the film showed you that you'd never seen before in the same way. Now write down one more thing: if you could change one thing about yourself because of the film, what would it be?

Discuss: Did you spot the analogy between John Coffey and Jesus Christ in the film? Which similarities strike you in particular? What did the portrayal of John Coffey's life and death help you to understand about Jesus?

Read: Mt. 27:32–56.

Act: When reading the Bible, it's sometimes hard to really place yourself at the scene. We can become too familiar with the text seeming so far removed from our own life. The words can almost dry up. But imagine, for a few moments, what it must have been like for John Coffey to walk the 'Green Mile' to his death as an innocent man. Now, try writing a short note to Jesus. Tell him that you've watched this film, and explain to him why it's helped you to understand a little bit more about how he must have felt. Perhaps you could keep the note in your Bible, to remind you.

Discuss: John Coffey asked for a final meal of meat loaf, mashed potatoes, gravy, okra, corn bread ... What would you eat for a final meal?

Read: Mt. 26:26–29. Jesus himself ate a famous final meal or 'last supper', at which he shared bread and wine with his disciples.

Act: Share some bread and a wine together as you reflect on the miracle of Jesus' life and death. As you taste the bread and wine, thank God for going through what he had to go through on our behalf. Remain quiet and reflective as you do this. You might like to play some contemplative music.

Discuss: Jesus' life was miraculous, and he performed many miracles of healing. Have you ever been healed of anything? If so, share this – if you feel happy to – with the group. Do you know of other people – first hand – who have been healed?

Act: Write down on your coloured strip of paper a prayer for healing – it might be for you, it might be for someone you know. In the quiet, stick the piece of paper to the branch – to create a 'prayer tree'. Once everyone who wants to has contributed, someone can close with a short prayer, offering these various requests to God.

Discuss: What other depictions of Christ have you seen in the movies? What other 'Christ-like figures'? Why should we use stories like this to explore who Jesus is and was? How can films like this help us as we read the Gospels?

10

Searching for Love
Bridget Jones's Diary

J. JOHN

UIP, 2001

Directed by SHARON MAGUIRE
Screenplay by HELEN FIELDING

RENÉE ZELLWEGER as *Bridget Jones*
HUGH GRANT as *Daniel Cleaver*
COLIN FIRTH as *Mark Darcy*

CLASSIFICATION: 15

Bridget Jones's Diary is the film of the book of the newspaper column – a romantic comedy, documenting a year in the life of a single, 30-something woman in London, played by Renée Zellweger.

It's the beginning of the new year for Bridget Jones, who works at a London publishing house as a marketing assistant. Determined to improve her life by losing weight, cutting down on cigarettes and alcohol and finding Mr Right, Bridget begins a diary to record her uncensored thoughts.

She starts by making a list of thirty-three resolutions (of which, in the end, she manages to keep only one). Bridget has two main fixations: to create the right image for herself, and to find a responsible man who will be truly committed to her, instead of just using her and leaving.

Her affections are torn between her boss, the dangerous, exciting and attractive Daniel Cleaver (Hugh Grant) and the haughty, mysterious human-rights barrister, Mark Darcy (Colin Firth). The love triangle that follows draws loose parallels with Jane Austin's *Pride and Prejudice.*

Bridget Jones's Diary (together with its sequel *The Edge of Reason*) was written by Helen Fielding, and has sold over 10 million copies in 30 countries. It was an overwhelming and instant success, capturing the plight of the contemporary woman in a remarkably familiar and endearing light.

Many people saw flashes of themselves as they followed the delightfully dysfunctional Bridget through 'performance anxiety' at work, ever-failing diets and her insatiable longing for love. I smiled at the one-liners, laughed at the subtle and not-so-subtle comedy and nodded in sympathy with Bridget's all-too-familiar plight – and I'm male. Imagine the female reaction!

It was, perhaps, encouraging to find that you can be a domestic disaster, a social embarrassment, a professional no-hoper and a little overweight, and still have two handsome hunks fighting over you... But beneath the humorous surface of the film lie glimpses of real sadness. This movie successfully combines comedy and truth, but the humour masks the real emotion.

Laughter can often be an antidote to the things that make us sad. The film communicates reality, however fictional. Whether we are single or married, we can relate, to some extent, with Bridget's frustrations. They prompt an examination of our own lives and relationships. It's a movie that makes us realise that what – or *who* – is on the inside is far more important than having the perfect body, the perfect career or saying all the right things at the right time.

It is completely natural that we – both women and men – want to fall in love and get married. After all, Bridget is living out the desire that God has planted in most people to find a life partner. It was God (not a grumpy Adam) who declared, 'It is not right for the man to be alone.' Desire for companionship is quite a legitimate need, and God recognises this.

Bridget's desire to find a life partner who loves her is a virtue, not a flaw. It is the way she goes about it – leaving herself sexually open for exploitation – that is the problem.

The director of the movie, Sharon Maguire, suggests that 'primarily, this film is about loneliness, dressed up as a comic anecdote.' The theme is established from the very start, as Bridget is alone in her flat, drinking, depressed, wearing her penguin-patterned pyjamas, and listening to Jamie O'Neal's song 'All by Myself'. The film opens expressing this fear ...

Film clip 1

All by myself. Intense loneliness is at the root of all of Bridget's actions. It's the end of a winter's evening. Bridget Jones is alone in her flat, wearing her penguin-patterned pyjamas. A fire is struggling to stay alight in the hearth, and Frasier is coming to an end on the TV. She has a glass of red wine in one hand, a cigarette and magazine in the other. Jamie O'Neal's song 'All by Myself' blasts from her stereo. Her magazine doubles as an air-guitar. She checks her answer-phone: 'You have no new messages,' announces the electronic voice. She downs her wine, as the music soars

'When I was young, I never needed any one
And making love was just for fun ...
Those days are gone.
All by myself. Don't wanna be all by myself, anymore.'

The drums crash in, Bridget smashes a pretend kit, kicks the air and sings into her rolled up magazine. 'Don't wanna be all by myself, anymore ...'

As Bridget records in her diary, 'Loneliness, far from being a rare and curious phenomenon, is the central and inevitable fact of human existence.' And she is not alone in thinking what she thinks. It was Emily Carr who remarked, 'You come into the world alone and you go out of this world alone. Yet it seems to me that you are more alone while living than even going and coming.'

Mother Teresa observed that 'loneliness and the feeling of being unwanted is the most terrible poverty.' Even Albert Einstein once said, 'It is strange to be known so universally and yet be so lonely.'

Each of us feels lonely at times, and wants to be understood. We fill our time with events and pack meeting after meeting into our schedules, and phone call after e-mail. Yet despite all the people that surround us and all the activity we engage in, we rarely connect deeply with others. We seem to have become a society of acquaintances, living vicarious 'friendships' instead through characters on the TV like those on the popular US sitcom *Friends*.

The rapid urbanisation of the world – a modern phenomenon that has spawned over 300 cities of more than 1 million people – has meant that people are packed closer together physically, yet live in greater isolation. London is like a thousand suburbs in search of a city. We are little islands of self-absorbed, self-contained individuals, cast adrift from the solid continent of community.

Society is characterised more by fear and suspicion than by friendship and neighbourliness. Loneliness assumes many forms, each equally undesirable – an unsatisfied inner ache, a vacuum, a craving for satisfaction. The human heart has an insatiable longing to be loved.

Loneliness is the feeling that you don't really matter to anyone, that you are not significant, that you are isolated. It can occur at any time in our lives, affecting the young and the elderly, the busy and the leisurely. A person can feel very lonely and yet be lost in a crowd; on the other hand, you can feel physically alone and yet have a strong sense of personal connection.

Research shows that the experiences which really trigger acute loneliness are the death of a life partner or other family member, a separation or divorce, a broken engagement and leaving your home for study or work. All these can prompt deep emotional trauma.

So it's not without reason that loneliness has been termed the most desolate word in the English language. The single person in particular lacks one of the most obvious antidotes to loneliness: a loving partner. It's made all the harder thanks to the unhelpful yet popular idea – or myth – that everyone should get married and live happily ever after. The implication is that if you're not married, you have somehow failed. Curiously, this myth still abounds, despite the fact that our culture also looks suspiciously on institutions such as marriage.

Her friends are constantly telling Bridget Jones that she should find a man and settle down. Certainly, loneliness can lead to discouragement and even despair – yet the good news is that it doesn't have to. It can bring about, much more positively, greater insight, deeper understanding, a more realistic lifestyle and unselfish loving.

We can't always control our feelings, of course, but we can control the decisions and choices we make because of them. Bridget is dissatisfied with herself, and even seems discontent with her own aims and values in life. Lurking beneath is a mass of insecurities. Every embarrassing moment serves to reinforce the critical view she holds of herself. This is a typical human tendency, one that we all seem to share.

Bridget believes that exercise and clean living is the key to her change, as many of us do. She changes her goals and the content of her bookshelf to adapt herself to a new set of rules. Her books fluctuate between *What men want* and then *How to get what you want*.

Film clip 2: Throwing things away

Bridget is turning over a new leaf. 'At times like this,' she records in her diary, 'continuing with one's life seems impossible, and eating the entire contents of one's fridge seems inevitable. I have two choices: to give up and accept permanent state of spinsterhood and eventually be eaten by Alsatians. Or not. And this time, I choose not. I will not be defeated.'

So, into the bin go the self-help books, which counsel what men want and how to get them. And onto the shelves, instead, go the new books about how to live without men. Cut to Bridget pedalling defiantly at the gym ... and falling off her bike. Cut to Bridget looking in the papers for jobs in TV. Cut to Bridget walking over a London bridge, head up, on a sunny day. She will not be defeated.

Many of us never seem satisfied. Jason Lehman once wrote:

> 'It was Spring, but it was Summer I wanted –
> The warm days and the great outdoors.

It was Summer, but it was Autumn I wanted –
The colourful leaves and the cool dry air.

It was Autumn, but it was Winter I wanted –
The beautiful snow and the joy of the holiday season.

It was Winter, but it was Spring I wanted –
The warmth and the blossoming of nature.

I was a child, but it was adulthood I wanted –
The freedom and the respect.

I was 20, but it was 30 I wanted –
To be mature and sophisticated.

I was middle-aged, but it was 20 I wanted –
The youth and the free spirit.

I was retired, but it was middle-age I wanted –
The presence of mind, without limitations.

Then my life was over, and I never got what I wanted.'

We seek more pleasure, more treasure and more leisure. Today we idolise sex, wealth, fame, pleasure, power and physical beauty. 'How do I look?' has become the predominant question in life. We worship the profane trinity of me, myself and I.

Bridget kept account of her weight and calorie intake every day. Do we treat scales like an idol, bowing to see what they say about us, and letting their verdict determine how we feel?

The 23rd Psalm for Dieting

My diet is my shepherd, I shall be in want,
It makes me jog quietly round and round green pastures,
It leads me to quietly drink water,
And jump on and off the scales.
It guides me to resist all pleasurable food

For my figure's shape.
Even though I walk through the aisles of Sainsbury's
I will buy no Bovril
For you are with me;
Your measuring tape and your calorie counter
They confuse me.
You prepare a table before me
In the presence of the Tellytubbies.
You cover my lettuce with low-fat mayonnaise,
My diet coke overflows.
Surely a rumbling stomach and a feeling of irritability will be with me
All the days of my slimming plan
And I will worry about my weight forever.

(Dr Debbie Lovell)

Like Bridget, we strive to measure up, while wishing we could be known and loved for who we really are. It's a search, ultimately, for the unconditional love of God.

Clip 3: I like you just as you are

[Bridget is leaving a dinner party early. Darcy has followed her out, stopping her on the stairs. The Christmas lights glow in the background; a taxi hoots outside the doors]

DARCY. I hear it didn't work out with Daniel Cleaver.
BRIDGET. No.
DARCY. I'm delighted to hear it.

At which point, Bridget spews words at Darcy. She feels like an idiot. She always feels like an idiot. She always puts her foot in it. She always says the wrong things. She always messes up. And people like Darcy know it.

Darcy says he's sorry for being so rude the first time they met at her mother's New Year's curry. In fact, he says he likes her.

DARCY. Despite appearances, I like you very much.

[And just as Bridget is spewing forth some more – yes, apart from the drinking and smoking, the vulgar mother and the verbal diarrhoea ... – he stuns her]

DARCY. I like you just the way you are.

[Bridget Jones is dumbstruck.]

When Mark Darcy tells Bridget that he likes her just the way she is, he shows that he's the right choice because he's not asking her to compromise herself to meet his selfish needs. Instead, he's offering her unconditional love.

As a result, Bridget grows in self-respect, so that she is able to turn down the manipulative, self-centred Cleaver and finally turn to the man who quietly offers her respect and friendship, as well as romantic love.

The psychologist Freud wrote, 'People are hungry for love.' The psychologist Jung wrote, 'People are hungry for security.' The psychologist Adler wrote, 'People are hungry for significance.' *Bridget Jones's Diary* is about a woman who is hungry for all three – love, security and significance.

We were all created with two major needs: fellowship with God and companionship with other human beings. There's no substitute for either. The spiritual and social instinct lies deep within every human being, and when this need remains unsatisfied, the seeds of loneliness can grow and flourish.

Jane Austen once wrote, 'Friendship is certainly the finest balm for the pangs of disappointed love.' Blaise Pascal believed that in every heart there exists a God-shaped vacuum. And centuries before him, Augustine wrote, 'God created man for Himself and our hearts are restless until they find rest in Him.' For this reason, the greatest need of every person is to seek after an authentic relationship with God, the Great Physician, who has the remedy for every disorder of the human heart.

We are hungry for God and in him, ultimately, we find love, security and significance. Bridget, meanwhile, seeks a meaningful relationship to fill the space in her life, and she is restless and anxious. We need a relationship with God to fill the space, and then we need to place God at the centre of our relationships.

Like Bridget, we need to realise that we are never really alone. People may let us down. Friends may disappoint us. Families sometimes fracture. But God is looking out for us. God sees, God knows, God cares, God loves. And God forgives.

Clip 4: Buying a new diary

[The snow outside is falling, Darcy is in Bridget's flat, and everything, finally, seems right with the world. She's next door in the bedroom, changing into some sexier underwear. Darcy, on his own, sees a book resting on the table. It's her diary. And it's open at the wrong page]

'Mark Darcy is rude. He's unpleasant. He's dull. No wonder his clever wife left him. I hate him! I hate him!'

DARCY [*says to himself*]. I see.

[And at that, he walks out. Bridget hears a door slam shut. She looks out the window and sees him trudging down the snowy street. She calls out, but he doesn't hear her, or won't hear her. Bridget runs into the dining room and sees the open diary. Help. Immediately, it all makes sense.

Without stopping to get dressed (she simply flings a cardigan around her shoulders), she runs into the street]

BRIDGET [*she shouts*]. Mark!.

[At which point, Mark emerges from a shop. The snow is still falling heavily]

BRIDGET. I'm so sorry. I didn't mean it. Well, I did, I suppose, but I didn't mean what I meant. Everyone knows diaries are so full of crap.

DARCY. I know that. I was just buying you a new one. Time to make a new start, perhaps.

In Jane Austen's *Pride and Prejudice*, the hero's pride is levelled, the heroine's prejudice turns out to be unfounded and the two come together to live happily. Why not discard last year's diary and begin again with God?

Whether you are married, divorced, widowed or single, you are being proposed to. Jesus is proposing to you. God is always trying to give good things to us, but our hands are too full to receive them. So why not lay down our pain, pride, prejudice, preoccupations, possessions, and pursue Christ? Be assured: if you walk with him, look to him and expect help from him, he will never fail you.

How much does Jesus Christ love us? The apostle Paul, in his letter to the Ephesians, prayed that they would 'grasp how wide and long and high and deep is the love of Christ' (Eph. 3:17,18, NIV). Wide, long, high and deep – that's four amazing ways in which Jesus' love grows for us.

Let's take them one at a time, starting with *wide*. Jesus' love is wide enough to include everybody who wants to receive it. The Bible tells us that 'God so loved the world ...' – but who does that include? Everybody. I take tremendous comfort in knowing that God's love for me is utterly realistic; and because he already knows the worst about me, no discovery can make him disillusioned about me, in the way I can become disillusioned about myself (and others).

There is nothing we can do to make God love us more. But the good news is that there's nothing we can do to make God love us less. He loves each one of us, as if we were the only one. One writer put it this way: 'If God had a fridge, your picture would be on it. If he had a wallet, your photo would be in it. He sends you flowers every spring, and a sunrise every morning.'

Whenever you want to talk, he'll listen. He can live anywhere in the universe, and still he chose your heart. Because Jesus loves me, I don't have to prove my own self-worth.

Second, God's love is *long* enough to last for ever. He says, 'I have loved you with an everlasting love' (Jer. 31:3, NIV). That is so different to our kind of love. Human love wears out – that's why we have divorces. That's why we need God's love; for God's love never wears out. It is patient, persevering.

It's good news that God never gives up on us. He loves us on our good days and on our bad days, because God's love is not dependent on our response. God is love.

Third, God's love is *high* enough to be everywhere. The Bible says, 'neither height, nor depth ... will be able to separate us from the love of God which is in Christ Jesus.' There is no place we can go to hide from God's love – because it reaches the parts other loves can't reach. Being a Christian is all about being in a relationship with God – so we never have to be alone.

Fourth, God's love is *deep* enough to meet my needs. 'My only hope is your love. For my problems are too big for me to solve and are piled over my head,' writes the psalmist (Ps. 40:11,12). It's not hard to identify with that. No matter how big the problem, God's love runs deeper.

Some people are in deep despair; some are in deep trouble. Some people are in deep distress; some are in deep loneliness. God's love is deeper still.

Where is God when you hit rock bottom? The Bible says: 'The eternal God is your refuge and underneath are the everlasting arms' (Deut. 33:27, NIV). God can catch us and support us if we will let him. Sometimes, God sends the brilliant light of a rainbow to remind us of his presence, lest we forget in our personal darkness his great and gracious promises to never leave us alone.

When we look at these four words – *height, depth, width* and *length* – we have the four dimensions of the cross. We cannot talk about the love of God without talking of the cross of Jesus Christ, because the ultimate demonstration of love is when someone gives their life for you. Jesus said, 'Greater love has no one than this, that he lays down his life for his friends.' God demonstrated how much he loved us by dying for us.

Notice that he doesn't show his love by sending a romantic poem or dropping a bunch of red roses onto our doorstep. Instead, 'God showed his great love for us by sending Christ to die for us while we were still sinners.'

He shows he cares, not by a poem, but through cries of agony and excruciating pain. It's not champagne he drinks, but bitter wine. He doesn't bear roses in his arms, but a crown of thorns on his head. He doesn't bathe us in fine smelling perfume, but saves us through sweat and blood. God's proposal was nailed to a cross. And he did it for us – that's true love.

I have found that many people – including Christians – find it easier to tell someone else that God loves them, than to say it to themselves. It probably has something to do with lingering feelings of guilt or inadequacy. But when you look at all that Jesus has said and done to show you how much you mean to him, such feelings will disappear. We may always sense the pangs of loneliness in our lives. But no matter, ultimately, for we all are of value to God.

DISCUSSION STARTERS

Personal reflection: How did the film make you feel? Was your laughter mixed with tinges of sadness? How, in particular, could you identify with Bridget? Do you feel 'All by yourself'? Do you know people who do?

Discuss: The film and books have been incredibly successful. Why do you think that is? What is it, in particular, that people like about Bridget Jones? Does the film appeal to both sexes? What might we learn – first, as women, and then, as men – from the film?

Read: *Bridget Jones's Diary* focuses closely on the way others see us, and the way we see ourselves. As we turn to think about this for a few minutes, read Ps. 139:1–18,23,24 together, in the light of the film.

Act: Either imagine you are standing in front of a mirror, or else actually use one! Stand and stare into your own eyes. Look at your face. The lines. The hair. The details. And now ask yourself – honestly – three questions. Take as much time as you need:

1. How do other people see this face that's staring back at me?
2. How do I see myself?
3. How does God see me, when he looks into these eyes?

As you finish, repeat the line from Psalm 139: 'I am fearfully and wonderfully made.' And thank God for it, in your own heart.

Read: 1 Sam. 16:7 and also Mt. 23:25,26.

Discuss: Are we part of the problem or part of the solution? How do we look at other people? Do we judge them by their outward appearance? And how, as Christians, might we be like the Pharisees – by putting the emphasis on how we look to others, rather than how we actually are?

Act: Bridget Jones started a diary in her attempt to change her life. It wasn't always successful, but at least it kept her to account. Journals – and in particular spiritual journals – can be really useful. They can help us to chart our walk with God, remind us of how far we've come along the journey, and what we've heard, seen, felt and learned along the way.

Try writing a first entry today. Think about what you'd like to record, and why. Even if you don't want to continue with it, write your first page as if you were going to.

Discuss: J. John writes, 'The human heart has an insatiable longing to be loved.' To what extent is loneliness a problem in today's culture? What can we do to prevent people from becoming lonely? How do we show people that God loves them, even if others don't? What might we do to become God's hands and feet in today's world?

11
Choices and Consequences
Unfaithful

J. JOHN

> *20TH CENTURY FOX, 2002*
>
> Directed by ADRIAN LYNE
> Screenplay by ALVIN SARGENT and
> WILLIAM BROYLES JR
>
> DIANE LANE as *Constance 'Connie/Con' Sumner*
> RICHARD GERE as *Edward 'Ed' Sumner*
> OLIVIER MARTINEZ as *Paul Martel*
>
> CLASSIFICATION: 15

Unfaithful is directed by Adrian Lyne, and set in the suburbs of New York City. That's where Edward and Connie Sumner (played by Richard Gere and Diane Lane) live with their 9-year-old son, Charlie (Erik Per Sullivan).

Edward and Connie have been happily married for 11 years; they clearly love one another. Edward's career may be demanding, but it has provided a beautiful home and an affluent life for them, without losing the affection of his wife who, he believes, is the most wonderful part of every day. They both adore their son, Charlie.

Clip 1

One very windy day, however, while Connie is out in the city, she struggles to keep her footing, and is blown straight into a dashing French man who's carrying a pile of books. They land together in a heap on the floor.

This is Paul Martel (Olivier Martinez), a sickeningly good-looking 28-year-old who deals in rare books. After picking themselves up, and chasing around for his books and her shopping, Connie asks him to hail her a cab for her, which he tries – and fails – to do. She has badly grazed her knee in the fall, so he invites her up to his apartment to clean up the cut.

First, she says no; but then, hesitating, and just as an empty cab passes, she accepts his invitation …

Paul asks Connie to accept a gift, and directs her specifically along an aisle to the last book at the end of the second shelf from the top. He tells her which page to turn to, and then joins her in reciting the words: 'Be happy for this moment, for this moment is your life.' Has Paul planted this book for just such a moment as this? Feeling awkward and sensing trouble, Connie beats a hasty retreat home.

The next day, however, she decides to return to Paul's apartment, and phones him from a payphone at the train station. She wants to see him again – and, even though she is painfully aware of how she could hurt her husband and son, she chooses to be unfaithful.

The phrase in the book – 'Be happy for this moment, for this moment is your life' – really sets the tone for the rest of the film. Connie has chosen to live for the moment, yet her choice, whether she likes it or not, will define the rest of her life.

After her first adulterous encounter, she feels conflicting emotions of pleasure and regret. On the train home she seems tormented, but at the same time, she revels in what she's just experienced. Connie struggles with the choice that she made, yet decides that passion – and the fulfilment of desire – are worth the risk, even though she already has a happy relationship with her husband.

As soon as she decides to sleep with Paul, however, the lies begin, and Connie starts to lead a double life. Adultery isn't just about who you lie with, it's also about who you lie to. Anyone who builds a relationship on anything less than openness and honesty is building on shifting sand. There are moments in our lives that change everything.

This film shows powerfully how adultery can be irrational, and can cause irretrievable damage to those involved. It explores the hurt and devastation that everyone goes through. Connie is not in love with Paul – she knows nothing about him, in fact, and their relationship is based simply on lust. Paul is naive, too, because he believes there'll be no price to pay if his actions are discovered.

Connie's passion, once unbridled, becomes almost like an obsession; it's a compulsive urge which begins to consume her. Her desire overrides the guilt she feels initially. The passion is like a drug and her highs come from pushing the affair to the very point of discovery.

Unfaithful is about one decision which affects the rest of Connie's life, and the people connected to her. Take her son, for example: in one instance, Connie fails to pick him up from school on time; in another, he gets out of bed to find her crying and is left confused as to why this is. Gradually, he becomes aware of the growing separation between his parents. His anxiety is revealed through small, poignant details, like wetting the bed.

Edward senses that he's losing his wife's affections, and when he discovers that Connie is not at the hair appointment she's meant to have arranged, he smells a rat. As if her lies and deception weren't enough, he, too, quickly falls into a downward spiral of suspicion and secrecy. He hires a private investigator who discovers the truth about Connie's affair. In the end, Edward confronts his wife's lover, and in a momentary fit of despair, accidentally kills him. Desperately, he tries to cover up his actions.

He disposes of the body, but as the police investigate, Connie gradually guesses that he's the murderer. The consequences will reverberate for ever. In the end, then, Edward and Paul, also become victims of a poor choice. The film clearly shows that our negative actions do have irreversible and damaging effects. In fact, this movie is very sobering. It's a powerful parable about the corrosive effects of adultery.

No matter how many horror stories we might hear, many of us still choose to get embroiled in relationships that we know will end in tears. Most of us have made choices that are wrong. And many people have experienced the subsequent pain in the breakdown of relationships, as a direct result of those choices. Of all the behaviour that can attack a marriage, adultery is clearly the most serious.

Adultery seems to promise pleasure, love and fulfilment, but in the end there is only shame, deceit, betrayal, ugliness and hurt. Adulterous love appears to be free; but it comes with a painfully high price. It shatters trust and severs friendship.

Marriage is about giving, but adultery is about taking. It denies love, degrades people, destroys families, defiles marriage and defies God. That's why God gave us the seventh commandment, which says, quite simply, 'Do not commit adultery' (Ex. 20:14, NLT).

God says 'No' to adultery because it attacks marriage. Jesus held marriage in high regard – 'a man leaves his father and mother and is joined to his wife,' he said, 'and the two are united into one. Since they are no longer two but one, let no one separate them, for God has joined them together' (Mt. 19:5,6, NLT).

Adultery breaks the unity of two people in marriage. Sex, after all, is a total giving of oneself, so we can't make love to one person and then expect no consequences if we choose to sleep with someone else. Many people end up feeling trapped by guilt, which they think might even be God's way of punishing them. But they're wrong. We bring it on ourselves.

Some people deal with guilt by denying it, others try to drown it with alcohol or drugs. Still others try deflecting it; they blame other people for their failures and faults. But we cannot escape the consequences of our own guilt.

'No amount of soap can make you clean,' said the prophet Jeremiah. 'You are stained with guilt.' Guilt is the corrosion of the soul. But how can we get rid of it? Ultimately, we can't deny it, drown it or deflect it. We can only dissolve it in the blood of Jesus Christ. Mercifully, hope abounds, because adultery is sin and Jesus Christ came to rescue sinners.

John's Gospel tells of how a crowd brought an adulterous woman to Jesus.

> '"Teacher," they said to Jesus, "this woman was caught in the very act of adultery. The law of Moses says to stone her. What do you say?"
>
> They were trying to trap him into saying something they could use against him, but Jesus stooped down and wrote in the dust with his finger. They kept demanding an answer, so he stood up again and said, "All right, stone her. But let those who have never sinned throw the first stones." Then he stooped down again and wrote in the dust.

When the accusers heard this, they slipped away one by one, beginning with the oldest, until only Jesus was left in the middle of the crowd with the woman. Then Jesus stood up again and said to her, "Where are your accusers? Didn't even one of them condemn you?"

"No, Lord," she said.

And Jesus said, "Neither do I. Go and sin no more."'

(Jn. 8:4–11, NLT)

Jesus forgave the woman, but expected her to learn and not do it again. In fact, Jesus was the only person who could have thrown a stone, being 'without sin', but he didn't. Instead, he forgave her. We have seventeen different instances recorded in the Bible in which Jesus forgave people and showed mercy.

If you have committed adultery, or you know someone who has, there's a prayer of confession in the Bible, written by King David after he committed adultery with Bathsheba. It's preserved for us as Ps. 51:

> 'Loving and kind God, have mercy. Have pity on me and take away the awful stain of my sin. Wash me, cleanse me from this guilt. Let me be pure again, for I admit my shameful deed – it haunts me day and night. It is against you and you alone I sinned, and did this terrible thing. You saw it all and your sentence against me is just ... Don't keep looking at my sins – erase them from your sight. Create in me a new clean heart, filled with clean thoughts and right desires ... Restore to me again the joy of your salvation and make me willing to obey you. Then I will teach your ways to others.'

God answered David's prayer.

A notice hangs in every Registrar's office in the country. It reads: 'Marriage, according to the law of the country, is the union of one man with one woman, voluntarily entered into for life, to the exclusion of all others.' Adultery can happen because no marriage, of course, is perfect; all of us have a sense in our lives of an unfulfilled need of love, acceptance and intimacy. But God still wants our marriages to be satisfying.

Agatha Christie once remarked that 'an archaeologist is the best husband any woman can have; the older she gets, the more interested he is in her.' The bonds of matrimony aren't worth much unless the interest is kept up. So, how do we maintain the interest over the years? How do we stay faithful?

First, get a grip on your thought-life! The Great Wall of China was built over many hundreds of years to keep China's enemies from invading. It is so wide that chariots could ride across the top of it, and is one of the few man-made objects that astronauts can see from space. But the Great Wall did not keep the enemy out. All they had to do was bribe a gatekeeper. Despite the massive defences, there was an enemy on the inside that let the one on the outside in. So it is with our lives.

The gatekeeper of our hearts must be faithful, otherwise God's instructions will do us no good. You are the gatekeeper. Beware of what you let in! Even if you haven't committed adultery, Jesus has a message for us all:

> 'You have heard that it was said, "Do not commit adultery." But I tell you that anyone who looks at a woman lustfully has already committed adultery with her in his heart. If your right eye causes you to sin, gouge it out and throw it away. It is better for you to lose one part of your body than for your whole body to be thrown into hell. And if your right hand causes you to sin, cut it off and throw it away. It is better for you to lose one part of your body than for your whole body to go into hell.'
>
> (Mt. 5:27–29, NIV).

Many of us (especially men) have sex on the brain, and it's the worst place to have it. How often do you take a second look? A man and his wife were in a department store and a stunning woman walked by. The man's eyes followed her. Without looking up from the item she was browsing, his wife asked, 'Was it worth it, for the trouble you're now in?' Adultery can begin to play itself out on the stage of the imagination long before it occurs in real life.

Jesus says, 'If your eye causes you to sin, gouge it out.' He doesn't mean literally –after all, you can still look through the other eye. What he's saying is, take drastic action. The problem is not actually in the eye but in the heart. Jesus demands that we deal decisively and severely by radical spiritual surgery.

So, rather than pluck out your eye, don't surf the Internet for pornography. Rather than cutting off your hand, cancel an adult channel on cable television. Watch your thoughts: they become words. Watch your words: they become actions. Watch your actions: they become habits. Watch your habits: they become character.

A mind that persistently schemes is a mind that needs cleansing. Jesus calls lust 'adultery in the heart'. If we don't confess and turn away from it, it will eventually consume our thoughts. And if we encourage it with sexually stimulating films, books, magazines or social settings, then fantasy will become reality.

Perhaps you could follow the practice of Job, who said: 'I made a covenant with my eyes not to look with lust upon a young woman' (Job 31:1, NLT).

The second thing to do if you want to stay faithful is to avoid dangerous liaisons. Watch how and when you are alone with someone of the opposite sex. Watch how you touch them. Watch out for that long lunch, that after-work drink, the times when you stay late and work together on a project. A newspaper editor once ran a competition for the best answer to the question: 'Why is a newspaper like a good woman?' The winning answer was: 'A newspaper is like a good woman because every man ought to have one of his own, and not look at his neighbour's.'

Clip 2

Connie is having a flashback. She's back on the street in which she first ran into Paul. The wind is raging, her knee is grazed, and Paul has just invited her into his apartment. But in the split second in which last time she hesitated and things turned out so badly, this time, she sees the taxi coming along the road and calls for it. It draws up, she gets in, and waves Paul goodbye. He stands at his door, smiling; his pile of books stacked up to his chin. Connie waves from the car, and smiles, as she turns her back on the 'moment'.

The third way to stay faithful is to try, at all times, to meet your partner's needs. The apostle Paul wrote about this very frankly in his first letter to the Corinthians: 'The husband should not deprive his wife of sexual intimacy, which is her right as a married woman, nor should the wife deprive her husband. The wife gives authority over her body to her husband, and the husband also gives authority over his body to his wife' (1 Cor. 7:3,4, NLT).

A happy marriage is not so much about how compatible you are, but how you deal with your incompatibility. We all have different needs, and some experts suggest these break down along gender lines: women in particular need affection, conversation, honesty, openness and integrity. They are looking for trust, responsibility and reliability. Men place sexual fulfilment higher up the list, as well as friendship and support. But of course, all our needs vary, according to who we are. The goal in marriage is not to think alike, but to think together; and the key to a good marriage is to understand that it's a union of two forgivers.

Lastly, to stay faithful, value your marriage. Prove your faithfulness to your spouse.

There was a minister who always hoped he'd become a principal of a Bible college. Eventually he did. But as he fulfilled his dream and vocation, Alzheimer's disease struck his wife. Her health degenerated to the point where he could not take care of her and stay on as principal of the college. The man decided to give up his position, even though his colleagues could not believe it. 'What are you doing?' they asked. 'She doesn't even know who you are.' The man replied, 'She might not know who I am, but I know who she is. She's the woman I made a promise to – until death do us part.'

A successful marriage requires falling in love many times with the same person. In a marriage it is important to treat all disasters as incidents and none of the incidents as disasters. As it says in the Book of Common Prayer, we accept our spouses 'to have and to hold from this day forward, for better, for worse, for richer, for poorer, in sickness and in health, to love and to cherish, till death us do part.'

For a good marriage, walk with the Master – 'But if we walk in the light, as he is in the light, we have fellowship with one another' (1 Jn. 1:7, NIV). And work on the marriage – as Paul commanded the Colossians, 'Whatever you do, work at it with all your heart.'

DISCUSSION STARTERS

Personal reflection: Movies don't just help us to escape from our everyday lives, they also shine a light back on them. This film might have stirred up some unhappy memories, guilty feelings or anxious thoughts in you. Even if you are not currently in a relationship, it is worth reflecting on the message of *Unfaithful*. So think, before we begin, about what the film has said to you. And if you know, already, that you need to act to change for good, then try to resolve to do so before the end of the session.

Discuss: 'Be happy for this moment, for this moment is your life.' That's what Paul Martel says to Connie. Our culture encourages us to 'live for the moment'. That can mean two things: that we make decisions without much thought for their consequences; and, we strain forward at every opportunity, looking for the next 'moment' to enjoy. But what is the difference between living *for* the moment, and living *within* the moment? How can we learn to live within the 'present' – living life now, not in the past or the future yet still make decisions in the light of their consequences?

Act: Small decisions or actions can have long-lasting consequences. Privately, draw a map starting from a decision that you took, through to its effect in the present day – whether it was good or bad. Try and trace on the map all of the people your decision or action has affected. You don't have to share this with everyone else if you don't want to!

Read: 2 Sam. 11.

Discuss: Even great people like King David make selfish decisions which have disastrous consequences. Do you find this encouraging or discouraging? If people back in David's day were making the same mistakes that we're making, is there any hope for us? Where does our hope lie?

Read: Ps. 51 (this is the psalm of repentance David wrote in response to his actions).

Personal reflection: In a few moments of quiet, examine yourself and ask whether you are being unfaithful to God or your partner (if you have one) in thought, word or deed. Try to resolve to put this situation right.

Act: And then, all together, say the following words from the psalm:

> 'Create in me a pure heart, O God,
>   and renew a steadfast spirit within me.
> Do not cast me from your presence
>   or take your Holy Spirit from me.
> Restore to me the joy of your salvation
>   and grant me a willing spirit, to sustain me.'

Read: Jn. 8:3–11.

Act: Try to get 'inside' this passage by splitting into smaller groups which represent the characters within it – Jesus, the woman, her accusers, the onlookers. In your groups, discuss how these people might have been feeling, what they looked like, how they were acting, what they were seeing and sensing ... Reconvene and present your character's perspective of the story – perhaps through a short 'meditation' or reflection.

Discuss: Why is Jesus' reaction so powerful, and so disarming? How often are you tempted to judge others, when you know that you yourself are guilty as charged? In what ways does this show itself?

Jesus said, 'Go and sin no more.' While he is ready to forgive, he also expects us to be transformed through the process. What can we do to strengthen our relationships, so that we can avoid temptation? What have you done that has successfully improved your relationship? Share your wisdom together.

Pray: If it's appropriate, pray a short prayer: 'Lord, thank you that you were faithful to us, and faithful to God's will for your life. Help us to be faithful – to your call, to each other and to ourselves. May we live with integrity in such difficult times, and shine your light within a dark world. Amen.'

12
It's What You Are on the Inside
Shrek

J. JOHN

DreamWorks SKG/PDI, 2001

Directed by ANDREW ADAMSON and VICKY JENSON
Screenplay by TED ELLIOT, TERRY ROSSIO, JOE STILLMAN and ROGER S.H. SCHULMAN

MIKE MYERS as *Shrek*
EDDIE MURPHY as *Donkey*
CAMERON DIAZ as *Princess Fiona*
JOHN LITHGOW as *Lord Farquaad*

CLASSIFICATION: U

Shrek is directed by Andrew Adamson and Vicky Jenson, and is based on the children's book by William Steig. This is an astonishing, delightful computer animation, and it's no surprise that the film took five years to make.

At the very start, we are introduced to Lord Farquaad. He is a small man with a big head – an authority figure who ranks low on the scales of integrity and bravery. This contemptible lord lives in Duluc, a sterile and manufactured 'reality'.

He has ordered all the 'misfit fairy tale creatures' to leave his realm, and they have been forced to relocate in a solitary swamp. The problem is, the swamp is home to a green ogre, who lives all alone in the middle of it.

He has made his home in the base of a large, broken tree. The tree is a symbol of Shrek himself: a giant with a broken heart. Shrek has isolated himself in his swamp. He has built layers around his heart, like those of an onion.

His frightening appearance has resulted in people judging and rejecting him without ever getting to know him. As a consequence, he doesn't want to get to know anyone else – especially all the creatures who have invaded his space. So, in an attempt to get rid of them and regain his solitude, Shrek agrees to go on a quest for Lord Farquaad, in return for the removal of his new, unwanted neighbours.

His mission is to rescue the lovely Princess Fiona from a castle guarded by a fire-breathing dragon, so that she can marry Farquaad, who can then become king. A loyal, talkative donkey accompanies Shrek. And donkeys, as it happens, are symbolic of humility, patience and burden bearers.

A story in the Bible's Old Testament also contains a donkey who finds he can speak, and who promptly rebukes the spiritual blindness of its master (Num. 22:27–33). This is exactly what Shrek's donkey does – he speaks words of wisdom and words of rebuke. 'Friends forgive one another,' he tells Shrek. He's certainly no ass …

In fact, the donkey doesn't judge by outward appearances, and he brings the best out of everyone, including the fire-breathing dragon. The love and friendship nurtured by the donkey are able, in the end, to set both Shrek and Princess Fiona free from the 'kingdom of self'.

Shrek is released from his swamp of rejection and Princess Fiona is released from her stronghold of fear. They ride off in an onion coach to live happily ever after. Only the proud, selfish Lord Farquaad remains unaffected.

The underlying themes in Shrek all question our traditional ideas of beauty. We have been brought up in a world dominated by beautiful popstars, glamorous actresses and striking supermodels. In the eyes of our all-pervasive media, those who are beautiful seem to have it all. And as sad and superficial as this may sound, this view is actually fairly traditional. Indeed, fairy tales present a similar theme: the beautiful princess, after initial obstacles, marries her Prince Charming in shining armour and they live happily ever after. Of course, these wonderful ideals appeal to us all; every man would like to be the hero, while most women have dreamed of becoming the beautiful princess.

Sometimes (even subconsciously) our perceptions of beauty are driven by how we imagine they could be in an ideal fairy tale world. In order to help us question these deeply rooted ideas, *Shrek* wonderfully turns the idea of fairy tale on its head. On the surface, the film has all the elements of the archetypal story: a beautiful princess, a fire-breathing dragon and a scary green ogre. It even opens with the classic storybook beginning.

However, things are not always as they seem. Lord Farquaad is not your typical villain – he's short, for a start. Princess Fiona is not a fairy tale princess: besides turning into an ogre every night at sunset, she proves more than capable of rescuing herself; and among other things, she burps, and she sings so piercingly that she causes a bluebird to explode. The dragon doesn't get slain, and turns out to be a 'good girl'. The ogre, in turn, becomes the 'knight in shining armour' and the object of the princess' affection.

The many parodies serve to prove the moral of the tale – that the beautiful story does not have to be conventional. In line with the rest of the film, at the end, Shrek and Fiona are not transformed into a picture-perfect couple. Instead, they remain as they are. The point is, Shrek and Fiona are beautiful despite their appearance, and their story is a confirmation that happy endings do not rely on beautiful exteriors.

Clip 1

[Donkey and Shrek are sitting on a rocky outcrop in the middle of nowhere. There is a tumbledown house behind them. Shrek tells Donkey how everyone judges him before they even meet him and get to know him]

DONKEY. That's not quite true. After all, I didn't judge you on appearances alone, did I?

[Donkey goes to make sure the Princess is all right. He creeps into the house where she is meant to be resting, and looks around for her in the dark, feeling more and more frightened and calling out for her. Then he gets the fright of his life, as he finds himself face-to-face with an ugly girl – an ogre, in fact]

DONKEY. You've eaten the princess. Don't worry Fiona! [*he shouts at the ogre's tummy*] Keep breathing! I'll get you out of there.

PRINCESS FIONA. I am Fiona.

[And, as Donkey slowly realises that this is, indeed, Fiona, he tries to calm down, while she explains that every night, as the sun goes down, she changes into her ugly self. It always happens, without fail. And she won't ever take on 'love's true form' until she experiences true love's first kiss]

Throughout the film, both Shrek and Princess Fiona embark on a journey of self-acceptance, or – put another way in the film – 'becoming comfortable in the skin you're in'. We see very clearly that Shrek struggles with his appearance: 'People take one look at me and say, "Ahhh, look, big, stupid, ugly Ogre,"' he complains.

As a result of his feelings of rejection, Shrek has shut himself away, and decided to live a lonely, solitary existence. Similarly, her 'night time' form repulses Fiona. Despairingly, she cries to the donkey, 'I'm ugly, OK?' She describes herself as 'this horrible, ugly beast', but knows this isn't how it's meant to be: 'I'm a princess, and this is not how a princess is supposed to look,' she explains. 'Princess and ugly don't go together.' She doesn't believe that anybody could ever love her: 'Who could love a beast so hideous and ugly?'

What about us? We work hard to make things appear different to how they really are. Think about how much money we spend on the 'outside': we wash it, brush it, comb it, spray it, curl it, colour it, tan it . . . We try to smooth its wrinkles, lift it, make it smaller, make it bigger – and still we don't like it.

Short people want to be taller, tall people want to be shorter and large people want to be smaller. Light-skinned people try to get darker and dark-skinned people feel they'd be better liked if they were lighter. Perfectionists, let's face it, are never perfectly happy.

However much we try to guard against it, we tend to shape ourselves in the image others have of us. It is not so much their example we imitate, as the reflection of ourselves in their eyes and the echo of ourselves in their words. We mould our faces to fit our masks. And all the time we're fussing over the external parts, while the internal parts are neglected.

As Shrek so wisely comments, 'Sometimes things are more than they appear.' He describes ogres like onions – 'they have layers,' he says, and insists that 'there's more to ogres than people think.' The message, that we shouldn't judge people before we get to know them, is both timeless and true. If we judge a book by its cover, we are often proved to be wrong. There's much more to a person than mere surface appearance.

Even an ogre like Shrek, who freely withdraws from having any contact with other creatures, has a suppressed desire for companionship. Appearances are very deceitful.

It's a theme that is picked up by the Bible. 'Don't judge by … appearance or height … The Lord doesn't make decisions the way you do! People judge by outward appearance, but the Lord looks at a person's thoughts and intentions' (1 Sam. 16:7, NLT).

In fact, the Bible says that all humans are made in the image of God. In an image-obsessed world, that's something to think about. The Bible wasn't talking about what God looks like, but how he is – a Creator God who loves others for who they are, and seeks their love in return.

God looks beyond our nose, which we think is too long, and our feet, which we think are too big. He looks beyond whether we think we are too tall or too short or too heavy or too thin. He looks inside the heart and sees what is there.

So, what *does* God look for in us? He searches for a heart that will accept his love. God is no respecter of persons. It doesn't make any difference what you look like. He wants a heart that is ready to receive his love, and reflect that love to others.

I remember walking down the corridor of a hospital, when I saw someone in a wheelchair. I couldn't tell if they were male or female, because their body was so twisted and bent. It turned out he was a boy, and he was in one of those motorised wheelchairs that can be controlled by the movement of just a finger or two.

This boy was motoring up and down the corridor, going faster than all the people walking along. He went to the end of the corridor, turned around and came back. As he raced along, I looked into his face and saw a great big smile and a look of exhilaration. It was clear that he'd just got the wheelchair, and all of this was the expression of joy in his new-found mobility. When I saw his face, I forgot about his body. I only saw the big smile, the sparkling eyes and a look of wonder.

I think God is like that. He doesn't see the imperfections, the scars and scrapes. He looks straight into the heart. Is there love inside of you that reflects the love of God so that others can see?

Jesus once said, 'Blessed are the pure in heart, for they will see God' (Mt. 5:8, NIV). When we think of the heart, we tend to think of our emotions. We say things like, 'I love you with all of my heart' or 'I have a broken heart'. Yet in the Bible, the word 'heart' refers to more: it refers to our emotions, our intellect and our will.

That is why Solomon urges us in the book of Proverbs (4:23, NIV) to 'Above all else, guard your heart, for it is the wellspring of life.' The heart is the control centre of our lives. According to Jesus, 'purity of heart' isn't about believing the right things. It isn't about going through the right motions. It's doing the right things with right motives.

St Augustine once wrote, 'Before God can deliver us from ourselves, we must undeceive ourselves.' We need unmixed motives, and transparent integrity.

Abraham Lincoln, when told that someone had called him 'two-faced', said: 'If I were two-faced, would I be wearing this one?'

Purity of heart isn't just the absence of certain negative things in your life; it's *positively* the very presence of God in you. It begins with the shedding of pretence, which leads to an absolute inner awareness of who you really are. 'Pure' is translated from the Greek word *katharos*, from which we get 'catharsis'. It literally means 'to make pure by cleansing from dirt, filth or contamination'.

In classical Greek, the word was most often used to describe metals that had been refined in the fire, until they were 'pure' – free from impurities. Jesus wants us to have a 'pure', 'clean', 'unmasked' heart. A pure heart is a forgiven heart. It's a heart that has been cleansed by the purifying blood of Jesus Christ.

A pure heart is one that is in a relationship with God, that repents of sins and seeks inward purity. Purity of heart cleanses the eyes of the soul so that God becomes visible. When Jesus said, 'Blessed are the pure in heart', he was pronouncing blessing on those who are pure at the very centre of their being, at the very source of their every activity, not those who appear pure on the surface. In fact, he berated the Pharisees for metaphorically washing the outside of their lives, while leaving the inside dirty.

Clip 2

[Shrek and Donkey are standing outside a beautiful cathedral. Inside, Lord Farquaad and Princess Fiona are at the top of the aisle, as a packed congregation looks on. They are about to get married and are preparing to say their vows]

[Donkey urges Shrek to get inside and, at the right moment, object. He should tell her how he really feels and stop the marriage. So, just as Fiona is about to kiss the nasty Lord, Shrek bursts in]

SHREK [*shouting*]. I object!

[Shrek walks down the aisle, as the on-lookers gasp. To Farquaad's consternation, he tells Fiona how he really feels. Outside, the sun is about to set. This is the moment of truth for Fiona. She walks to the window and says that she's been waiting to tell Shrek the truth – to show him who she really is. The sun sinks below the horizon and she transforms again into her 'ugly' self]

SHREK. That explains a lot.

[Lord Farquaad screams, calls his guards and commands that she be locked back in the tower. At that moment, the dragon crashes through a huge stained-glass window, the guards wither in fright, and the dragon promptly swallows the evil lord whole]

SHREK [*Shrek and Fiona look into each others eyes*]. I love you.

PRINCESS FIONA. I love you.

[They kiss – for Fiona, it is true love's first kiss, the kiss that she has waited for all her life, to transform her into 'love's true form']

[In a huge explosion of light and stars, which is so fierce that all the windows smash with the force, she is lifted up and caught in a magical, beautiful cloud. Then she falls softly to the floor]

SHREK. Are you all right?

PRINCESS FIONA. Yes, but I'm still ugly. I thought I would be beautiful.

SHREK [*looking at her lovingly*]. But you are beautiful.

[Cue the celebrations ...]

As *Shrek* progresses, we discover that the characters find acceptance. Shrek is accepted and befriended by Donkey, and Fiona grows fond of him. Slowly, he finds that he can accept himself and be content with who he is. It is in the penultimate, wedding scene that Fiona reveals her true identity to Shrek. In the knowledge that Shrek still loves her as she is, she can then accept herself.

Fiona says, 'I don't understand, I'm supposed to be beautiful.' Shrek replies, 'But you *are* beautiful.' This acceptance is confirmed in the final words of the film. 'And they lived ugly ever after.' Not only are they content, but happy.

A 6-year-old boy with an ugly birthmark on the side of his face was once brought to one of Mother Teresa's orphanages. He appeared fearful, unloved and uncared for. He immediately went and sat in the corner and wouldn't talk to anybody.

Mother Teresa walked over and knelt down beside him in the corner and said, 'Well, what do we have here?' Then she embraced him in her arms and kissed him right on the birthmark on his face.

The other children started clapping because they knew that if Mother Teresa kissed the birthmark, it was all right. It made it beautiful, just because Mother Teresa said it was.

That is what God has done. He has embraced us and kissed us, through the death of his son Jesus on a cross. It's another one of those topsy-turvy fairy tales – God became human, and not even a very handsome one at that (so the Bible says). The all-powerful king of the universe made himself weak, gave himself into human hands and died for us, so that we could be made beautiful in God's sight.

If you are experiencing loneliness and rejection, then know that God looks beyond all those things that people might consider ugly and unattractive. He looks at your heart. He looks for love. He looks for purity.

If you have those things, you're beautiful in God's sight. If you don't have them, God wants to take you in his arms, the same way Mother Teresa took the little boy in hers, and embrace you with love and acceptance.

DISCUSSION STARTERS

Personal reflection: *Shrek* is a charming animation with a message for us all. What struck you most about the film? Which characters did you find yourself able to identify with? How did the film leave you feeling? If you could sum it up in a phrase or sentence, what would it be?

Discuss: On the surface, *Shrek* seems like your average fairy tale. But it's not. Sometimes, the power of a work of art lies in its ability to surprise us, and to help us see the world differently, through different eyes. How did this film defy your expectations? Can you think of other works of art that do similarly?

Read: Is. 52:13–15.

Discuss: What does Jesus look like? We tend to have a picture book image of Jesus – as white, Western, bearded, smiling. But the prophet Isaiah suggests that God's 'suffering servant' would not be attractive, physically. Why do we prefer our heroes to be good looking and attractive? To what extent have Christians bought into the Hollywood myth that leading characters are like film stars? How much have we sanitised Jesus, along with the suffering that he went through?

Act: Try to think of someone you admire who defies the convention for being 'good looking' or attractive. It might be a hero, or a sporting figure, an author or a politician. What do you admire about them? Each person in turn should spend a minute presenting the person they admire to the rest of the group. As you go, try to remember that true character – and the inclination of our hearts – counts for so much more, in the end, than the surface appearance.

Act: How well do you know each other? It's amazing how we often remain at quite a shallow level within our relationships. Think of one thing about yourself – a character trait, an event or an achievement – that might surprise people about you. Everybody should write one thing down anonymously on a piece of paper. Then let the group try to decide which description fits which person.

Discuss: Now spend a few minutes discussing how carefully we listen to each other within a group, and whether we even listen at all. Do we, instead, simply wait to get our own word in without listening to others? How much have we missed out on, by presuming we know each other, while not really getting down to the business of 'active listening'?

13

Confessions
Phone Booth

J. JOHN

20TH CENTURY FOX, 2002

Directed by JOEL SCHUMACHER
Screenplay by LARRY COHEN

COLIN FARRELL as *Stu Shepard*
KIEFER SUTHERLAND as *The Caller*

CLASSIFICATION: 15

Does art imitate life or life imitate art? Joel Schumacher's wonderful thriller *Phone Booth* was originally set to be released in November 2002, but as a result of the terrifying shooting spree by the notorious 'Washington Sniper', 20th Century Fox chose to delay its release.

Colin Farrell, who plays the film's star, Stu Shepard, described *Phone Booth* as an exploration of a 'complex character's life-and-death struggle for redemption whilst undergoing a terrifying ordeal'. The film raises many serious issues which we can reflect positively on, and which provoke us to think harder about who we are, and who we might become.

Shepard is a man at the very top of his game – or, so he thinks. He's in his late twenties, with beautiful hair, manicured nails, a Donna Karan suit and silk Armani tie. He's got the gift of the gab, and struts confidently down Broadway as if he owns the place. He somehow seems to represent so much about our fast-paced and skim-the-surface culture. There's no depth to his life; no substance to his dealings with other people.

He's a highly-strung, fast-talking manipulator; a New York publicist who fakes his own success. Stu spends his days pacing the street, hyping himself to clients on his mobile phone and telling them what they want to hear, so that they do exactly what he wants them to. He doesn't have much use for the truth, which he bends, twists and breaks at every opportunity.

Clip 1: Who do you think you are?

Stu and his young assistant Adam are walking down the streets of Manhattan, each speaking into a mobile phone. Stu is persuading 'Donny' that he'll get him the front cover scoop he's after. 'No means yes to these people, Donny,' he argues. At the same time, Stu is getting Adam to ring big-name magazines, to play them off against each other, telling each one that the other is going to run a picture of Donny on their cover.

Suddenly, Adam raises the alert – it's Mario's restaurant! They always walk quickly past Mario's, where Stu has been dining out on false promises of publicity for the restaurant for months. But it's too late. Mario appears on the pavement beside them. Before Mario can finish his complaint ('No more free drinks. No more free meals'), Stu is promising him the biggest celebrity party of the month, to be held at his restaurant with TV coverage and stars … And Mario is thanking him, as if he really believes him.

Stu gives Adam some further instructions about the magazines and sends him off to go and get a suit. And once alone, Stu checks his watch, and sidles up to a phone booth – the same one, in fact, that he approaches at the same time every day. Stu, who's married to Kelly, always uses this booth in Manhattan to call a pretty, aspiring actress called Pamela who he's stringing along because he's attracted to her. In a cell-phone world, it's one of the last remaining 'booths' of its kind in the city, 'one of the last vestiges of privacy in Manhattan', as the narrator says. Stu calls Pam from the booth so that his wife, Kelly, doesn't find her number on his mobile phone bill. Conveniently, Pam doesn't know that Stu is married.

As he starts to dial Pam's number, he fiddles with his wedding ring, and then takes it off. But before he can make the call, a pizza delivery man appears at the booth, and knocks on the door. The pizza's for the man occupying the phone booth, he says. But Stu – who is confused by this surprise gesture – is rude, callous, insulting and instructs him: 'Please return to sender' with a final cutting remark about the man's weight.

He dials Pam, and proceeds to string her along with empty promises of acting parts and press conferences. But when she refuses to come down and meet him at a hotel for the afternoon, his manner changes, and he ends the call. As he picks up the wedding ring, the phone rings. Curious, Stu answers it immediately.

'Isn't it funny? You hear a phone ringing and it could be anybody. But a ringing phone has to be answered, doesn't it?'

It's his judgement call. As the film's tagline would have it, his life 'is on the line'.

On the other end is a man's voice; terrifyingly, it's a mad sniper who has decided to become Stu's judge and jury.

The man announces to Stu that his time is up, and that, if he values his life, he had better not hang up.

A sign on the wall by the phone booth says, in huge letters, 'Who do you think you are?' and for the rest of the film, Stu has no choice but to set upon a course of self-discovery. The voice on the other end seems to know all about his personal life and his myriad lies. He has watched him act without respect to all the people around him.

Judgement day

During the call, the sniper tries to get Stu to realise that he is 'guilty of inhumanity to (his) fellow man' and the 'sin of spin – avoidance and deception'. He also explains that he has a high-powered rifle trained on the phone booth from one of the many buildings, and if Stu tries to leave it, he will be killed. His scope is so good that he could find Pam's number from watching Stu dial it.

And to prove he is deadly serious, he shoots a bystander. Panic breaks out everywhere and the police quickly arrive, assuming that Stu is the killer. They try to force him to put the phone down and come out of the booth. Stu finds himself in a life-and-death struggle, while being forced to re-examine his life and his priorities.

The mystery caller is a self-proclaimed enforcer of morality, who is set on teaching his 'immoral' target at any cost. He also warns how he shot two other businessmen who had committed similar 'sins' to Stu and who had refused to repent.

This is an avenging angel who manages to stir Stu's conscience, offering him the opportunity to repent from past mistakes and to start a new way of life. 'You have a choice to make things right,' he tells him. The caller then takes Stu through three different phases – of judgement, confession and redemption.

First, he's forced to acknowledge his wrong doings. The sniper calls several things into question in Stu's life, such as his self-inflated image.

Stu genuinely believes himself to be at the centre of his world; nothing else matters to him. At first, he thinks the man might be a failed actor in need of his help, and he threatens him: 'A lot of people know who I am... You won't ever get work in this town again ... I can turn people into gods and I can turn people into losers ...'

The caller highlights his lack of respect for others, which has been clear from the film's onset. It is also shown most dramatically in his dealings with a pizza delivery man. Stu has become used to being able to pay people off with money. And as the voice reminds him, 'Everyone has their price.'

Another aspect of Stu's character the voice calls into question is his countless lies. As he later admits, Stu lies to everyone: to the people he works for or with; to his friends; to both Pamela and Kelly; and to his assistant, who he bribes with the empty promise of a pay-cheque he never intends to give.

It is Stu's inability to tell the truth that concerns the voice most: 'Why don't you try telling her the truth?' he asks. 'You're in this position because you're not telling the truth.'

Phone Booth's director, Joel Schumacher, has said of our society that 'we accept lying and lying to the most important people in our life and that rules aren't for us. We are showing the selfishness and decadence of this generation.'

Second, the sniper forces Stu to acknowledge the consequences of his wrong decisions. At first, he cannot understand why this has happened to him and he is told, 'If you have to ask, you're not ready yet.'

Later, the voice intones, 'You are guilty and therefore take responsibility. Your sins have been noticed. Life has given you your fair share. Deception can't go unrewarded.'

It continues, 'Your choices still jeopardise other people. When are you going to realise that?' The caller teaches him a lesson when he goes back on his word, telling him: 'You can't know the pain of betrayal until you've been betrayed.' Ominously, Stu is told, 'Your sins have finally caught up with you.'

Third, Stu is offered redemption as the voice always gives him a way out: 'You could confess your sins and beg for absolution,' he reminds him. The voice explains that he is doing 'all this to get you to do what is right ... I'm offering you a chance to redeem yourself. Humble yourself in front of your loved ones,' he commands. 'Tell Kelly about the real Stu.'

Clip 2: Confession time

Stu is in the phone booth. He's looking flustered, upset. Nothing like the confident PR man who walked into it minutes earlier to call Pam. 'Your sins have finally caught up with you,' says the sniper.

'Tell me what you want!' begs Stu.

'What everyone wants: for the bad guy to get what he's always deserved.'

Police, following the shooting of the bystander, surround him. And there's a gun in the phone booth, planted by the sniper. Unless Stu confesses 'everything' to the watching media, he will be forced to pick up the gun, thus provoking the police marksmen to shoot him.

The sniper tells Stu that he's talking 'prime time material, now. So no more excuses or half truths ... TV seems to bring out the worst in people, so you should be fine.'

Stu is perplexed, though, at this call to confession. What has he done that makes him any worse? He's just a publicist who fantasises about pretty little actresses; he hides himself behind expensive suits, and doesn't waste his time being nice to people who aren't useful to him.

'I know your crimes,' interrupts the sniper. 'Tell them!'

So, Stu leans out of the booth, and looks at the cameras all lined up, alongside the TV cars and officers and reporters and public. He sees his wife, Kelly. And then he turns and sees Pamela. Both are there, as he begins to list his 'crimes':

'I never do anything for anyone unless they can do something for me. I string along an eager kid because he looks up to me. I lie to the magazines, papers and my friends. I feel that I need my expensive clothes, because underneath I feel like the Bronx. My $2,000 watch is a fake and so am I. I should be alone.'

He talks directly to Kelly: 'I've been dressing up as something I'm not for so long. I'm so afraid you won't like what I am underneath. But here I am, I'm just flesh and blood and weakness. I love you so much. I take my ring off [when I talk to Pam] only because it reminds me how I've failed you. I don't want to give you up, but it may not be my choice anymore. You deserve better.'

Stu is distraught. Kelly stares. Pam cries. The world watches.

The dynamics of true repentance

Stu becomes a changed man immediately after his confession, when he realises that 'I didn't confess for you' (the sniper). He has seen for himself the value in honesty.

Instead, he realises that his marriage is really worth fighting for. 'I neglected the things I should have valued the most,' he admits.

Stu is being forced – however bizarrely – to recognise a spiritual reality that will eventually face us all. 'For,' the Bible says (in 2 Cor. 5:10, NLT), 'we must all stand before Christ to be judged. We will each receive whatever we deserve for the good or evil we have done.'

Obviously repentance cannot be coerced. And neither is God a mad sniper with a long-range rifle. A change of heart must come from within. Still, we should know that a day is coming when we will be held accountable for all that we say or do. Our lives are already like an open book to God.

After his confession, Stu comes out of the phone booth and adopts a crucified position. He is felled by a policeman's rubber bullet. But then, he experiences new life – a resurrection, if you like – in his wife's arms, the woman he has come to realise as the most important figure in his life. She forgives him. Heartfelt confession brings new life. The voice warns Stu: 'Lets hope that your new-found honesty lasts, because if it doesn't, you'll be hearing from me.'

The example of King David

In the Bible we find a very personal prayer of confession, self-examination and a cry for forgiveness. Psalm 51 is a confession by David, who committed the double sin of adultery and murder while he was king of Israel. David was on his palace roof one day while his army had gone out to battle and he saw a beautiful woman bathing. He sent messengers and ordered her to be brought to him. He slept with her while her husband, a soldier in his army, was away fighting for his king. Later, when David learned that she was pregnant, he panicked and tried to cover up his actions. He ordered Bathsheba's husband, Uriah, to be sent home from battle, hoping that he would sleep with his wife and the child would then be accepted as his own.

But Uriah was a faithful soldier, committed to battle, and would not go to his own house, but stayed at the palace and returned to the battle the next day. David knew that what he did would be found out, so he ordered Uriah, the husband, to be put in the forefront of the battle where he would most certainly be killed. When news of Uriah's death reached David he felt he was off the hook, he had safely covered his sin.

However, David's conscience continued to bother him. In Psalm 32 (NLT), David describes how he felt during the time he was trying to cover up what he had done. 'When I refused to confess my sin, I was weak and miserable, and I groaned all day long,' he writes. For about a year, he tried to live with a guilty conscience. But God loved David too much to let him go on covering up and damaging himself and his entire kingdom by this hidden sin. So God sent the prophet Nathan to David. And when Nathan confronted the king, he acknowledged the terrible thing he had done. He fell on his face before God, and out of that experience of confession came Psalm 51 (NLT), with its beautiful line, 'Create in me a clean heart, O God, and renew a right spirit within me.'

The need for cleansing

It reminds me of two students who were chatting. One of them said, 'I was given a cookbook for Christmas, but I can never do anything with it.'

'What, too much fancy work in it?' asked the other.

'No,' replied the first. 'Every one of the recipes begins the same way: 'Take a clean dish.'

Like both King David and Stu Shepard, our lives need cleansing. God says, 'Take a clean life,' and that's a problem, because the Bible tells us that we 'all fall short of God's glorious standard' (Rom. 3:23, NLT).

In fact, we're a bit like snowflakes. Their crystal formations are beautiful. Each is unique, with a different shape and size; but they all have one thing in common: they have dirty hearts. In fact, the centre of every snowflake has a formation of dirt, which holds it all together.

Every one of us has a dirty heart. We are the greatest of all creation, God's pride and joy, and every single one of us is – amazingly – unique. Yet we all have a common thread: sin. Every one of us is also marked by sin. And sadly, sin is dirty. It's filthy, and it stains our lives.

We try to deal with our guilt in a lot of different ways. Some people try to cover it up with a lot of good works, thinking, 'If I do enough good deeds, I can balance the scales in my favour.' But good deeds won't, in the end, dispense with our guilt.

Our tendency is to rationalise, explain, excuse, defend or justify our actions.

The great author and scholar C.S. Lewis once wrote that 'we have a strange illusion that mere time cancels sin, but, mere time does nothing either to the fact or guilt of sin. The guilt is washed out not by time, but by repentance and the blood of Christ.'

Only what God has done for us through the sacrifice Jesus offered on the cross can take away the sin and the guilt. The Bible says, 'The blood of Jesus Christ … cleanses us from every sin' (1 Jn. 1:7, NLT). It's very good news for us, when there is no other way to find forgiveness and redemption.

So, David says, 'Purge me, purify me, and wash me.' He says, 'God, that's what I want you to do to me. I've got myself dirty. I've been messing with some things I shouldn't have been. I need you to clean me up. He describes forgiveness as a cleansing: 'Create in me a clean heart, O God,' he writes. 'Wash me clean from my guilt …

Purify me from my sins, and I will be clean; wash me, and I will be whiter than snow' (Ps. 51:2,7, NLT).

Contrition before confession

We can see from the Psalms that before David could be cleansed, God wanted him to be sorry, and even 'contrite'. 'The sacrifice you want is a broken spirit. A broken and repentant heart, O God, you will not despise,' David writes (Ps. 51:17, NLT).

To be contrite does not mean merely feeling bad or remorseful about sin. It means that we experience a genuine and deep-down sorrow for our actions against God and against others. We must also show a determined desire to be different, unlike the man who wrote a letter to the Inland Revenue saying, 'I am having trouble sleeping because of my conscience: so please find enclosed £100. If this doesn't cure my insomnia, I'll send you the rest.'

That's not an attitude of contrition! A contrite heart does not seek to blame circumstances or other people or God for our own failure. And in the biblical account, David doesn't blame God or Bathsheba. He doesn't say, 'Lord, if you hadn't made me king I wouldn't be walking on this palace roof in the first place. And besides, did you see what she wasn't wearing?'

In Las Vegas, there is a call-in 'confession line' which you can ring to confess your sins to a recording. It costs $9 for three minutes to record your sin; but if you want to pay $18, you can listen to other people's confessions. One of the phone line's directors has commented: 'It's a technological way to get something off your chest without the embarrassment that comes from confessing one-on-one.' But do you know what it really is (besides a nice little earner for some entrepreneurial spirit)? It's confession without accountability.

If we ever hope to have a clean heart, we must experience contrition. And then, just as with King David and Stu Sheppard, we must confess what we've done. The reason most people don't find God is the same reason that most criminals don't find a policeman.

The two sides of confession

There is a part of us that finds it very difficult to go to God and honestly admit doing wrong. In fact, we can be freed by confession or locked in by denial. The choice is ours. It's been that way since Adam and Eve sinned in the Garden of Eden. They tried to hide from God and when that didn't work they tried to shift some of the blame for their sin on to someone else. And that's exactly what continues today. We see it throughout our society, whether it's in politics, sport, education, the BBC …

In Ps. 51:3,4a, David writes, 'For I recognise my shameful deeds – they haunt me day and night. Against you, and you alone, have I sinned; I have done what is evil in your sight.' There are two sides to his confession. First of all, he confesses to himself. He acknowledges his guilt: 'I realise that I have sinned. I can't deny it or escape it or forget it. I recognise what I've done.' Then he confesses his sin to God: 'Against you, you only, have I sinned.'

Along with his admission of guilt is a confession of God's justice, and God's right to judge him for what he has done. David makes no plea for lenience, no claim that God is being too hard on him, no appeal for a lighter sentence. Simply put, he says, 'You're right, I'm wrong.' Genuine confession demands that we take sin as seriously as God takes it.

It's not about excusing ourselves, about thinking it's just a slip-up, a mistake. It's about us developing the right attitude towards sin; we need to loathe it, to find it disgusting. Just like Stu and the sniper, this is deadly serious. And armed with disgust for sin, we must determine to turn away from our sin. The Bible says, 'if we confess our sins to him, he is faithful and just to forgive us and to cleanse us from every wrong' (1 Jn. 1:9, NLT).

David was contrite and confessed his sins, so God cleansed him. And wonderfully, God is willing to do the same for any of us. We don't have to be a king. We don't even have to have committed adultery, or killed a man, to experience the amazing sense of forgiveness, which comes with confession. God delights in having the opportunity to forgive us all, for whatever we have done, whether big or small. And when he forgives, he doesn't continue to hold it over our heads. Sometimes we have a harder time forgiving ourselves than God does.

We sometimes feel weighed down with the burden of guilt long after God has removed it from our backs. If we follow God's instructions to be contrite and to confess, we can then trust that God has kept his promise to forgive. Ps. 103:12 (NIV) puts it beautifully: 'as far as the east is from the west, so far has he removed our transgressions from us.'

Have you asked yourself recently whether you need the cleansing that God offers? Are you covering up the guilt in your life through good works or denial? Or are you labouring under an enormous burden of guilt? Either way (and many of us are somewhere in between), have you received God's forgiveness? Have you forgiven yourself?

Do you need to let go of your regrets about the past, and experience God's healing for the previous poor choices you have made?

Like the film, our lives are on the line. And like the film, we need a wake up call, to contrition, confession and redemption. Thankfully, we don't need a sniper to trap us in a phone booth. This movie will make you think hard enough. But the words of King David, who confessed and experienced forgiveness, will show you where to go next for the source of all life. There is always hope.

DISCUSSION STARTERS

(You'll need some plain and coloured paper, pens, pencils and some painting implements if you have them.)

Personal reflection: The sign by the telephone booth says, 'Who do you think you are?' For a few moments, stop to reflect on that question before we start. Who *do* you think you are? Do you see anything of yourself in Stu Sheppard?

Discuss: *Phone Booth* is a shocking film. How did you respond to the unfolding events? If the sniper were to trap you in the phone booth, would he have much to go on? How might you react?

Act: Stu asks the sniper what he has done that makes him worse than anyone else. It's a good question. We might, in turn, ask, 'What makes us as bad as Stu?' Write down as many ways or situations you can think of in which you 'spin the truth' like Stu. They don't have to be spectacular – in fact, the more mundane, the better.

Discuss: Share these together, so long as they aren't too personal! Which subjects arise most frequently? Can you address this as a group? Is there any way you can make yourselves a bit more accountable to each other – without the use of a gun?!

Act: Stu rings Pam from the phone booth because he doesn't want his wife to find out. But we can reclaim the phone booth for positive reasons. Write down your telephone number on a few strips of coloured paper, and give them to a few members of the group (of the same sex) that you would like to be more accountable to.

Put any numbers you are given in your wallet or purse. It's unusual for us to use phone boxes these days – but each time you see one, try to let it remind you of your commitment to ring your numbers at least once a week. Take the time to go into the phone box, pray for the person you need to ring, then spend a few minutes calling and asking how they are. It is an act of commitment to go into the phone box; try to do this instead of squeezing in a call on the train.

Read: Read Ps. 103.

Act: The Bible says, 'as far as the east is from the west, so far has he removed our sins from us.' The sun rises in the east and sets in the west. Draw or paint a picture of a sunrise or sunset, that you can take home and keep. Each time you look at it, let it remind you that God's mercies are 'new every morning' – with every new sunrise – and that no matter how often we do bad things, God will forgive us if we confess our sins. With every sunset, remember that it's in completely the opposite direction from the sunrise, and thank God that your sins are going down with the sun, being removed from sight by a loving and merciful God.

Pray: If it's appropriate, pray this short prayer to end: 'Father you know everything. You know my thoughts, and you know my deeds. You know the way I spin my words to suit each situation and to use it for my advantage. Thank you that you are not holding a gun to my head. But help me to respond to your loving invitation to help me to change, for good. Amen.'

14

You've Got the Power
Bruce Almighty

MARK STIBBE

UNIVERSAL PICTURES, 2003

Directed by TOM SHADYAC
Screenplay by STEVE KOREN, MARK O'KEEFE and STEVE OEDEKERK

JIM CARREY as *Bruce Nolan*
JENNIFER ANISTON as *Grace Connelly*
MORGAN FREEMAN as *God*

CLASSIFICATION: 12A

In June 2003, America Online ran a poll asking the following:

> What would you do if you were God for the day:
> Change the climate in Britain to one on a par with the Mediterranean?
> Fix the Lotto so you win it – every week for a year?
> Let the Big Brother four pass a task again?
> Make Justin Timberlake or Jennifer Lopez your slave who will obey your every wish?

Something a little more serious, like eradicating world poverty or curing cancer?

The results were interesting:

Let the Big Brother four pass a task again? 2 per cent

Change the climate in Britain to one on a par with the Mediterranean? 4 per cent

Make Justin Timberlake or Jennifer Lopez your slave who will obey your every wish? 9 per cent

Fix the Lotto so you win it – every week for a year? 24 per cent

Something a little more serious, like eradicating world poverty or curing cancer? 56 per cent

I wonder what you and I would do if we had all of God's attributes for a day or for a week. That's the question posed by our movie in this chapter.

Bruce Almighty tells the story of Bruce Nolan, acted by Jim Carrey, an eyewitness news TV reporter in Buffalo, New York. He is well known for doing humorous, human interest stories in the local area and these make everyone happy except him. He is profoundly frustrated by the triviality of his stories and his existence. Bruce would rather be taking the place of retiring anchorman Pete Fineman or reporting hot news stories from other parts of the world.

One day Bruce is handed a news opportunity when asked to do a story on the twenty-third anniversary of Niagara Falls' famed *Maid of the Mist* boat – to go live on air. But just as Bruce is about to speak he hears that the anchor position he wanted is going to his great rival, Evan Baxter. In front of a live audience, Bruce has a complete meltdown punctuated by four-letter words. One disaster follows another on this, the worst day of Bruce's life. He's fired from the TV station and beaten up by a gang of youths, who then vandalise his car. Bruce now falls into a depression. He goes back home in the evening to his flat and starts to complain to his girlfriend Grace in their apartment. Feeling victimised and hard done by, Bruce begins to rail against God. Bruce is adamant that God has it in for him. 'He's ignoring me completely,' he says. 'God is a mean kid sitting on an anthill with a magnifying glass and I'm the ant. He could fix my life in 5 minutes if he wanted to but he'd rather burn off my feelers and watch me squirm.'

Railing against his mediocre job, his mediocre apartment and his mediocre life, Bruce takes off with his car keys. He drives along the freeway complaining against God. In the end he takes hold of the prayer beads given to Grace by the kids in her day care job. He asks God for a sign. He even tries praying.

Clip 1: Prayer, the last resort

[It's night time and it's raining now. Bruce drives, going nowhere in particular. His frustration is turning to desperation]

BRUCE. OK, God. You want me to talk to you? Then talk back. Tell me what's going on? What should I do? Give me a sign …

[Bruce passes a blinking yellow caution light, doesn't notice …]

BRUCE. I'm right here. Speak to me. All I need is some guidance. Please send me a signal.

[A truck transporting various road signs pulls in front of Bruce. Four ways, blinking. The varied signs read. Yield, Wrong Way, Dead End, Do Not Enter, Stop]

BRUCE. Oh well, I guess you don't care.

[Bruce spots the prayer beads hanging on the rear view mirror]

BRUCE. OK, we'll do it your way.

[Pulls the beads from the mirror]

BRUCE. Lord, I need a miracle. Please help me.

[He hits a bump and the beads drop to the floor. Bruce reaches down, fishes for the beads ...]

BRUCE. Come on, where'd you go?

BRUCE [*holds them up in triumph*]. Aha! AHHH!

[And bam! Bruce's car slams into a light post]

[Bruce stumbles out, surveys his demolished car, then looks at the beads in his hands. He begins to laugh maniacally. He spots the lake, starts running toward it like a madman, heaves the prayer beads into the lake. He looks heavenward, challenging the Infinite]

BRUCE. OK, if that's the way you want it. The gloves are off, pal! Let me see a little wrath! Smite me, oh mighty smiter. What, no pestilence, no boils? Come on, you got me on the ropes, don't you want to finish me off?! You're the one who should be fired! The only one around here not doing his job is YOU! What are we, your little pet project? A hobby you tinker with now and again? Answer me. ANSWER ME!!!

[A beat of silence then Bruce's beeper goes off. He cynically chuckles at the timing, checks it, sees 772-5623]

BRUCE. Sorry, don't know you, wouldn't call you if I did.

[Bruce walks off toward his wrecked car, it beeps again.]

Who's driving your car?

A man really hated his wife's cat and one day decided to get rid of it. He drove 20 blocks away from home and dropped the cat there. As he arrived home the cat was already walking up the driveway. The next day, he decided to drop the cat 40 blocks away but the same thing happened. He kept on increasing the number of blocks but the cat kept on coming home before him. At last he decided to drive a few miles away, turn right, then left, past the bridge, then right again and another right, and so on and so on, until he reached what he thought was the perfect spot, and pushed the cat out of the door. Hours later, the man called his wife at home and asked her, 'Jen, is the cat there?'

'Yes, of course, why do you ask?' answered the wife.

Frustrated, the man said, 'Put him on the phone, I am lost and I need directions.'

Bruce Nolan is a man who is totally lost and without direction in his life; he asks for a sign from God and, when confronted by a whole truck load (literally) of them, he continues to steer the car in the wrong direction. What a picture.

So many of us live our lives with ourselves in the driving seat not God – and, like Bruce, we hold on to the steering wheel stubbornly and possessively. We set the route and determine the destination. Then we get surprised when we find that we're lost or we've ended up wrapped around a lamp-post.

Bruce's life is like that; he's in the driving seat but he's taken a wrong turn and now he's crashed. With his life falling apart, like so many people, he turns to prayer as an absolutely last resort. He asks God to speak to him and, when he feels that God has not answered in the way he was expecting, he rails against him saying, 'The only one around here not doing his job is YOU!'

Are you listening?

In the Old Testament there is a story told of a man called Job whose whole life falls apart. Job eventually starts moaning and a friend responds by saying:

> 'You have said it in my hearing. I have heard your very words. You said, "I am pure; I am innocent; I have not sinned. God is picking a quarrel with me, and he considers me to be his enemy. He puts my feet in the stocks and watches every move I make."
>
> 'In this you are not right, and I will show you why. As you yourself have said, "God is greater than any person." So why are you bringing a charge against him? You say, "He does not respond to people's complaints." But God speaks again and again, though people do not recognise it. He speaks in dreams, in visions of the night when deep sleep falls on people as they lie in bed. He whispers in their ear and terrifies them with his warning. He causes them to change their minds; he keeps them from pride. He keeps them from the grave, from crossing over the river of death.'
>
> (Job 33:8–18, NLT)

Job's friend tells him that he is not right to complain that God does not respond to our cries for help. He points out that God speaks to us again and again, but that we neither see nor listen.

In an episode of the TV series *X-Files* entitled, 'Revelations', Dana Scully is asked the question, 'What are you afraid that God isn't speaking?' Dana Scully replies, 'No. I'm afraid that he *is* speaking but that no one is listening.'

Bruce Nolan has yet to realise that God is omnipresent – he is present everywhere – but that you have to look in order to find him. And he is found in unexpected places, such as the tramp who appears throughout the film holding signs.

In the second of our extracts Bruce has answered the call on his pager and makes his way to a warehouse for a firm called Omni Presents where he meets a stranger.

Clip 2: The boss, the electrician and the janitor

[Bruce's demolished car enters frame. He studies the area and building suspiciously. Bruce cautiously moves towards the structure and then, steps in a puddle. He sinks up to his knee]

BRUCE. Perfect.

[He gets out, shakes off his sopping leg, and heads inside. Bruce enters and checks the building directory. It reads, Omni Presents Unltd.]

[*Personnel Rm. 7*]

[*Accounting Rm. 7*]

[*Security Rm. 7*]

[*Creative Rm. 7*]

VOICE [*off-screen*]. You're looking for room 7.

[Bruce turns to see a janitor mopping the floor. He looks at Bruce's wet leg, offers the mop]

JANITOR. Want me to even those up for you?

BRUCE [*feigns a smile*]. How would I get to room 7?

JANITOR. That'd be on the seventh floor. Stairs are right over there.

BRUCE. What about the elevator?

JANITOR [*he points to an elevator bank a couple of steps away*]. Out of order.

[*Bruce heads for the stairs*]

JANITOR. You mind giving me a hand with this floor?

BRUCE. What? Yeah, I mind.

[He continues on]

[Seventh floor. The stairwell door opens up to a large room with a single desk at the end of an otherwise empty space. Bruce hears someone tinkering atop a tall ladder extending into a hole in the ceiling]

BRUCE. Excuse me. Hello. I'm, ah, looking for whoever runs this joint ...

MAN. Be right with ya, just fixin' a light. Tell me if it's working?

[Click and an insanely bright white light illuminates, shining down blinding Bruce]

BRUCE. Yep, seems to be. [*Wiping his eyes*] Kinda bright, though.

[An electrician, silhouetted in the bright light, descends the ladder]

MAN. Yeah, it is for most people. They spend their lives in the dark ...

[As he talks he steps down next to Bruce and we see that it is the same janitor]

JANITOR. ... thinkin' they can hide from me.

[The two stand, angelically illuminated. Bruce tries to put everything together]

BRUCE. Oh, the elevator's broken, huh?

JANITOR. Yeah, but I'll get around to it.

[The janitor claps his hands twice and the light goes off]

BRUCE. You installed a clapper?

JANITOR. Nope. Catchy jingle, though.

[sings] Clap on. Clap off. Clap on, clap off. The clapper.

[claps twice]

You can't get it out of your head.

BRUCE. I gotta go.

JANITOR. OK, but the boss'll be right out.

[The janitor unzips his uniform, revealing a very nice suit. He extends his hand to Bruce]

JANITOR. You must be Bruce. I've been expecting you.

BRUCE. Oh, this is hilarious. So you're the boss and the electrician and the janitor.

JANITOR. Nothin' wrong with rollin' up your sleeves, son. People underestimate the benefits of good 'ol manual labour. There's freedom in it. Happiest people in the world stink like hell at the end of the day.

He strolls down the room, takes a seat behind the big desk.

JANITOR. Your father knew that. He was a damn good welder.

[Bruce approaches the desk]

BRUCE. How do you know my father? And how did you get my pager number?

JANITOR. Oh, I know a lot about you, Bruce. Pretty much everything there is to know. Everything you've ever said, done or thought about doin', is right there in that file cabinet.

[He points out a single drawer file cabinet]

BRUCE [*sarcastic*]. Wow, a whole drawer. Just for me? Mind if I take a look?

JANITOR. It's your life.

[Bruce pulls the drawer and it flies open, dragging him the full length of the room.]

Our image of God

I don't know how you personally picture God. In the scene above there are some very interesting things to note about how director Tom Shadyac – a devout Christian – sees God. Perhaps the most notable thing is the fact that Shadyac's God appears in three guises – or, as Christians would put it, in a Trinity of guises.

He first of all appears as the cleaner. This may well be a reference to the Holy Spirit, the third person of the Trinity. He is associated with cleaning up our lives as the adjective 'Holy' shows.

In the last chapter we looked at the movie *Phone Booth*, and J. John used Ps. 51 in his analysis; here are some lines from that psalm that show how closely connected the Holy Spirit is with cleaning up our lives:

> 'Create in me a pure heart, O God,
> and renew a steadfast spirit within me.
> Do not cast me from your presence
> or take your Holy Spirit from me.'
>
> (Ps. 51:10,11, NIV)

Later on in the film the cleaner, or janitor, will say, 'No matter how filthy something gets you can always clean it up.'

The second guise in which God appears is as the electrician. Bruce finds him up a ladder fixing the lights. The electrician switches on the light and comes down the ladder. This represents Jesus, the second person of the Trinity, who came down from heaven as the Light of the World. As the song puts it:

> 'Light of the world you stepped down into darkness
> Opened my eyes let me see.'
> ('Here I am to Worship')

The third guise is as the boss. The electrician takes off his outer overalls and steps out in a white suit. This points to the first person of the Trinity, described by Christians as God the Father Almighty.

So Tom Shadyac's God is a God who appears as three persons, the same yet different. Shadyac's God is also personally interested in Bruce's life even though he is omnipresent. When Bruce cries out to God, God answers Bruce personally by calling him on his pager. God knows the most intimate details of Bruce's past history and has everything on record in a deceptively small filing cabinet.

It is one of the Bible's greatest truths that the God who created the universe and who holds all things together is also personally interested in each one of us. As St Augustine once said, 'God loves each of us as if there were only one of us.'

When someone challenged Galileo to explain how God could be so powerful and yet care for every person, he replied: 'The sun, with all those planets revolving around it and dependent on it, can still ripen a bunch of grapes as if it had nothing else in the universe to do.'

God loves us personally. He is always ready to answer when we call. God answers Bruce's cry and he answers him personally by giving Bruce all his divine powers for a week with two conditions: first, he can't tell anyone he is God. Second, he can't override anyone's free will. God challenges Bruce to see if he can do a better job than him.

In our third extract we see Bruce using God's power in order to win back his girlfriend Grace who has now left him.

Clip 3: Grace and free will

[Grace goes out for a run and notices something carved on a tree; it reads: 'Grace + Bruce'. Carved in the next tree, 'A couple for the ages'. Carved in the next tree, 'Come on already, give him another chance'. She does a double take, continues on. She enters a coffee shop. Grace reaches in her purse to pay for her coffee and a bunch of photos fall out. They are all of Bruce and Grace. She thinks, 'Definitely didn't put them there']

[She notices something outside the window. It's a cloud formation that strangely looks like Bruce (in profile) holding

hands with Grace. She reacts as the imagery melts away into a very faint 'Forgive him']

[She presses on to the Small Wonders day care where she works. She is talking with one of the other teachers. The kids, playing dodge ball in the background, laugh and scream louder and louder. Grace turns and sees Bruce getting pelted by multiple balls]

BRUCE. OK, surrender, surrender.

[He walks over to Grace]

BRUCE. Hi.

GRACE. Hi.

BRUCE. I miss you.

GRACE. I don't know what to say.

BRUCE. How about you love me and you'll take me back.

GRACE. No, Bruce.

BRUCE. Come on, what about all the signs?

GRACE. What? How do you know about that? Did you talk to Debbie?

BRUCE. Would it help if I told you I acted like an ass?

[Martin is standing nearby]

MARTIN. Hey, you said ass.

BRUCE. It's OK as long as you mean a donkey. I didn't add 'hole'. It's only bad when you say 'ass-ho–'

GRACE. Alright, inside, Martin.

GRACE [*to the others*]. OK everyone, inside.

[The kids race in. Grace starts to follow]

BRUCE. Grace, please. None of this seems right without you.

GRACE. I have to go ...

[She starts off ...]

BRUCE. Wait.

[Bruce dramatically raises a hand towards Grace, like putting a love spell on her]

BRUCE. Now how do you feel?

[She looks at him, oddly]

GRACE. ... Are you out of your mind? Have you been drinking?

BRUCE. Drinking? Sure. I'm drunk with power.

[Bruce raises his hands ...]

BRUCE. LOVE ME!

GRACE. I did.

[She heads back inside. Bruce throws his hands in the air, frustrated. Looks heavenward]

BRUCE. Yeah, I know. Free will.

Amazing grace

Just before this scene starts, Bruce talks to God and asks, 'How do you make someone love you without affecting their free will?' To which God replies, 'Welcome to my world, son.'

Bruce has all the power in the universe and yet he cannot affect Grace's free will. He cannot force Grace to love him. So Bruce confronts his powerlessness. He was powerless before he met God, when he was in the driving seat, running his life on his own steam and in his own strength. Now, even with God's power, he is powerless because he cannot use that power to make the person he adores love him in return. And it is here that the film reveals itself to be such a powerful parable. Nothing reveals this more clearly than the name of Bruce's girlfriend, Grace. In the New Testament, grace is defined as God's unmerited love and favour towards us. It is supremely demonstrated in the death of Jesus, where the Son of God gave us a gift we don't deserve, the gift of forgiveness for all our sins. The cross is the ultimate expression of God's amazing grace – or unmerited love. But note this: God chose the path of powerlessness. Jesus Christ gave up the divine attributes he had enjoyed in heaven and was born as a frail infant. He lived as a servant even though he was the King of kings. And he died the death reserved for the lowest of the low. In Jesus Christ, God gave up everything for you and me.

Why did God go to such dramatic lengths? Because he knew that he could not force us to love him, so he decided to woo us by demonstrating the extraordinary depths of his commitment to us. And this is grace – the free gift that we don't deserve. As we read in the New Testament, in the letter to the Ephesians:

> 'But because of his great love for us, God, who is rich in mercy, made us alive with Christ even when we were dead in transgressions – it is by grace you have been saved. And God raised us up with Christ and seated us with him in the heavenly realms in Christ Jesus, in order that in the coming ages he might show the incomparable riches of his grace, expressed in his kindness to us in Christ Jesus. For it is by grace you have been saved, through faith – and this not from yourselves, it is the gift of God – not by works, so that no-one can boast. For we are God's workmanship, created in Christ Jesus to do good works, which God prepared in advance for us to do.'
>
> (Eph. 2:4–10, NIV)

This is what John Henry Newman, in his most famous hymn, called amazing grace. Or, as I was taught when I became a Christian, G–R–A–C–E – God's Riches at Christ's Expense. As someone has said: 'When someone works an eight-hour day and receives a fair day's pay for their time, that is a wage. When someone competes with an opponent and receives a trophy for the performance, that is a prize. When someone receives appropriate recognition for long service or high achievements, that is an award. But when someone is not capable of earning a wage, can win no prize, and deserves no award – yet receives such a gift anyway – that is a good picture of God's unmerited favour. This is what we mean when we talk about the grace of God.'

In *Bruce Almighty*, Grace simply loves Bruce; it's a gift that he doesn't deserve. And it's only when Grace leaves him that Bruce realises what a fool he's been. So Bruce experiences an awakening, realising that he has been incredibly foolish. He thought at the start of the film that God was to blame for his mediocre life so he shook his fist at heaven and told God he wasn't doing his job. He then met God face to face and was given a week with God's power to see if he could do any better. During that time he exercised power without wisdom. At one point, trying to impress Grace, he lassoes the moon in order to create a more romantic mood and in the process he causes a tidal wave in Japan. He grants everyone's prayers with a blanket yes, and causes 400,000 people to win the Lottery simultaneously – with a prize of just $17 each – causing riots in Buffalo.

Bruce at last wakes up and the lights come on. He surrenders to God and meets him again face to face, after being run over on the freeway.

Clip 4: Now that's a prayer!

[City street – night]

[Rain droplets splash on the river where Bruce first raged at God. He stands in the middle of the street, looks up heavenward, weakly. Humble]

BRUCE. You win. I'm done. Please. I don't want to do this anymore. I don't want to be God.

[Sighs]

BRUCE. Please, help me.

[And with that beams of light cut through, shining down upon Bruce as ...]

[HONK! HONK!]

[A truck mows Bruce down]

[We move to a huge white room – no walls, just white as far as the eye can see. Bruce finds himself standing there. He looks around and when he turns behind him, he sees God]

BRUCE. Am I ...?

GOD. You can't expect to kneel down in the middle of a highway and live to talk about it.

BRUCE. But why? Why now?

GOD. I work in mysterious ways, son.

[Bruce takes everything in]

BRUCE. You knew it all along. You knew if I got everything I wanted, I would ruin my life.

[God doesn't respond, just listens]

BRUCE. So I'm dead ... OK. If this is what you want. OK, OK ...

[God holds up the prayer beads, tosses them to Bruce]

[Bruce looks at the beads, then up at God, puzzled]

GOD. Go ahead, use 'em.

BRUCE. Alright ... I've learned that I don't know as much as I thought I did ...

GOD. Boy, you can say that again.

BRUCE. Hey, I'm praying here.

GOD. Sorry, go.

BRUCE. If I could have just one thing in the world. It would be for Grace to live a happy, joyful life. And that she finds someone ... [*getting emotional as he realises what he's saying*] ...that she finds someone that will treat her with the love and respect that she so deserves.

[God smiles the most satisfied of smiles]

GOD. Now that is a prayer. Well, I better get on to that one.

Total surrender

What a scene that is. Bruce declares, 'You win. I surrender to your will. I want you to decide what's right for me.' In the end, Bruce discovers true powerlessness – the powerlessness that leads to new life. He has known three kinds of powerlessness in the film. The powerlessness of not being able to fix his life in his own strength. The powerlessness of not being able to fix his life using God's power. And now the powerlessness of surrendering his whole life to God, handing control back to the one who created and redeemed him.

Truly, the lights have come on in Bruce's life. All the time, he had the power to change things. All he had to do was choose to surrender and to hand his life over to loving God and loving others. Once he surrendered his life, he received what he had wanted deep down all along – Grace!

C.S. Lewis once said, 'There are two kinds of people: those who say to God, "Thy will be done," and those to whom God says, "All right, then, have it your way."' In the end, Bruce learns to say, 'Your will be done.' He had the power to choose to change. And he chooses wisely.

And this, in the end, is the message of the film. God has given us the power to choose – to choose to respond to his overtures of love and build an eternal friendship with him. And the power to choose to put others before ourselves and to see other people through God's eyes. In the end we all have the power to choose whether to become passive and moan, or whether to become active and make a difference. As actress Minnie Driver said: 'There is absolutely no point in sitting around and feeling sorry for yourself. The great power you have is to let go ... focus on what you have, not that which has been mean or unkindly removed.' Or, as God says in *Bruce Almighty*:

> 'Parting your soup is not a miracle, Bruce. It's a magic trick. A single mum working two jobs and still finds time to take her kid to soccer practice – that is a miracle. A teenager who says no to drugs and yes to an education – that is a miracle. People want me to do everything for them but what they don't realise is that they have the power. You want to see a miracle son? Be the miracle!'

And that's the message. Instead of looking all the time for God to give you a miracle and whining when you don't get one, why not resolve to *be* a miracle by choosing to love God and love others? In the end, all of us have freedom to choose – to choose whether to be a misery or to be a miracle.

Bruce Nolan is a sad figure at the start of the film – a Homer Simpson-like figure who whines about relatively minor problems, thereby colluding with the blame culture. But he is redeemed, and we can be, too.

We too can surrender our lives to God and choose to receive his grace – the love that we don't deserve. We can choose to live a God-centred rather than a self-centred life, seeing the world through God's eyes rather than our own. At the end of the day, it's our decision. We can either carry on clutching to the steering wheel and living our lives our way. Or we can hand over to Jesus Christ, surrendering control to him, and let him decide the direction of our lives. As someone has said:

> 'The road to success is not straight. There is a curve called Failure, a loop called Confusion, speed bumps called Friends, red lights called Enemies, caution lights called Family. But,

if you have a spare called Determination, an engine called Perseverance, insurance called Faith, a driver called Jesus, you will make it to a place called Success.'

DISCUSSION STARTERS

(You'll need a bunch of grapes or bottle of wine, a flip chart and pen and if possible a copy of U2's song 'Grace' from the album *All That You Can't Leave Behind*.)

Personal reflection: What did you learn about yourself and about God from this film? How would you like to let this film affect you? Spend a few moments quietly contemplating this, before starting.

Discuss: Mark points out that Bruce turned to prayer as an absolutely last resort. When was the last time you prayed a 'last resort' prayer – or an 'I'd like to win the lottery' prayer? How do you think God feels about getting both types? What should prayer be like? And what do we actually expect of God?

Act: Mark writes that when someone challenged Galileo to explain how God could be omnipresent but still care for each of us, he replied: 'The sun, with all those planets revolving around it and dependent on it, can still ripen a bunch of grapes as if it had nothing else in the universe to do.'

Take a bunch of grapes and pass them round the room. You should each take a few grapes and pass them on. Hold them in your hands. Think about the sun that has ripened them slowly, in the vineyard. Close your eyes, and imagine the warmth of the sun on your face. And with your eyes closed, eat the grapes, and taste the goodness of God's love for each of us, as individual human beings. (You could supplement the grapes with a glass of wine if you wished.)

Discuss: God may be everywhere, but sometimes we struggle to see him. Share with each other the unexpected places that you may have 'seen' God over the last few days or weeks. You might like to write a list together on a flip chart.

Personal reflection: It's hard to make people love you. Think about a time when you loved someone else but they didn't love you back. It was probably a painful experience. Now try to think how it must be like for an all-powerful God to allow us the free will to love him.

Act: Write a letter to God, in which you explain what you have learned from *Bruce Almighty* about him. Let it be a prayer that's not a wish-list, but an act of true communication. Keep the letter, and when you get home, read it before you go to bed as a prayer.

Read: Eph. 2:1–10.

Act: If you have a copy of U2's 'Grace' – from the album *All That You Can't Leave Behind* – play the song and listen closely to the lyrics. Finally, if you feel happy to, close by singing together 'Amazing Grace'.

> 'Amazing grace, how sweet the sound
> That saved a wretch like me!
> I once was lost, but now I'm found
> Was blind, but now I see.'

15

Family Ties

My Big Fat Greek Wedding

J. JOHN

IFC Films, 2002

Directed by JOEL ZWICK
Screenplay by NIA VARDALOS

NIA VARDALOS as *Toula Portokalos*
JOHN CORBETT as *Ian Miller*

CLASSIFICATION: PG

I am Greek. And if you've seen *My Big Fat Greek Wedding,* you'll have seen some of my relatives – including my mother, who is a travel agent for guilt trips. (Recently, she returned the Christmas presents that my wife and I bought for her.)

You'll have probably heard of lots of Greeks. There's Homer (not Simpson, but the giant of ancient literature); the playwrights and dramatists Aesop, Sophocles, Aeschylus and Euripides; Pythagoras, the mathematician; Thales, the first person to measure pyramids; the father of modern medicine, Hippocrates; Herodotus, the historian;

Socrates, Plato, Aristotle, the great philosophers; the Parthenon (OK, it's a building, but it's still Greek); and Pilavachi, the youth worker.

Although *My Big Fat Greek Wedding* is about a Greek family, its story has universal appeal – not least because, as the famous nineteenth-century poet P.B. Shelley once said, 'We are all Greeks. Our laws, our literature, our arts all have their roots in Greece.'

Released in April 2002, this film became a surprise hit. It was produced on a very small budget with no major stars, but still managed to out-gross many of the more expensive and heavily promoted films.

The reason for such astonishing success is because *My Big Fat Greek Wedding* is a modern day Cinderella story; it's a movie that touches our hearts, and is based on a true account. Nia Vardalos, who grew up in a Greek family and describes the story as an autobiography, wrote the script. 'I believe that the movie is about any family that loves you to the point of smothering,' she wrote.

And she's right. Many of us will relate directly to her experience, whether we're Greek or not. (Personally, I was so smothered by the Greek culture that when I went to school, aged 5, I couldn't even speak English. By 8, I was working in my father's Greek restaurant.) Every family surely has its challenges.

The movie opens at 5 o'clock on a dark, rainy Chicago morning. Toula (played by Vardalos) and her father are driving to the family restaurant he owns and where she has always worked. Toula yawns, rather unattractively, as they sit side by side in the car. Her father looks over, frowns, and says (in his thick Greek accent), 'You better get married soon. You starting to look old.'

Toula and her family are from Greece, but live in Chicago. Toula is a frumpy, dowdy 30-something, quietly wasting away as a waitress in her father's restaurant Dancing Zorba's. She wears thick-rimmed glasses and seems outwardly, at best, to be utterly unremarkable.

According to her parents, Gus and Maria, Toula's purpose in life should be 'to marry a Greek boy, make Greek babies and feed everyone'. But having failed to fulfil her cultural mandate so far, they are worried that she will wind up as a lonely old maid.

Toula may be ready for change. Unfortunately, the rest of her family are not. Since birth, she has struggled with the heritage her parents will not allow her to forget; and she despises the duty of having to 'be Greek'.

'You should be proud to be Greek,' her family tell her. 'There are two kinds of people ... Greeks, and those who want to be Greek.'

The Portokalos family clearly demonstrate that Greeks take immense pride in the history of their civilisation and their achievements – such as astronomy, philosophy and democracy.

In fact, they are so proud of their culture that it completely dominates their identity. Take their house, for example: it's set in what Toula describes as 'a normal, middle-class neighbourhood of tasteful, modest houses'. But they've added Corinthian columns at the front, the garage door is entirely painted in the Greek flag, and statues of the Greek gods litter the garden, 'guarding the house'.

They stand out a mile for 'being Greek' and for everything associated with it, clinging desperately to their traditions and roots. They are set in their ways. And although this seems to bind them together as a family, it also blinds them. With tradition comes great expectation. Tradition can create a narrow set of attitudes and way of life. It does not leave room for individualism and creativity.

Clip 1: Dreaming of a better life

[The restaurant is open but quiet. Toula, who is getting on with setting up for the day, narrates, while her father tucks into breakfast, chatting to another man]

TOULA. I wish I had a different life. Prettier, cleverer, braver. But it's useless to dream. Nothing ever changes.

[Toula is trapped in the seemingly hopeless situation of a world from which she cannot escape. Her heart is screaming to be liberated, while at the same time she is losing all hope. As she pours milk from a huge jug, her Aunt Voula – 'If nagging were an Olympic sport, she would have a gold medal' – joins the men at the breakfast table]

[They are discussing Toula, lamenting the fact that she won't go to Greece to find a husband. Nikki, Toula's handsome brother, sits down and tells his father not to worry, as he plans to get married one day]

GUS. That's OK. You've got plenty of time.

[As if this weren't enough, Aunt Voula assures Gus, within earshot of her niece]

AUNT VOULA. You'll always have Toula in the restaurant.

[Horrified by the very thought of such a life-sentence, Toula escapes to the back alley for some air. She sits among the bins, where she finds a leaflet called 'Add to Your Life'. Like a prayer, she makes a wish for a different life; one in which she is braver and prettier. Returning to the restaurant, she chides herself for dreaming and realises that nothing will ever change. But at that moment, a man opens the door and walks in. She turns to look. It's Ian Miller.]

Determined to change

Toula makes a resolution to change and break out from the smothering confines of her family. She becomes determined not to waste her life trying to conform to a script written for her by somebody else. And she summons up the courage to challenge her father: 'Don't you want me to do something with my life?' she asks him.

Regardless of his reaction, she decides to enrol on a computer class at a college; she discovers contact lenses and make-up and starts working in a travel agency owned by another of her aunts.

And then Ian Miller, who she had seen and served one day in the restaurant, comes to the shop. He is a teacher who is tall and definitely not Greek. Ian provides the spark that begins a whole process of change.

They begin dating, fall in love and are soon engaged. However, when the news reaches the rest of the Portokalos family, there is complete uproar. Ian Miller is, in their eyes, a 'xenos' (foreigner). Instead of being happy for her that she has finally met her true love, they cannot believe that she is contemplating marrying a non-Greek. And on top of that, he is a vegetarian!

At various points in the film, racial differences and unacknowledged prejudices are exposed. The Portokalos family regard Ian's parents as 'dry toast'. Meanwhile, Ian's parents seem not to be able to distinguish between Greeks and Guatemalans. Both parties regard the other as 'different' and at times their worlds seem too far apart. We can all be fearful of what is unfamiliar and unknown, of course. We can all become set in our own traditions.

Clip 2: A weird family

[One night, Toula and Ian are walking and talking as they cross a bridge in Chicago. Ian is telling Toula about his family]

IAN. I have only two cousins. They live in Wisconsin. What about you?

[Toula seems reluctant to answer]

IAN. What do you do at Christmas?

TOULA. My mum roasts lamb …

[Toula goes on to explain the madness of Christmas lunch, and how Aunt Voula chases her to make her eat the lamb's brain, while cousins abound and uncles argue]

TOULA. I'm Greek, right? I have 27 first cousins alone. The only people Greeks are meant to marry is Greeks. So that they can breed more 'Greek eaters'.

[Toula feels doomed; surely they can't pursue a serious relationship under these circumstances?]

TOULA. You're wonderful, but I just don't see how this is going to work out.

[Thankfully, Ian remains undaunted]

IAN. Work out? What's to work out? You've got a weird family. Who doesn't?

A love that brings liberation

The romance between Ian and Toula culminates with a huge wedding. But as with most weddings, the day doesn't arrive without its associated mishaps and complexities.

On the surface, *My Big Fat Greek Wedding* describes a comical situation in which Toula escapes from being just her Greek father's daughter to discover another life and be transformed. But it also shows how you can come to terms with your own heritage and family in the midst of enormous pressure and expectations.

It is the story of how love not only transforms Toula, but also liberates her. It is a contrast between two men and two kinds of love.

Her father judges her by her outward appearance. He tells her that she's starting to look old, wounding her with words and wanting her to conform to his wishes. Ian, on the other hand, sees her inner beauty, heals her with kind words, and allows himself to be conformed to her. Gus whines, Ian woos. Gus uses her, Ian pursues her. Gus pouts, Ian praises. Gus is proud, focusing on himself and using his family as a tool of emotional blackmail to hold onto her. Ian, meanwhile, praises her, focuses on her, is humble, and accepts her family as well as her. In doing so, he helps to release her.

In her relationship with her father, Toula is trapped in a soul-killing life of duty and obligation in which she sees herself only as a frump. With Ian, however, she is released into a life of liberation and love; her heart is free and her beauty naturally shines as a result.

A parable of all conquering love

The contrast between these two loves is profound. Whether we will admit it or not, we are all like Toula. We are imprisoned in a world we can't seem to escape from. The book of Genesis describes how Adam and Eve were banished from their original home in the Garden of Eden, and Adam was 'to work the ground from which he had been taken' (Gen. 3:22–24).

Adam and Eve, after they had eaten from the tree of the knowledge of good and evil, realised they were unclothed and so hid their nakedness with fig leaves. We still hide behind fig leaves today – not literally, of course, but metaphorically. Toula hid herself behind the counters at the restaurant and the travel agency. And we hide behind things. On the inside, we might feel like the frumpy girl, and quite often find ourselves sitting out in the alley having lost all hope.

The good news is that someone loved us enough to suffer for us. As Phil. 2:5–11 (NLT) tells us:

> 'Your attitude should be the same that Christ Jesus had. Though he was God, he did not demand and cling to his rights as God. He made himself nothing; he took the humble position of a slave and appeared in human form. And in human form he obediently humbled himself even further by dying a criminal's death on a cross. Because of this, God raised him up to the heights of heaven and gave him a name that is above every other name, so that at the name of Jesus every knee will bow, in heaven and on earth and under the earth, and every tongue will confess that Jesus Christ is Lord, to the glory of God the Father.'

At the end of the film, Toula herself comes to accept her family for what they are: 'My family is big and loud, but they're my family. And yes, we fight and argue and whatever I do, wherever I go, they will always be there.' And when Toula comes to have her own daughter, she too sends her to Greek school and continues some of the traditions and customs instilled in her for so long as a child. She does not move away from them completely, having learned instead to value them for what they are.

The message of the film is that love conquers all, and that you can find happiness despite your family's meddling! Gus' speech at the wedding reception summarises much of what the characters and we learn throughout the film.

Clip 3: In the end, we're all fruit

> *[It's the big day, and both families are crammed in to the reception. Toula looks beautiful as she sits beside her brand new groom. Her proud – but slightly shaky – father has risen to make his speech. He looks nervous, and speaks slowly, in his strong Greek accent]*
>
> *[Gus welcomes both sets of families: the Millers and the Portokaloses. He then proceeds on to explain how 'Miller' actually has its roots in a Greek word (could it be any other*

way?). And that the word means 'apple'. Then, he explains, 'Portokalos' has its roots in a Greek word that means 'orange']

GUS. So here tonight we have apples and oranges. We're all different ... but in the end, we're all fruit.

[His audience smile, then laugh, at the profundity and wit of his statement. Gus has grasped the beauty of difference; unity through diversity.]

The chance to be re-shaped

Ultimately, Toula's change has a positive effect on the rest of her family; her brother Nick also decides to pursue his passions and take up painting and art at evening classes. 'Don't let your past dictate who you are, but let it be part of who you will become,' he advises.

Towards the end of George Bernard Shaw's life, a reporter asked him, 'If you had your life to live over again and could be anybody you've ever known, who would you want to be?'

'I would choose,' replied Shaw, 'to be the man George Bernard Shaw could have been, but never was.'

What would have been your answer? Who is it you want to be? What do you want your life to become?

J.N. Kelly wrote, 'In the tribunal of relentless history, the Greek is intelligent, but also conceited; active, but also disorganised; with a sense of honour, but also full of prejudices; one moment the Greek fights for truth and the next hates the person who refuses to serve a lie. A strange creature, untameable, inquisitive, half-good, half-bad, fickle, of uncertain mood, self-centred, foolish, wise – the Greek.'

Greeks will always be Greeks. But as Shelley said, in a way, we are all Greeks. There is something about us all that is foolish and wise, half-good, half-bad. We have all been sent from the Garden, banished, imprisoned.

And we all have the opportunity to be reshaped by Jesus Christ. When we enter a relationship with Jesus, we start becoming the people God created us to be in the first place. No longer bound by all those things that trap us – expectations, tradition, pressure, self-image, duty, and the like – we start to fulfil our human potential as people who were made in the image of a loving, caring God.

A rose only becomes beautiful and blesses others when it opens up and blooms. Its greatest tragedy is to stay in a tight-closed bud, never fulfilling its potential. Whatever your past has been, you can have a spotless future if you turn to your Heavenly Father. He doesn't want to enslave you; he doesn't want you to live in yesterday. Instead, he wants you to be freed from the unforgiveness which so often binds us.

If you are struggling to forgive your parents, or family or friends for that matter, you can be set free. If you're a parent, have you stopped to ask whether you're domineering, demanding and manipulative with your children? If so, you can find forgiveness, from them and from God.

Since Jesus, the Son of God, came to live with us and to die for us, there is no longer any need for any of us to be consumed by the disappointment of wasted years. In fact, the prophet Joel assures us that God can make up for 'the years the locusts have eaten.'

Family matters. Your family matters. You might be an apple, and I might be an orange, but don't forget: we're all fruit. We're part of a heavenly family, thanks to Jesus. Which means that our earthly families, and our relationships, can be transformed ... for good.

DISCUSSION STARTERS

(You'll need a selection of fruit – the stranger the better!)

Personal reflection: None of us can choose our families, and often we end up feeling hurt by what they've said or done in years gone by. Spend a few moments of quiet, trying to reflect positively on the good times you have enjoyed with your family.

Discuss: The writer of *My Big Fat Greek Wedding* said, 'I believe that the movie is about any family that loves you to the point of smothering.' What was the movie about for *you*? Is the film pessimistic or optimistic about human nature and relationships?

Act: J. John writes, 'Tradition can create a narrow set of attitudes and way of life. It does not leave room for individualism and creativity.' Using your own individualism and creativity, draw, paint, write or 'craft' anything that reflects a tradition you've become a part of. It can be either negative or positive (or somewhere in between).

Discuss: Share your creativity with the rest of the group. Explain how you've become part of a tradition, and how this affects you.

Read: Rom. 9:25,26.

Discuss: We all have the opportunity to join a new family, to become 'sons and daughters of the living God' through Christ. But this family cuts across traditions, nationalities, prejudice – and celebrates the fact that we're all different. What should the hallmarks of this new family be? Do we live up to our calling? If not, how could we welcome the Ian Millers of this world more readily into our family?

Act: In his wedding speech, Ian says, 'So here tonight we have apples and oranges. We're all different ... but in the end, we're all fruit.' Take several pieces of fruit – the more unusual the better – cut them up and taste them. Try to describe the various flavours, textures, colours and so on in ways that go beyond saying, 'It tastes and looks orange.' And see if you can guess the correct fruit.

Thank God for the richness and variety of his creation as you taste the fruit. Which fruits would you associate with different people in your group?

Personal reflection: We're all different, but that's not a bad thing. In fact, it's a very good thing, and the film helps us to understand that more fully. Stop to reflect personally, for a few quiet moments, on how you differ from other family members. Think about why that can be a good thing. After all, you are uniquely made by the Creator God – in his image. What unique part of you reflects the creator in a unique way to other people?

Discuss: J. John writes that George Bernard Shaw was once asked, 'If you had your life to live over again and could be anybody you've ever known, who would you want to be?' Who, and why?

Pray: Pray this short prayer to end: 'Lord Jesus, thank you for our families – for the people we've grown up with, for local groups like this which are part of the family of God, and for the wider, international family of which we are a part. Please help us to celebrate each other's differences as well as our similarities. And help us to show, through your kind of love, that the world around us can become a very different place. Amen.'

16

Does Everything Happen for a Reason?
Signs

MARK STIBBE

TOUCHSTONE PICTURES, 2002

Directed by M. NIGHT SHYAMALAN
Screenplay by M. NIGHT SHYAMALAN

MEL GIBSON as *Rev. Graham Hess*
JOAQUIN PHOENIX as *Merrill Hess*
RORY CULKIN as *Morgan Hess*
ABIGAIL BRESLIN as *Bo Hess*

CLASSIFICATION: 12

In July 2003 the BBC ran a news story with a headline that caught my attention; it said, 'Lightning hits preacher after call to God.' The report went on to say, 'A congregation in the United States was left stunned when lightning struck a church moments after a visiting preacher asked God for a sign. Church members in the town of Forest in the state of Ohio said the preacher had been emphasising the importance of penance when, in the course of his prayers, he called on the heavens above. The lightning struck the steeple, then hit the preacher himself when it travelled through electrical wiring to his microphone. Local authorities said he was not injured.

'"It was awesome, just awesome," said church member Ronnie Cheney, who was among the congregation when the strike hit. "You could hear the storm building outside ... the preacher just kept asking God what else he needed to say. He was asking for a sign and he got one."'

Signs have always fascinated people. For some, the lightning hitting the preacher was a supernatural sign. For others, it was merely a coincidence with a purely naturalistic interpretation. Signs have always intrigued people, and they have always divided them.

It is with this polarising fascination that the movie *Signs* deals. It stars Mel Gibson and is written and directed by M. Night Shyamalan, who also wrote the stories behind *The Sixth Sense, Unbreakable* and *The Village*.

Signs tells the story of Graham Hess, an Anglican priest in rural Pennsylvania, who loses his faith and stops exercising his ordained ministry. The reason for this is because his wife Colleen is tragically killed while going out for a walk on a remote road. A vet called Ray Reddy, acted by M. Night Shyamalan in the film, is driving along the road at precisely the same moment that Colleen is taking an evening stroll. He falls asleep at the wheel, veers off the road, runs into Colleen, pinning her to a tree, leaving her fatally injured. She dies leaving her husband Graham Hess, and their two children, a boy Morgan (acted by Rory Culkin), and his younger sister called Bo (acted by Abigail Breslin).

At the time the film opens, Graham is still living on the same family farm, bringing up the two children with his brother Merrill, acted by Joachim Phoenix. Graham regards his wife's death as a sign – as evidence – not that God does exist but proof that he doesn't, and that there is no one watching over them. But things are about to happen that may suggest otherwise.

The opening scenes of the film show Reverend Graham being woken up one morning by the sound of his daughter Bo screaming outside. The camera tracks him running from his house to his daughter:

Clip 1: I think God did it

We are looking out of a second storey window of a house. The backyard is surrounded by crops 6 feet high. Everything is perfect. Like a postcard. And then we hear a child scream.

We cut to a bedroom. Graham Hess wakes up from his sleep. He thought he heard something. He listens. He climbs out of bed. He moves towards the bedroom door. Graham stands in the hall landing where three bedroom doors meet. He moves to the door that has children's drawings taped to it. A bathroom door is open. Outside the bathroom on the bedroom wall is the sun-faded outline of where a large cross used to hang.

A child screams.

Graham steps into the doorway. Toothbrush and foam in his mouth. He becomes very still. Graham steps into his children's room. Graham's eyes move to the small messy beds. They're both empty.

We hear the screams again.

In the adjacent barn, Merrill Hess throws the bed sheets off himself as he swings onto his feet in one quick motion.

Graham bangs open the back screen door and runs into the backyard. He spins as he looks around. Merrill, now with a T-shirt and jeans, rumbles down the side stairs adjacent to the garage building. Merrill and Graham make eye contact as they approach each other across the yard.

MERRILL. Where are they?

[Graham looks around – panic growing in his eyes]

CHILDREN [*yelling in the distance*]. Daaaad!

[Graham and Merrill in unison turn in the direction of the yelling. They look away from the house, across the yard and into the thick wall of crops]

[The tall stalks of corn smack Graham and Merrill's faces as they run through the crops. A little girl appears in the crops 30 feet ahead of them like an apparition. She is in her nightgown. She is 4 years old. They reach her fast. She stands unaware of them in a daze. Her hair is messed from sleep]

GRAHAM. Bo where's Morgan?

[Bo stands peacefully lost in her thoughts]

GRAHAM. Bo?

[Bo finally looks at her father. She smiles softly]

BO. Are you in my dreams, too?

GRAHAM. This isn't a …

MORGAN. Dad!

[Graham looks in the direction of the boy's voice. Graham picks up Bo and rushes through the crops. He finds Morgan standing with his hands in the pockets of his pyjama bottoms]

GRAHAM. Morgan what's happening?

[Graham puts Bo on the ground and moves right in front of Morgan. The 10-year-old boy looks deep in thought. Graham takes hold of Morgan's chin and turns his face so he's looking straight at him]

GRAHAM. Are … you … hurt?

[Morgan's eyes reveal he's come to some answer]

MORGAN. I think God did it.

GRAHAM. Did what Morgan?

[Morgan takes hold of his father's unshaven chin and turns his face. Graham is forced to look to his right. Graham Hess

slowly rises to his feet. He starts moving forward. He walks through a thin layer of crops and emerges in a clearing. Two German Shepherds are running back and forth. They are clearly agitated. Graham looks around at the thousands of corn stalks lying flat on the ground in a gigantic crop circle, 100 feet wide. Graham Hess looks around in a daze as he walks out into the centre. Merrill, Bo and Morgan follow him. The dogs keep running and barking as we pull back and reveal the four members of the Hess family standing in the middle of a gigantic circle.]

Seeing and believing

The story opens with a perfectly-formed set of crop circles appearing in the fields next to the Hess' farm. Morgan, Graham's son, turns his father's head to see, uttering the words, 'I think God did it.'

Already we are being introduced to the major theme of the movie: seeing and believing. Morgan interprets the crop circles as a sign from God. In spite of his mother's death, he still holds onto his faith with resilient simplicity. Graham is not so easily persuaded, however. He regards the crop circles as a prank by local kids. So father and son are divided; does this a sign have a heavenly explanation or an earthly one?

This kind of polarisation has always been with us. When Jesus ministered in Galilee he performed many signs and wonders, and these divided opinion, too. In John's Gospel seven miracles are described and these are all called 'signs'.

John 2: Jesus turns water into wine
John 4: Jesus heals the official's son
John 5: Jesus heals a paralysed man at the pool of Bethesda

John 6: Jesus feeds the 5,000
John 6: Jesus walks on water
John 9: Jesus heals a man born blind
John 11: Jesus raises Lazarus from death

John's Gospel, on 15 occasions, describes these miraculous events as 'signs'.

By definition, a sign is something that points you to something else bigger than itself. In this case, the signs of Jesus point to who he really is – the Son of God. On the one hand, some see this and put their trust in him; so we read in Jn. 2:11 (NIV), after Jesus has changed water into wine, that 'This, the first of his miraculous signs, Jesus performed in Cana of Galilee. He thus revealed his glory, and his disciples put their faith in him.' But while the disciples see and believe, the Pharisees see but do not believe. And so we read in Jn. 12:37 (NIV), 'Even after Jesus had done all these miraculous signs in their presence, they still would not believe in him.'

Signs have always had the potential to polarise opinion. When is a sign something we have to explain supernaturally? When is a sign something that has a perfectly natural explanation? Why do some people think in miraculous terms while others think in materialistic terms?

In October 1977, Maria Rubio was rolling up a burrito for her husband Eduardo's breakfast when she noticed a thumb-sized configuration of skillet burns on the tortilla that resembled the face of Jesus. Needless to say, Eduardo went hungry that meal as Maria told family and neighbours. All this happened in the small town of Lake Arthur, New Mexico, 40 minutes south of Roswell. Thousands of visitors have visited the Shrine of the Miracle Tortilla, regarding it as a sign – though today the merciless south-western heat has destroyed the image. Other miraculous tortillas have since been discovered. Scientists on the one hand call this 'pareidolia' – a perception of pattern and meaning from natural randomness. Mrs Rubio and her family call it a sign.

Whether a proposed 'sign' really merits any supernatural interpretation has a great deal to do with issues of cultural context and personal background. Some people easily resort to a miraculous interpretation (too easily, if the example above is anything to go by). Some more readily employ a scientific theory.

This point is well made in the next clip when Graham and his brother Merrill discuss 'signs'. At this stage, events have progressed since the discovery of the crop circles. Lights have now been seen in the night sky and these are causing worldwide discussion and even wonder.

Clip 2: A sign of God's existence?

[The family room lights are off now. The TV is still on. The fourteen lights are still hovering on the screen. Morgan is asleep on Graham's lap. Bo is asleep on Merrill's shoulder]

MERRILL [*whispers*]. Some people are probably thinking ... this is the end of the world.

GRAHAM [*whispers*]. That's true.

[Merrill looks his brother in the eyes]

MERRILL. Do you think it's a possibility?

GRAHAM. Yes.

MERRILL. How can you say that?

GRAHAM. That wasn't the answer you wanted?

MERRILL. Can you at least pretend to be like you used to be? Give me some comfort?

[Graham thinks it over]

GRAHAM. People break down into two groups when they experience something lucky. Group number one sees it as more than luck, more than coincidence. They see it as a sign, evidence, that there is someone up there, watching out for them. Group number two sees it as just pure luck. Just a happy turn of chance. I'm sure the people in group number two are looking at those fourteen lights in a very suspicious way. For them, the situation isn't 50–50. Could be bad, could be good. But deep down, they feel that whatever happens, they're on their own. And that fills them with fear. Yeah, there are those people. But there's a whole lot of people in the group number one. When they see those fourteen lights, they're looking at a miracle. And deep down, they feel that whatever's going to happen, there will be someone there to help them. And that fills them with hope. See what you have to ask yourself is what kind of person are you? Are you the kind that sees signs, sees miracles? Or do you believe that people just get lucky? Or, look at the question this way: Is it possible that there are no coincidences?

The two types of people

Graham talks about two different types of people: type A and type B. Type A see life as meaningful, type B see life as meaningless. Graham used to be type A but now, because of the bitter pill of personal tragedy, has become type B. Indeed, Graham goes on to ask Merrill, 'Do you know what Colleen's last words were? She said, "See," and then her eyes glazed a bit and she said ... "Tell Merrill to swing away." Do you know why she said that? Because the nerve endings in her brain were firing as she died, and some random memory of us at one of your baseball games popped into her head. There is no one watching out for us Merrill. We're all on our own.'

Graham has simply let go of his faith in God. He no longer sees life as meaningful but as meaningless. God does not exist, and there is no one providing either direction or protection. 'We are all on our own.'

Some people have always taken this view. Marcus Aurelius once summed up human existence in these memorable terms: 'Yesterday a drop of semen ... tomorrow a handful of ashes.' Noel Coward wrote a song about the human condition to the tune of 'Old kit bag':

> 'There are bad times just around the corner
> There are dark clouds travelling through the sky
> And it's no good whining about a silver lining
> For we know from experience that they won't roll by
> With a scowl and a frown
> We'll keep our faces down
> And prepare for depression doom and dread
> We're going to unpack our troubles from our old kit bag
> And wait until we drop down dead'

Some certainly see the world without reference to God and life as meaningless. These are type B people who see signs as sheer luck or mere coincidences.

Type A people, on the other hand, see signs as evidence of God's activity in their lives – as evidence of his power and his existence. As the Bible says,

> 'From the time the world was created, people have seen the earth and sky and all that God made. They can clearly see his invisible qualities – his eternal power and divine nature. So they have no excuse whatsoever for not knowing God.'

According to this verse there are signs of God all around us all the time; God is speaking to us, calling to us, trying to catch our attention. Some of these traces of divinity may be more imagined than real. But not everything can be explained rationalistically and in terms of our humanistic and naturalistic philosophies.

Returning to the movie, we now reach the point where it becomes clear that the crop circles are not signs from God but landing markers for alien spaceships. The aliens have now begun their attack and Graham's family are holding out in the basement of their farmhouse, in scenes reminiscent of Alfred Hitchcock's *The Birds*. Morgan, Graham's son, has an asthma attack and falls unconscious. The family hold out till dawn when they learn that the aliens have been defeated and are leaving. Hess and his family go back upstairs only to find that there is an alien waiting for them in the sitting room. The alien grabs hold of Morgan – still unconscious – threatening to fill his lungs with poisoned gas. As Graham looks on in horror, he remembers the last words of his wife Colleen.

Clip 3: Tell Graham to see

Graham straightens and turns around slowly, facing the alien creature who is holding Morgan a few feet off the floor. It is close to seven feet tall and standing in the middle of the family room. Its powdery skin has taken on the shades, lines and colours of the room so perfectly it almost disappears. It blinks. Graham and Bo have turned to stone. Bo stands frozen in the front hall.

Merrill has been to find Morgan's inhaler. He comes out of the doorway from the kitchen. He takes two steps into the room and comes to a stop next to the fireplace. The inhaler and syringe in his hand fall to the ground. The creature is between Graham and Merrill in the middle of the family room.

Morgan is dying. The creature's hand moves to Morgan's face. It tilts its fingers and palm back. A small pore opens up on its wrist. A yellowish gas starts to leak out of the opening. Graham looks up from the leaking poison gas to the face of the creature. Its large empty black eyes lock on Graham's. Graham experiences a flashback.

It's a country road, late at night. A car door opens. Graham Hess steps out. He is wearing a black shirt and black trousers. A priest's white collar sits under the lapel of the black shirt. Graham looks around in a daze.

[Officer Paski walks up to Graham]

OFFICER PASKI. What do you know?

GRAHAM. There was an accident. Drunk driving. They weren't sure.

OFFICER PASKI. He wasn't drinking. Ray fell asleep at the wheel.

[Officer Paski gestures in the direction of one of the ambulances. Ray Reddy sits to the side on the grass. His arms rest on his bent knees]

GRAHAM. Is he OK?

OFFICER PASKI. Yes … That's the first thing Colleen asked, too.

[Graham smiles a little smile]

GRAHAM. She's talking … which ambulance is she in?

OFFICER PASKI. She's not in an ambulance, Father.

GRAHAM. Why not?

OFFICER PASKI. See Father, Ray's truck swerved off the road and ah … hit Colleen and then a tree. She was pinned between the two.

GRAHAM. Pinned? What does that mean?

OFFICER PASKI. The truck … the truck has severed most of her lower half.

GRAHAM. What did you say?

OFFICER PASKI. She won't be saved. At this point she's alive, because the truck is holding her together. She doesn't feel much, and she's talking almost like normal. We didn't pull the truck out, cause we wanted you to come down here to be with her, as long as she's awake. That won't be very long. Father, you understand what I've told you?

GRAHAM [*he starts crying*]. This is the last time I'm going to talk to my wife.

OFFICER PASKI. Yes it is.

[The other officers turn and look as Graham walks by them. He walks on, unaware of the stares. He slows as he reaches the back bumper of the truck. It sticks out onto the road a few feet. He comes around the side of the vehicle]

[Colleen Hess leans over the front bumper of the truck onto the hood. Her head rests on her arms like a child resting on a school desk. Her back is against a tree. The lower half of her is obscured by the truck. She's able to raise her head and shoulders as Graham walks up to her. She is shivering slightly]

COLLEEN. Hi sweetie.

GRAHAM. Hi baby.

COLLEEN. I was just taking a walk before dinner.

GRAHAM. You love walks.

COLLEEN. I guess it was meant to be.

GRAHAM. Does it hurt?

COLLEEN. I don't feel much.

GRAHAM. Good.

[Graham touches her cheek. She starts crying. Graham starts crying with her]

COLLEEN [*crying*]. Tell Morgan to play games – it's OK to be silly.

GRAHAM [*crying*]. ... I will.

COLLEEN [*crying*]. ... Tell Bo to listen to her brother. He'll always take care of her.

GRAHAM [*crying*]. ... I will.

COLLEEN [*crying*]. ... Tell Graham ...

GRAHAM [*crying*]. I'm here.

COLLEEN [*crying*]. ... Tell him ... see. Tell him to see.

[Colleen presses her cheek on top of Graham's hand. She rests on it. Her eyes are distant]

COLLEEN [*soft*]. And tell Merrill to swing away.

[We cut back to the family room]

[Graham stares at the baseball bat on the wall]

GRAHAM [*soft*]. Swing away, Merrill.

GRAHAM [*loud*]. Merrill.

[Merrill turns and looks to Graham]

GRAHAM. Swing away.

It was meant to be

Merrill swings away and beats the alien to the floor; as the alien falls over he knocks a glass of water over; the water falls on him, burning and eventually killing him. This is significant because Bo, Graham's daughter, is hydrophobic; she has a fear of water – particularly contaminated water – and she has been leaving glasses of water all over the house. And so an apparently meaningless act – the random pouring of glasses of water by the daughter – turns out to be what destroys the alien. And the apparent meaninglessness of the son's asthmatic condition – hinted at throughout the film – turns out to be what saves him. And thus a whole string of coincidences come together in Graham's life.

If Merrill had not stopped playing baseball, his baseball bat would not have been hanging on the wall.

If Colleen hadn't have said, 'Swing away', just before she died Graham wouldn't have known what to do.

If Bo had not been obsessed with drinking water, there would not have been glasses of water in the sitting room.

If Morgan hadn't have been asthmatic, his lungs would have been open and he would have been poisoned.

Graham sees in his own words that 'it can't be luck', that 'it was meant to be'. Even the very bad things that happened in his life, though at the time they seemed so meaningless, were used by God for a redemptive purpose. As it says in Romans 8:28: 'And we know that God causes everything to work together for the good of those who love God and are called according to his purpose for them.'

Jewish psychologist Victor Frankl once wrote, 'He who has a why to live for can bear with almost any how' (*Man's Search for Meaning*, 1959). Hess begins to see the why in the midst of his suffering. He sees that his wife's last words were in fact prophetic (she, like her daughter, dreamed dreams about the future). He sees that his daughter's hydrophobia and his son's asthma were no accidents. He begins to see how even bad things in his life had some redemptive purpose. In short, he sees the deeper meaning in the apparent madness.

Clip 4: 'Did someone save me?'

In the final clip we are back in the garden of Graham's house, the alien is dead but Morgan is still in trouble. He is lying in his father's arms. Merrill and Bo find Graham kneeling in the grass. Morgan lies limp in his arms. They kneel down in the grass with him. Merrill sees the empty syringe in Graham's hand. He looks to Morgan.

The boy's head is tilted back. His tiny mouth hangs open unnaturally.

GRAHAM. His lungs were closed. His lungs were closed. No poison got in ... No poison got in.

[Merrill stares at Morgan. His body is utterly still]

GRAHAM. His lungs were closed.

[Merrill reaches for Morgan's still hand]

GRAHAM. Don't touch him.

MERRILL [*soft*]. Graham.

[Morgan lies lifeless]

BO. Daddy.

GRAHAM. Don't touch him.

[Bo is crying]

MERRILL. Graham.

GRAHAM. Don't.

MORGAN'S VOICE. Dad.

[Graham starts crying. Every bit of sadness trapped in his body is released. He looks down through tears and stares at Morgan]

MORGAN. Did someone save me?

GRAHAM. Yeah baby. I think someone did.

The camera cuts to a morning scene months later. We look out through the bedroom window. It's snowing. There is the sound of children laughing. Graham comes out of the bathroom, in his full clerical outfit, priestly collar and all. He puts on his jacket and walks purposefully out of the room.

Never separated from God's love

And so, after terrible suffering, an Anglican priest regains his faith.

The aliens that tried to invade his home and destroy his life have been thwarted. In the end, like his doubts, they tried to overwhelm him but they were beaten back. While Graham lost his faith in God, God never lost his faith in him. While Graham lost his hold on God, God never lost his hold on Graham. Graham discovered that God is faithful to his promises even when we are not so faithful to ours.

One of my favourite passages in the Bible is Rom. 8:35–39 (NLT):

> 'Can anything ever separate us from Christ's love? Does it mean he no longer loves us if we have trouble or calamity, or are persecuted, or are hungry or cold or in danger or threatened with death? … No, despite all these things, overwhelming victory is ours through Christ, who loved us.
>
> And I am convinced that nothing can ever separate us from his love. Death can't, and life can't. The angels can't, and the demons can't. Our fears for today, our worries about tomorrow, and even the powers of hell can't keep God's love away. Whether we are high above the sky or in the deepest ocean, nothing in all creation will ever be able to separate us from the love of God that is revealed in Christ Jesus our Lord.'

Terrible things happen to people. Being a Christian is no inoculation against the ills and the mysteries of life. But God gives us signs of his purposes in the midst of the mess. All we have to do is see.

Most of M. Night Shyamalan's films feature a main character who's suffered a loss – the death of a loved one in *Signs,* the emotional separation of the lead character from his wife and son at the beginning of *Unbreakable*, the loss of a parent through divorce in *The Sixth Sense*. What I really like about *Signs* is the way it teaches us to look for spiritual meaning in the midst of mess. It encourages us to see.

Mel Gibson said this in a recent interview: 'I think there have been many experiences in my life [that were] unexplainable also. Where you couldn't rule out the idea of some supernatural or otherworldly kind of influence playing a part in the road you choose or in forcing you to go that way ... I don't really think it's about luck. I think most things are preordained. And I've always thought that, so that's OK.'

Jesus Christ was nailed to a tree outside Jerusalem 2,000 years ago in order to save us. In the movie *Signs*, Colleen is pinned to a tree and it is her words that ultimately save not just her son Morgan but her family, including Graham. But Graham has to see. And we are all invited to see. There are signs all around us of God's existence and power. God is trying to communicate with all of us. I believe this is especially true in times of great suffering. As C.S. Lewis once wrote: 'God whispers to us in our pleasures, speaks in our consciences, but shouts in our pains. It is his megaphone to rouse a deaf world.'

What you have to decide is: what kind of person are you? Are you the type who believes in miracles and looks for signs? Or are you the kind who believes things just happen by chance?

DISCUSSION STARTERS

(You'll need a star chart or Internet pictures of space, plus a copy of Coldplay's song 'Yellow'. Also, you'll need a few nightlight candles and a tray to put them on that won't burn.)

Personal reflection: Are you the sort of person who sees signs around you or just coincidences? Think on this for a few moments. There's not a right answer here – it's a question of being honest with yourself. Has anything happened in your life that seems too much of a coincidence?

Discuss: Discuss these moments with each other. Plus, how did the film help to draw out the tension between signs and coincidences? Was it a useful means of opening this discussion? Can we read too much into 'signs'? Or, can we go around with our eyes shut, oblivious to help?

Read: Ps. 19.

Act: Do all signs really have to be 'supernatural'? In the psalm we just read, the Bible says that the stars 'declare the glory of God' through their sheer, wondrous existence. If it's dark, go outside (if you can) and spend a few minutes looking up at them. Let them speak to you in 'the voice that goes out into all the earth', in the 'words that go to the ends of the world'. If you can't get outside, either get a star chart or else download some pictures of space from the Internet and show them to the group instead. Or, simply use your imagination.

Act: If you have a copy, play Coldplay's 'Yellow' at the end of this short session, and reflect on the line 'It's true – see how they shine for you'. Thank God for the different ways his creation speaks to us about what he's like. Otherwise, simply play an appropriate piece of music and ask God to help you be open to hear from him.

Discuss: How else does God speak to us? And how does he bring about his purpose for our lives? What is the relationship between our free will, and God's 'plan' for us?

Read: Rom. 8:35–39.

Personal reflection: Mark quotes C.S. Lewis, who said, 'God whispers to us in our pleasures, speaks in our consciences, but shouts in our pains. It is his megaphone to rouse a deaf world.' For a few, quiet moments, think of one time when everything seemed to be going wrong. What good came out of that time? What did you feel God was saying to you through it?

Act: Turn all of the lights out in the room, and sit, for a minute, in the darkness. Reflect on the fact that it needs to be dark in order to see the stars outside properly. And you only see a light burn brightly in the darkness. Now, anyone who wants to should light a nightlight, put it on the tray, and in a sentence, thank God for speaking to them through difficult times. You can be specific about the difficulty, or simply thank God for speaking. The lights together will speak, like stars, of God's grace and love to us.

Prayer: If it's appropriate, pray a short prayer: 'God who flung the stars into space, who speaks in signs and wonders, yet who came to live with us in poverty and humility, in flesh and blood, we ask you to speak to us in as many ways as you can; and we pray that we will be open to hear your voice, and not only that, but ready to obey you when you speak. Thank you for caring enough to speak in the first place. Amen.'

17

Forgive and Forget
Changing Lanes

J. JOHN

PARAMOUNT PICTURES, 2002

Directed by ROGER MICHELL
Story and screenplay by CHAP TAYLOR

BEN AFFLECK as *Gavin Banek*
SAMUEL L. JACKSON as *Doyle Gipson*

CLASSIFICATION: 15

This fast-moving, gritty thriller charts a single day in the lives of two men whose (very different) worlds collide after a minor car crash, which has major repercussions for them both.

Clip 1: A fateful collision

Doyle Gipson (played by Samuel L. Jackson) is a recovering alcoholic who is desperately trying to secure a mortgage in the hope that he can keep his family together. He's driving to a family court hearing, with no time to lose, and he's rehearsing his lines. He's decided to defend himself in court. 'Boys need their fathers,' he says to the imaginary judge, then starts writing the phrase down on an envelope on the passenger seat. His car swerves a little.

Meanwhile, Gavin Banek (Ben Affleck) is a Wall Street lawyer who's also heading for court, and is also cutting it fine. Banek is not concentrating on his driving either, looking up at the signs to see which route to take. As he tries to change lanes, he hits Gipson's car, which crumples into rubbish bins in the central reservation, seriously damaged. Banek's car is only scratched.

Fate could not have brought together two more different people. When their cars collide, we see their different approaches to life straight away. They are both in a rush, but while Gipson wants to see Banek's insurance card so that he can do things by the book. Banek, on the other hand, wants to follow the route of expedience, and tries to fob Gipson off with a blank cheque for the repairs. Gipson protests, 'I have to do this right, you know what I mean?'

'Yes, I think so …' replies Banek, as he receives a call from his secretary telling him he's late and the court is in session.

'Tell them I'm on the steps,' he says. And he drives off shouting, 'Better luck next time!' to Gipson who is stranded on the freeway with no chance of making his own court hearing on time. Gipson's hope of keeping his family together is disappearing before his eyes; in the end, he will arrive at court just in time to hear the judge award sole custody of his two children to his wife. But as he stands forlornly in the central reservation, Gipson looks down at the ground and sees that, in the rush, Banek has dropped a red file.

A bitter contest of wills

The incident not only thwart's Gipson, it also leaves Banek high and dry. The red file is, in fact, a crucial 'power of appointment' that gives Banek's senior partners control of a $107million trust fund. A dying philanthropist called Simon Dunn had signed control of his estate over to Banek and his partners – to the annoyance of the Dunn family, who are contesting the matter in court. Banek had manipulated the man on his deathbed, in an attempt to bring a lucrative deal to the law firm that recently made him a partner. But the only document that proves Banek's case is now in Gipson's hands; he only finds that he doesn't have it when he is in court, in front of the judge.

The judge gives him the rest of the day to produce it – otherwise the consequences will be disastrous for Banek. Without the document, Banek is in very big trouble with these senior partners, especially as one of them, Delano (Sydney Pollack), is his father-in-law. He will also be in big trouble with the courts, and could end up without a job and in jail. He has to retrieve the file from the man he has just left high and dry. The man to whom he wished 'Better luck next time!'

The stage is set for a bitter contest of wills between the two men, as they struggle to right the wrongs and settle the scores of the car crash. Both are driven to the very edge of themselves, with each man willing to stop at almost nothing to thwart the other's intentions.

By chance, Banek catches sight of Gipson walking down the street and tries to persuade him to return the file. But Gipson reminds Banek of his words on the freeway: 'You said better luck next time. I need you to give my time back to me. Can you give me my morning back?' Banek pleads with him for the file, but Gipson has thrown it away.

Back at his office, Banek despairs as to know what to do regarding Gipson and the file. His colleague Michelle (Toni Collette) reminds him of how he came by the file in the very first place. She acts, in some sense, as his conscience: 'Did you really think it was right to convince a dying man to sign a power of appointment?' she asks.

Banek begs her for help. 'There's this guy,' she says. 'This guy who helps out with things that need helping out with.' Banek is torn. He desperately needs the file, but at the same time he is reluctant to engage in all-out war with Gipson. 'Do you want what's right?' Michelle asks. 'Yes,' Banek replies.

Wanting to do the right thing

Banek is struggling to know 'what is right'. Is it right to put his own life, his own job and his own wife first and ruin someone else's life in the process, or to own up to his boss and face the consequences?

While Banek struggles with this dilemma, Gipson has a change of heart and, having retrieved the file from the bin he dumped it in, requests an envelope from a work colleague to courier the file to Banek. 'Is there a reward or something?' the colleague asks. 'Doing the right thing,' Gipson replies. 'That's the reward.' His colleague is surprised. 'Well, how about that?'

From the moment of the accident, Gipson has wanted to do the right thing: to exchange the right insurance documents, and now, even, to return the file to the man who has ruined his day and, by consequence, his life. But a threatening voicemail from Banek puts paid to his good intentions.

Gipson's wife has threatened to take his children to Oregon, which seems to him like the other side of the world. Effectively, it means he won't be able to see his children.

His last hope to at least keep his family in the area is to buy them a house – settle them in. He might even, one day, be able to move back in with them. Having found a house and arranged a loan, the bank calls him back to say that there has been a mistake – that his name is blacklisted. They can't therefore give him a loan, and he can't buy the house.

Banek has fixed it so that the one thing Gipson hoped might save his marriage is destroyed – securing a mortgage to buy a house. He displays his anger and bitterness as he goes in search of tools in a hardware store in order to tamper with Banek's car.

Later, Banek receives a fax of the 'power of appointment' with 'Better luck next time!' scrawled across it. It's from Gipson. Banek begins to grow disillusioned when he discovers that his senior partners have helped themselves to millions of dollars from the Dunn Foundation, and that he, as Dunn's attorney, is implicated.

Then, to top off his morning, a tense lunch meeting with his wife reveals that she knew all about an affair he conducted at work long before it ended. She also knows that the senior partners want to forge the missing document, and she presses him to do what they say. She seems less concerned with what is right, and more about what is expedient.

Gipson then phones to say that his credit's back on and he'll return the document. But just as things appear to be coming together for Banek, they fall apart again. Gipson has tampered with his car in revenge for blocking his loan, and the car spins out of control as he is speeding down the highway.

Revenge is not sweet

Scared and shaken, Banek scrambles out and walks along the road – to where Gipson's crumpled Daihatsu is sitting – where it crashed – in the rain. He is back where he started the day: standing on the freeway, only this time he is the one without a car. And he's back where he started regarding the document, too. Gipson still has it, and the clock is ticking.

Banek then gets even in a cruel act of revenge involving Gipson's children. He makes a hoax call to warn their school that Gipson is going to kidnap them, following the custody ruling. He then calls Gipson's office and leaves a message, saying that there has been an accident at the school: when Gipson turns up demanding to see his kids, he is arrested.

As Gipson is led away in a police car, Banek yells: 'You see that? I tried to make peace with you. You know who I am? You see what I can do to you? You tried to kill me.' But the scene exposes Banek at his weakest. Despite his boasts, he is undoubtedly the one in the worst position without the file.

He has to shoulder the burden of knowing that he's ruined Gipson's life, while trying to sort out his own. And this shouting, this jeering at Gipson masks a deeper insecurity.

Gipson's sponsor from Alcoholics Anonymous (played by William Hurt) challenges him after paying his bail. 'What's wrong with you? Keep doing the wrong thing and you could start a religion. Everything decent is held together by a covenant, an agreement not to go back to it. You broke the contract.'

'I didn't have a drink!' Gipson retorts.

'Well wow, thank you for sharing that,' Hurt mocks.

'That's the point isn't it?' Gipson asks.

'You know,' Hurt muses, 'booze isn't really your drug of choice anyway … you got hooked on disaster. You're addicted to chaos.'

Sorry seems to be the hardest word

Changing Lanes explores the themes of bitterness, revenge, forgiveness and a distorted sense of right and wrong.

At several points in the film, both Gipson and Banek try to say sorry, but each time they discover how difficult it is to truly forgive someone.

A certain story goes that an elderly, single woman preplanned her funeral. The funeral director was intrigued by the fact that she chose six female pallbearers. 'Are you sure you want all women to carry your casket to the grave?' he asked. 'I'm positive,' she responded. 'If those men wouldn't take me out when I was alive, I'm not going to let them take me out when I'm dead.'

How many people's lives have been destroyed because they were not willing to forgive? 'Forgiveness' means to dismiss, to release, to leave or abandon. We might hear of a judge that has 'dismissed' charges against a defendant, or a person who is released from an obligation such as a loan or debt.

The Bible contains a passage – in Mt. 18:21–35 – which suggests that a forgiving person will not count how many times they are called to forgive (verses 21,22). Peter asks Jesus, 'how often should I forgive someone who sins against me? Seven times?'

In fact, Peter was being generous, as the Jewish people felt that God only wanted them to forgive a person three times. (Their thinking came from the book of Amos, in which God pronounces judgements against the neighbouring nations of Israel. God says that he will revoke his punishment against them three times, not four. The religious teachers wrongly interpreted this to mean that they only had to forgive a person three times.)

So, Peter is willing to go the extra mile in saying 'seven'. But Jesus responds, 'No, seventy times seven.' In other words, set no limits when it comes to forgiving!

We are called to forgive like Jesus has forgiven us. Eph. 4:32 (NLT) says, 'be kind to each other, tenderhearted, forgiving one another, just as God through Christ has forgiven you.' The question is, how many times has Jesus forgiven you? And at what stage, exactly, did Jesus ever say that he would no longer forgive you?

When our children are born, we can't just say that we'll give them twenty-eight chances in their life before that's it. Col. 3:13 (NLT) says, 'Remember, the Lord forgave you, so you must forgive others.' In fact, when God forgives, he buries our sins and doesn't mark the grave.

Forgive your debtors

In the passage in Matthew's Gospel (Mt. 18:21–35), Jesus proceeds to tell a parable to illustrate what he means. A king starts to call to account all the people who owe him money. He wants them to settle up. One person in particular owes him a very large amount. He is in a hopeless situation, and seeks mercy from the king.

At this point, the man just wants more time so that he can figure out a way to take care of things himself. But he knows he has no way out. He is looking for anything to stall the inevitable.

The king's response would have surely been enough to end the parable beautifully at this point: 'The king was filled with compassion for him and he released him and forgave his debt.'

How would you have felt coming away from the king? Imagine you had lost your job and were out of work for six months. The bank phones and you plead with them for a little more time. Then they tell you, 'The £100,000 that you owe on the house has been forgiven you. And by the way, all your other loans and debts have also been written off.'

However, the story doesn't end there for the servant. As soon as this man leaves the king – forgiven – he goes in search of a man who owes him the equivalent of a couple of month's wages. The servant wants to find him to show forgiveness, doesn't he? Sadly, no. Instead, he has the man arrested and thrown into prison.

How many times do we hold on to a grudge because we want the other person to pay their due? A forgiving person will sow what they have received, as it says in Mt. 18:31–35. Verse 33 (NIV) is the key: 'Shouldn't you have mercy on your fellow servant just as I had on you?'

We must sow the seeds of forgiveness that we have reaped from God. In fact, the only request in the Lord's Prayer that comes with a condition attached is one about forgiveness (Mt. 6:12, NLT): 'and forgive us our sins, just as we have forgiven those who have sinned against us.'

In other words, if we want God to forgive us, we must forgive other people. It is very sad that some people will go through life holding a grudge because they think it somehow hurts the other person – when the blunt truth is, it hurts them instead. Resentment makes us 're-feel' our wounds, while forgiveness heals them.

Forgiveness frees us, while unforgiveness enslaves. It is better to forgive and forget than to resent and remember. To forgive others can be one of the toughest things that Jesus commands us to do, but still he demands it from us, and we must respond.

A mother brought her two arguing children together and insisted they make immediate amends. The siblings hesitantly apologised to each other, but one commented,

'I'm apologising on the outside, but I'm not on the inside.' At least he was honest.

Unfortunately, adults tend to go through the motions of forgiveness by covering up their real emotions. True forgiveness doesn't bury the hatchet while allowing the handle to remain exposed.

Acknowledging our hurts

So how do we forgive?

First, we must acknowledge that we have been hurt. Sometimes, we might pretend that something didn't really bother us, but we know that we're fooling no one, not least ourselves. We must be careful that we don't try to get rid of our hurt by covering it up – otherwise hurt can so easily turn into hate.

The rule of the world is, 'Do unto others as they've done unto you.' But when we forgive, we choose to lay aside whatever right we think we have for revenge. When we choose to forgive, we are leaving ultimate justice to God, and we are deliberately choosing the path of forgiveness for ourselves.

Acknowledging that we have been hurt gets us in the right place to begin, but surrendering our right to get even is the first step down the path. Some would argue that choosing such a path means that we are going to end up as a doormat. But a power is released by this decision that cannot come from any other source.

What does such a power look like? Albert Tomei was a Justice of the New York State Supreme Court. A young defendant was once convicted in Judge Tomei's court of gunning down another person in a self-styled 'execution'. The murderer had a bad record, was no stranger to the system, and only stared in anger as the jury returned its guilty verdict.

The victim's family had attended every day of the two-week trial. On the day of sentencing, the victim's mother and grandmother addressed the court. When they spoke, neither addressed the jury. Both spoke directly to the murderer. And they both forgave him.

'You broke the Golden Rule – loving God with all your heart, soul, and mind. You broke the law – loving your neighbour as yourself. I am your neighbour,' the grandmother told him, 'so you have my address. If you want to write, I'll write you back. I sat in this trial for two weeks, and for the last 16 months I tried to hate you. But you know what? I could not hate. I feel sorry for you because you made a wrong choice.'

Judge Tomei wrote: 'For the first time since the trial began, the defendant's eyes lost their laser force and appeared to surrender to a life force that only a mother can generate: nurturing, unconditional love. After the grandmother finished, I looked at the defendant. His head was hanging low. There was no more swagger, no more stare. The destructive and evil forces within him collapsed helplessly before this remarkable display of humanness.'

In choosing the path of forgiveness, the grandmother released a power that could not be tapped into any other way. And it was that power which caused the defendant to hang his head for the first time.

Look for the real person beneath the mask

When we have been wronged, we tend to caricature our wrongdoer; we emphasise all the bad things about them, twisting anything that looks remotely good. We are quick to discredit their every motive, and see them only and always in one way.

Forgiveness requires, however, that we look for the real person behind the caricature we've created in our minds.

Not only have they hurt, but also they have been hurt. We begin to see that they are weak, needy and fallible. And we can start to find reasons for our hearts to turn towards mercy instead of malice.

This doesn't mean we automatically grant them victim status and excuse all their wrong – we are forgiving, not excusing.

And what is our motivation for doing this? We are doing for them what God has done for us. God could have simply seen our wrongdoing and said, 'I've seen enough, that's all I need to know.' But God looked beyond our wrongdoing and saw something worth loving. And that's what we've been called to do as well.

Desire the best for your wrongdoer

It sounds almost impossible to hope for good things to happen to someone who has done bad things to you, but in the process of forgiveness, we move from dreaming of bad things befalling people toward hoping for good things in their life.

At this point, it might be helpful to consider a related question: does forgiving mean there's no punishment? The answer is no. Forgiveness does not necessarily mean that there should not be punishment. If someone remains unrepentant, punishment that leads to sorrow may be the desired option, because it will bring a person closer to where they need to be.

The key, however, is in our motive. Whereas before we might have prayed for them to be punished because of our anger and hatred, we might alternatively pray for them to be punished because we want to see their heart changed. We must seek to desire good things, not bad things, for those who hurt us.

Imagine that a thief breaks into my house and steals most of my belongings. He is caught and put on trial, but is completely lacking remorse. If I go to court and plead for his release, he will immediately return to more burglary. In that situation, the good things I want for the burglar's life are a change of heart and a change of lifestyle. As this is most likely to happen through punishment, forgiveness does not keep me from supporting such action – although I might well want to write or visit while they're in prison, for instance, to try to share the love of God.

When Chris Carrier was 10, he was abducted, stabbed, shot and left for dead. Amazingly, he survived, but the emotional and physical scars were very difficult to heal. Eventually, though, his commitment to Christ helped him to move on with his life. The perpetrator was never found.

Over 20 years later, on 3 September 1996, Chris received a phone call from a detective in the Coral Gables, Florida police department. He said that an elderly man in a local nursing home had confessed to being his abductor. The man's name was David McCallister.

Chris visited David the following day, and this is what he said: 'It was an awkward moment, walking into his room, but as soon as I saw him I was overwhelmed with compassion. The man I found was not an intimidating kidnapper, but a frail 77-year-old. David's body was ruined by alcoholism and smoking – he weighed little more than 60 pounds. He had no family, or if he did, they wanted nothing to do with him, and no friends.

'A friend who had accompanied me asked him a few questions that led to him admitting that he had abducted me. He then asked, "Did you ever wish you could tell that young boy that you were sorry for what you did?" David answered emphatically, "I wish I could." That was when I introduced myself to him.

'Unable to see, David clasped my hand and told me he was sorry for what he had done to me. As he did, I looked down at him, and it came over me like a wave: why should anyone have to face death without family, friends and the joy of life – without hope? I couldn't do anything but offer him my forgiveness and friendship.'

In the days that followed, Chris was able to share the love of Christ with David.

What is our motivation for doing such a difficult thing? We are doing for them what God has done for us.

If possible, enjoy a healed relationship

Sometimes the other person can't join us in moving toward reconciliation (for example, a parent we need to forgive might now have passed away) and sometimes the other person simply won't join us (such as someone who won't acknowledge that they have hurt us, for instance). In this case, for reconciliation to happen they must understand the pain that they've caused us and be remorseful about it. But when they are, we must make sure that we enjoy the healing and the renewed relationship that can only come through forgiveness.

Back to *Changing Lanes.* At the end of the film, Banek asks his father-in-law and senior partner Delano, 'How can you live with yourself?' – referring to the way they all handled the Simon Dunn affair. Delano replies, 'I can live with myself because, at the end of the day, I think I do more good than harm: what other standard have I got to judge by?' Delano sees morality as a kind of balance sheet of good and evil, a profit-and-loss account where as long as assets outweigh liabilities, you've done OK.

When he interviews a prospective associate, Banek finds the man's ideological approach to the law laughable. 'I believe in the law,' he says. 'I believe in order and justice. I believe that people are by nature good ...' – but he is interrupted by Banek's laughter. The youngster is wrong. People are by nature corrupt and evil: Banek has seen this firsthand in the events of that day, in himself and Gipson. And the law condemns us: it shows us how we ought to live, but also how we fail to measure up to it.

Clip 2: Changed lanes, changed lives

Gipson is in Banek's office. He has returned the red file, at the end of a long and traumatic day. 'I have to thank you,' says Gipson. Banek has tried – a little too late – to help him buy a house. But his wife has already left him, and taken the children. She's told him he won't ever see them again. 'But I will,' Gipson declares, with determination. In the meantime, a house seems too much for him right now. 'But I'll find a way to be their father again. What about you?' he asks Banek.

Banek starts thinking aloud. He has the file, but it's too late for him, too. His senior partners had to act fast to cover their tracks while he was trying to find the file. They forged the document, and now it's as if 'it never happened'. So now, he muses, he's going to go for dinner with his wife and his in-laws, and at the weekend go and look at a boat, and then come back in to work on Monday. 'Magically, this whole incredible day somehow becomes a memory,' he says. 'It's like meeting a girl in a fleeting moment, who you can't forget. After that day, you remember her – not every day, but she comes back to you as a memory of another life you could have had. Today's that girl,' he reflects.

'I'm sorry about what I did,' Gipson tells Banek.

'I'm sorry, too,' Banek replies.

Then we see Banek going to the restaurant, where, in an atmosphere you could cut with a knife, he joins his wife and her parents for dinner. Banek and his father-in-law exchange steely glares. But just as the small talk seems to be smoothing over the wrongdoing of the day, Banek whips out the crumpled red file from his pocket. 'This is Simon Dunn's power of appointment,' he says. 'I got it back.'

'This is behind us,' his father-in-law speaks through gritted teeth.

'Can you imagine how unpleasant it would be if the judge found this file?' Banek asks. He will not be moved; he will not be dispatched to Texas for a few months, as Delano has suggested, to do some charity 'pro-bono' work with poor men on death row. Instead, he has changed. He will stay at the office and stand his ground, and do the pro-bono work from there – starting on Monday by helping a man to buy a house.

'I've found the edge,' he tells his wife. 'Can you live there with me?'

It is only in these closing moments of *Changing Lanes* that true forgiveness is reached between Banek and Gipson. As a further act of reconciliation, Banek visits Mrs Gipson to explain what happened, and persuades her to give Gipson another chance. The closing shot is of Gipson coming out of his apartment and seeing his family waiting for him across the road.

If you want to be a forgiving person, set no limits on forgiveness. Seek the experience of forgiveness in your life through Jesus and sow what you have received from God.

Do not let anger; revenge and grudges destroy your life and the lives of those around you. Give it to Jesus. If you are holding a grudge, release it and ask Jesus to enable you to forgive the person who hurt you.

It's never too late to change lanes.

DISCUSSION STARTERS

(You'll need a brick or piece of rock (or something heavy) and enough feathers to go round. You'll also need a set of notelets.)

Personal reflection: Take a few moments to reflect personally on the film. It may have reminded you of someone you have yet to forgive; or, who has yet to forgive you. If it did, think about that person in the quietness, and try to think about them in a positive way.

Discuss: It's easy for one thing to lead quickly to another – especially something like road rage. Chat about a situation you've been in that has spiralled out of control, and talk about how you might have acted differently to prevent it. Why do you think it's so easy for things to snowball?

Read: Mt. 18:21–35.

Personal reflection: Have you ever been let off a debt? (It doesn't happen very often!) Have you got a debt you'd *like* to be relieved of?! How would you feel if you were? Sometimes it's hard to receive good things and good news – out of the blue – but we must learn to. Spend a few moments 'receiving' God's grace. You might find it helpful to sit with your eyes closed and your hands upturned.

Act: J. John writes, 'If we want to be forgiven, we must also forgive others.' Sometimes that's the hardest part – but clearly it's vital, according to the last verse in the passage we read from Matthew.

Pass the brick around, and feel its weight. It's like the weight of unforgiveness we carry around with us. Once you have held it and felt it for a few moments, pass it on. Then, go and take a feather. Feel its lightness in comparison. Think of the person you need to forgive, or who needs to forgive you. And consider the lightness that this act will bring. Keep the feather safe, and let it remind you of the need to forgive.

Read: Lk. 23:32–43.

Act: Hidden among this passage is a simple verse: 'Jesus said, "Father forgive them, for they do not know what they are doing."' Not only was Jesus willing to forgive his tormentors, but he died for us all so that we could be so much better off.

Can we, too, move from dreaming of bad things befalling people towards hoping for good things in their life? Take a notelet and write a short, positive note to someone you think bad things about. You may or may not have the courage to post it; if you don't, keep it with you to remind you to dream good things for those you need to forgive. While writing the note, try to think how you can do something positive for that person – like baking them a cake, or taking them a bottle of wine.

18

A Love that Won't Let Go
Finding Nemo

MARK STIBBE

DISNEY/PIXAR, 2003

Directed by ANDREW STANTON and LEE UNKRICH
Story by ANDREW STANTON
Screenplay by ANDREW STANTON, BOB PETERSON and DAVID REYNOLDS

ALBERT BROOKS as *Marlin* (voice)
ELLEN DEGENERES as *Dory* (voice)
ALEXANDER GOULD as *Nemo* (voice)
WILLEM DAFOE as *Gill* (voice)

CLASSIFICATION: U

In this chapter we are looking at a Walt Disney cartoon – the beautifully-crafted *Finding Nemo*. *Finding Nemo* is another product of the powerful collaboration between Disney and Pixar. The movie raked in $70 million in its opening weekend and outperformed *Toy Story, Toy Story* 2 and *Monsters Inc.* It is the most successful animated film of all time. And it's my favourite!

The movie begins with what is now a Disney cliché – the death of the mother figure. Marlin, a male clownfish, is married to Coral, a female clownfish. He has found them both a beautiful home on the edge of the Great Barrier Reef in Australia. Scores of their eggs glow in a shell in the undergrowth of the reef; they are expecting to hatch any time now. Everything seems perfect.

Clip 1: A perfect world

MARLIN. Wow.

CORAL. Mmm.

MARLIN. Wow.

CORAL. Mmm-hmm.

MARLIN. Wow.

CORAL. Yes, Marlin. No, I see it. It's beautiful.

MARLIN. So, Coral, when you said you wanted an ocean view, you didn't think that we were gonna get the whole ocean, did you? Huh? [*sighs*] Oh yeah. A fish can breath out here. Did your man deliver or did he deliver?

CORAL. My man delivered.

MARLIN. And it wasn't so easy.

CORAL. Because a lot of other clownfish had their eyes on this place.

MARLIN. You better believe they did – every single one of them.

CORAL. Mmm-hmm. You did good. And the neighbourhood is awesome.

MARLIN. So, you do like it, don't you?

CORAL. No, no. I do, I do. I really do like it. But Marlin, I know that the drop-off is desirable with the great schools and the amazing view and all, but do we really need so much space?

MARLIN. Coral, honey, these are our kids we're talking about. They deserve the best. Look, look, look. They'll wake up, poke their little heads out and they'll see a whale! See, right by their bedroom window.

CORAL. Shhh, you're gonna wake the kids.

MARLIN. Oh, right. Right.

CORAL. Aww, look. They're dreaming. We still have to name them.

MARLIN. You wanna name all of 'em, right now? All right, we'll name this half Marlin Jr. and then this half Coral Jr. OK, we're done.

CORAL. I like Nemo.

MARLIN. Nemo? Well, we'll name one Nemo but I'd like most of them to be Marlin Jr.

CORAL. Just think that in a couple of days, we're gonna be parents!

MARLIN. Yeah. What if they don't like me?

CORAL. Marlin.

MARLIN. No, really.

CORAL. There's over 400 eggs. Odds are, one of them is bound to like you.

CORAL. What?

MARLIN. You remember how we met?

CORAL. Well, I try not to.

MARLIN. Well, I remember. 'Excuse me, miss, can you check and see if there's a hook in my lip?'

CORAL. Marlin!

MARLIN. 'Well, you gotta look a little closer because it's wiggling.'

CORAL. Get away!

MARLIN. Here he is. Cutie's here! Where did everybody go?

MARLIN [*sees barracuda, gasps*]. Coral, get inside the house, Coral. No, Coral, don't. They'll be fine. Just get inside, you, right now.

MARLIN. No! [*barracuda attacks*].

MARLIN. Coral! Coral?

MARLIN. Coral? Oh!

MARLIN. Ohh [*looks at one surviving egg*]. There, there, there. It's OK, Daddy's here. Daddy's got you. I promise, I will never let anything happen to you … Nemo.

Living in a world ruined by evil

Over the course of this book, John and I have been looking at modern films from a Christian perspective. We both believe that films are often a window into how people think about spiritual things. Today's films reveal a great deal about God. The reason even non-Christian films can reveal something about God is because, as Dorothy Sayers pointed out, film-makers are creators. They are creators because they are made in the image of a Creator God. They are what Tolkien called, 'sub-creators'.

In many ways, *Finding Nemo* is a good example. The scene we have just described is reminiscent of where the Bible story begins. The first book of the Bible, Genesis, describes a perfect world. In the first three chapters we see God creating an idyllic world – a world of unparalleled beauty, with a luscious and exquisite garden at the centre. As we read in Genesis 2:8,9 (NLT):

> 'Then the Lord God planted a garden in Eden, in the east, and there he placed the man he had created. And the Lord God planted all sorts of trees in the garden – beautiful trees that produced delicious fruit. At the centre of the garden he placed the tree of life and the tree of the knowledge of good and evil.'

This is also an intimate world – a world where Adam and Eve live in the innocence of unspoiled intimacy, like Marlin and Coral. Here is Genesis 2 again:

> '"At last!" Adam exclaimed. "She is part of my own flesh and bone! She will be called 'woman', because she was taken out of a man." This explains why a man leaves his father and mother and is joined to his wife, and the two are united into one.'
>
> (Gen. 2:23,24, NLT)

This is indeed an idyllic and intimate world, but this is also an invaded world. At the beginning of Genesis 3 a serpent appears. This serpent is a symbol of the destroyer, Satan, and through his manipulation he causes God's perfect world to be ruined. Through his evil, the peace and harmony of Eden is lost; human beings will no longer inhabit this kind of world and will for ever harbour a longing for Eden.

Whatever your view of the opening of Genesis – a literal description of man's origins, or a parable of our beginnings – these chapters portray a perfect world ruined. That is the first spiritual truth you encounter in the Bible: we live in a world ruined by evil. And there's more – entering our world, the devil has tempted humankind to rebel against God. And it's to the theme of rebellion that we now turn, as we see Nemo, several years later, rebelling against his father's wishes on his first day at school.

Clip 2: A son's rebellion

NEMO. Hey guys, wait up! Whoa.

TAD. Cool.

TAD. Saved your life!

PEARL. Aw, you guys made me ink.

NEMO. What's that? [*looking up at the hull of a boat*].

TAD. I know what that is. Oh, oh! Sandy Plankton saw one. He called, he said it was called a … a butt.

NEMO. Whoa.

PEARL. Wow. That's a pretty big butt.

SHELDON. Oh, look at me. I'm gonna go touch the butt. [*sneezes*] Whoa!

SHELDON. Oh yeah? Let's see you get closer.

PEARL. OK. Beat that.

TAD. Come on, Nemo. How far can you go?

NEMO. Uh, my dad says it's not safe.

MARLIN. Nemo, no!

NEMO. Dad?

MARLIN. You were about to swim into open water!

NEMO. No, I wasn't going to go out – but Dad!

MARLIN. It was a good thing I was here. If I hadn't showed up, I don't know …

PEARL. Sir, he wasn't gonna go.

TAD. Yeah, he was too afraid.

NEMO. No, I wasn't.

MARLIN. This does not concern you, kids. And you're lucky I don't tell your parents you were out there. You know you can't swim well.

NEMO. I can swim fine, Dad, OK?

MARLIN. No, it's not OK. You shouldn't be anywhere near here. OK, I was right. You'll start school in a year or two.

NEMO. No, Dad! Just because you're scared of the ocean …

MARLIN. Clearly, you're not ready. And you're not coming back until you are. You think you can do these things but you just can't, Nemo!

NEMO. I hate you.

MR. RAY. There's … nothing to see. Gather, uh, over there. Excuse me, is there anything I can do? I am a scientist, sir. Is there any problem?

MARLIN. I'm sorry. I didn't mean to interrupt things. He isn't a good swimmer and it's a little too soon for him to be out here unsupervised.

MR. RAY. Well, I can assure you, he's quite safe with me.

MARLIN. Look, I'm sure he is. But you have a large class and he can get lost from sight if you're not looking. I'm not saying you're not looking –

FISH KID. Oh my gosh! Nemo's swimming out to sea!

MARLIN. Nemo! What do you think you're doing? You're gonna get stuck out there and I'll have to get you before another fish does! Get back here! I said get back here, now! Stop! You take one move, mister. Don't you dare! If you put one fin on that boat … are you listening to me?

Don't touch the bo … Nemo!

TAD [*whispering*]. He touched the butt.

MARLIN. You paddle your little tail back here, Nemo. That's right. You are in big trouble, young man. Do you hear me? Big … big –

NEMO [*Nemo is put in a net by a diver*]. Aaaah! Daddy! Help me!

MARLIN. I'm coming, Nemo!

KIDS. Aaaah!

MR. RAY. Get under me, kids!

NEMO. Ah! Oh no! Dad! Daddy!

MARLIN. Oh! Nemo! Unh! Nemo! Nemo, no! Nemo! Nemo! Nemo! No! No! Aah! Nemo! Nemo!

Our rebellion separates us from God

Rebellion is a strange thing; right from the earliest stages of our life human beings have a tendency towards rebellion. Where does a small child get that rebellious 'No!' from? Why is it that this rebellion never really leaves us?

In Nemo's case, rebellion leads to separation from his father, but there are some mitigating factors. His father Marlin is partly responsible; he is nervous because Nemo, on his first day at school, will be going near the drop-off, and the drop-off has some very painful memories. Marlin is understandably anxious and says, 'You shouldn't be anywhere near here. OK, I was right. You'll start school in a year or two.' This leads Nemo to shout, 'I hate you' – Nemo's last words to his father before he is taken.

I don't know a parent or a child that doesn't relate to this episode. The director of the film, Andrew Stanton, has some very interesting observations here:

> 'When my son was five, I remember taking him to the park. I had been working long hours and felt guilty about not spending enough time with him. As we were walking, I was experiencing all this pent-up emotion and thinking, "I-miss-you, I-miss-you," but I spent the whole walk going, "Don't touch that. Don't do that. You're gonna fall in there." And there was this third-party voice in my head saying, "You're completely wasting the entire moment that you've got with your son right now." I became obsessed with this premise that fear can deny a good father from being one.'

Marlin is overprotective of Nemo, and this causes him to shelter his son to an unnecessary degree. This in turn breeds anger and rebellion in Nemo and creates further pain for Marlin.

Now it would be all too easy in our culture to blame the father for Nemo's rebellion. This happens all the time in our society today. Someone rebels against their parents, against their school, against their government, and automatically people say, 'It wasn't their fault; it was their upbringing.' They are not to blame; someone else is!

Here's a poem I read once that says it all for me:

'I went to my psychiatrist to be psychoanalysed
To find out why I killed the cat and blackened my husband's eyes
He laid me down on a downy couch to see what he could find
And here is what he dredged up from my subconscious mind
When I was 1, my mummy hid my dolly in a trunk
And so it follows naturally that I am always drunk ...
At 3 I had a feeling of ambivalence towards my brothers
And so it follows naturally I poison all my lovers
But now I am happy, now I've learned the lesson this has taught
That everything I do that's wrong is someone else's fault'

(Jay Adams, *Competent to Counsel*, Baker Book House, 1970)

Whatever Marlin's anxieties in *Finding Nemo*, ultimately, Nemo made the choice to break the rules and rebel against his father's wishes. And the same is true of each one of us. The Bible teaches us not only that we live in a world ruined by evil, but also that our rebellion separates us from our Father in heaven. God has placed absolute moral laws in our universe and they are here not for our punishment but for our protection. When we ignore or break God's laws we sin, and when we sin we must take responsibility. We can't say, 'It's in my genes', 'It's my upbringing', 'It's my education', 'They made me do it'.

Remember the Garden of Eden? When God shows up after Adam and Eve have rebelled, Eve points to the snake and says, 'He made me do it,' and Adam points to Eve and says, 'She made me do it.' 'No,' says God, 'You chose, you sinned and now you must experience the just consequences.' And so we became separated from the Perfect Father, the God and Father of our Lord Jesus Christ.

And this leads to the third truth taught in the Bible, and also vividly illustrated in *Finding Nemo,* that we are unable to save ourselves . . .

Clip 3: There's no way out

[Nemo has been put in an aquarium in a dentist's surgery in Sydney. He finds there an assortment of aquatic friends and with their help tries to escape captivity]

GILL. You miss your dad, don't you, Sharkbait?

NEMO. Yeah.

GILL. Well, you're lucky to have someone out there who's lookin' for you.

NEMO. He's not looking for me. He's scared of the ocean.

GILL. Peach, any movement?

PEACH. He's had at least four cups of coffee, it's gotta be soon.

GILL. Keep on him.

GILL. My first escape, landed on dental tools. I was aimin' for the toilet.

NEMO. Toilet?

GILL. All drains lead to the ocean, kid.

NEMO. Wow. How many times have you tried to get out?

GILL. Aah, I've lost count. Fish aren't meant to be in a box, kid. It does things to ya.

BUBBLES. Bubbles! Bubbles, bubbles, bubbles–

PEACH. Potty break! Potty break! He just grabbed the Reader's Digest! We have 4.2 minutes.

GILL. That's your cue, Sharkbait.

BLOAT. You can do it, kid.

GILL. OK, you gotta be quick. Once you get in, you swim down to the bottom of the chamber and I'll talk you through the rest.

NEMO. OK.

GILL. Go on, it'll be a piece of kelp.

NEMO [*takes a deep breath*].

GILL. Nicely done! Can you hear me?

NEMO. Yeah.

GILL. Here comes the pebble. Now, do you see a small opening?

NEMO. Uh-huh.

GILL. OK, inside it you'll see a rotating fan. Very carefully, wedge that pebble into the fan to stop it turning.

NEMO. Aaah!

GILL. Careful, Sharkbait.

NEMO. I can't do it!

PEACH. Gill, this isn't a good idea.

GILL. He'll be fine. Try again.

NEMO. OK.

GILL. That's it, Sharkbait. Nice and steady.

NEMO. I got it! I got it!

PEACH [*sigh*].

BLOAT. He did it!

GURGLE. Whew!

GILL. That's great, kid! Now, swim up the tube and out.

NEMO. Oh no! Gill! Gill!

GILL. Sharkbait!

BLOAT. Oh my gosh!

GILL. Get 'im outta there! Get 'im outta there!

BUBBLES. Help him!

GURGLE. What do we do!? What do we do!?

PEACH. Oh no!

GILL. Stay calm, kid! Just don't panic!

NEMO. Help me!

GILL. Sharkbait! Grab hold of this!

NEMO. No! No!

GILL. Feed me more!

GURGLE. That's it!

GILL. Come on, Sharkbait! Grab it!

NEMO. I got it!

GILL. Pull!

PEACH. Gill, don't make him go back in there.

GILL. No. We're done.

We are unable to save ourselves

Nemo is trapped; he tries to escape but he can't get out. He knows that the ocean is just outside the window. He knows this is the place he is supposed to be – a place of freedom – but he is now imprisoned. And he is imprisoned as a direct consequence of his rebellion against his father. Look what happens to those who live like this. Look at his fellow inmates and what living in a tank, rather than the open sea, has done to them. One is obsessed with the bubbles coming from the treasure chest aerator. Another believes her reflection in the glass to be an annoying twin sister. As Gill poignantly concludes, 'Fish aren't meant to be in a box, kid. It does things to ya.'

Here again we see parallels with the Bible story. Bible truth no. 1: we live in a world ruined by evil. Bible truth no. 2: our rebellion separates us from the Father. Bible truth no. 3: we are unable to save ourselves.

Sin separates us from God and, aware of our separation, we have tried to get back to the Father using good works, religious rituals and animal sacrifices. But we are utterly helpless, unable to save ourselves from the self-destructive power within.

There is a story from Australia which illustrates this point. One day a snake managed to enter a house and saw a canary in a cage. It decided that the bird would make a tasty morsel, and so went through the bars of the cage and ate it. Unfortunately, once the bird was in its throat, the snake was too big to get back out of the cage again. It was a prisoner of its own appetite.

And so it is with us. We have refused to accept the moral limits which the Creator has placed on us. Determined to find our way through the bars, we now find ourselves not free at all but imprisoned. All our so-called permissiveness has brought us is a miserable bondage to self-indulgence. According to the Bible, we are unable to save ourselves. But thank God this is not the end of the story in the Bible any more than it is the end of *Finding Nemo.*

Let's get back to the film. Marlin and his wonderfully loopy friend, Dory, continue their odyssey, with menacing sharks, ravenous gulls, forests of deadly jellyfish and other dangers of the deep standing – or swimming – in their way.

Clip 4: The father's rescue

[We are nearing the end of the journey. Marlin is swimming with his friend Dory and talking to some sea turtles about his

quest to rescue his son. This starts an extraordinary chain of storytelling through the ocean right to the fish tank where Nemo is imprisoned]

SQUIRT. So where are you going?

MARLIN. Well, you see my son was taken. My son was taken away from me.

TURTLE KIDS [*gasp*].

DORY. No way.

SQUIRT. What happened?

MARLIN. No, no, no, kids. I don't wanna talk about it.

TURTLE KIDS. Awww! Please?

SQUIRT. Pleeeease?

MARLIN [*sighs*]. Well, OK. I live on this reef, a long long way from here.

DORY. Oh, boy. This is gonna be good, I can tell.

MARLIN. And my son, Nemo, see he was mad at me. And maybe he wouldn't have done it if I hadn't been so tough on him, I don't know. Anyway, he swam out in the open water to this boat and when he was out there, these divers appeared and I tried to stop them but the boat was too fast. So we swam out in the ocean to follow them …

TURTLE KID. They couldn't stop them. And then Nemo's dad, he swims out to the ocean and they bump into …

SMALL FISH. … three ferocious sharks! He scares away the sharks by blowin' them up!

BIG FISH. Golly, that's amazing!

SMALL FISH. And then dives thousands of …

LOBSTER. … feet straight down into the dark. It's like wicked dark down there, you can't see a thing. How's it goin', Bob? And the only thing that they can see down there …

SWORDFISH. ... is the light from this big horrible creature with razor sharp teeth. Nice parry, old man. And then he has to blast his way ...

DOLPHIN. So, these two little fish have been searching the ocean for days. On the East Australian Current.

FEMALE BIRD. Which means that he may be on his way here right now. That should put them in Sydney ...

MALE BIRD 1. ... Harbour in a matter of days. I mean, it sounds like this guy's gonna stop at ...

MALE BIRD 2. ... nothing until he finds his son. I sure hope he makes it.

MALE BIRD 3. That's one dedicated father if you ask me.

GULLS. Mine! Mine! Mine! Mine! Mine! Mine! Mine! Mine! Mine!

NIGEL. Oh, would you just shut up! You're rats with wings!

PELICAN. ... bloke's been lookin' for his boy Nemo.

NIGEL. Nemo?

PELICAN. He was taken off the reef by divers and this ...

NIGEL. There, take it! You happy?!

GULLS. Mine! Mine! Mine! Mine!

NIGEL. Hey, hey, hey! Say that again! You said something about Nemo. What was it?

GULLS. Mine! Mine! Mine!

CRAB. Whoooooaaa ... watcha!

GULL. Mine!

PELICAN. Last I heard, he's headin' towards the harbour.

NIGEL. Ho ho! Brilliant!

[Cut to Nigel the pelican flying towards the dentist's surgery and hitting the window]

NIGEL. All right! Hey, hey, hey, hey–!

DENTIST. What the!?

PATIENT. Aaaaaaaaah!!! Oooooh …

DENTIST. Well, uh, that's one way to pull a tooth. He he he he he! Huh, darn kids. Well, good thing I pulled the right one, eh, prime minister? He he he he!

NIGEL. Hey, hey. Psst!

PEACH. Oh, Nigel. You just missed an extraction.

NIGEL. Ooh! Has he loosened the periodontal ligament yet … oh, what am I talkin' about!? Nemo! Where's Nemo? I gotta speak with him.

NEMO. What? What is it?

NIGEL. Your dad's been fighting the entire ocean looking for you.

NEMO. My father? Really?

GILL. Really?

NIGEL. Oh yeah. He's travelled hundreds of miles. He's been battling sharks and jellyfish and all sorts of –

NEMO. Sharks? That can't be him.

NIGEL. Are you sure? What was his name? Some sort of sportfish or something. Tuna, uh, trout …

NEMO. Marlin?

NIGEL. That's it! Marlin! The little clownfish from the reef.

NEMO. It's my dad! He took on a shark!

NIGEL. I heard he took on three.

DEB / BLOAT / GURGLE. Three!?

GILL. Three sharks!?

BLOAT. That's gotta be forty eight hundred teeth!

NIGEL. You see, kid, after you were taken by diver Dan over there, your dad followed the boat you were on like a maniac.

NEMO. Really?

NIGEL. He's swimming and he's swimming and he's giving it all he's got and then three gigantic sharks capture him and he blows them up! And then dives thousands of feet and gets chased by a monster with huge teeth! He ties this demon to a rock and what does he get for a reward? He gets to battle an entire jellyfish forest! And now he's riding with a bunch of sea turtles on the East Australian Current and the word is he's headed this way right now, to Sydney!

The Father has come to our rescue

This is a wonderful scene in which we see a father coming to the rescue of his son. Marlin was quite timid, naturally displaying a nervous temperament. But he loved Nemo so much that it did not matter how big the ocean was, or how many obstacles and terrors there were. He was determined to save Nemo, and set out on an incredible adventure to seek and save his son. And his journey became the talk of all the fish and birds.

The good news of this heroic father travelling the ocean in search of his son reached Nemo through a pelican named Nigel. And this compelled Nemo to take a leap of faith.

What a father we see here! Marlin deserves the comment: 'That's one dedicated father.'

Now this is something of a departure for a Disney cartoon. Traditionally, father figures don't fare well. Father figures have fared particularly badly since the cartoon that revived Disney's fortunes and reputation, *The Little Mermaid*. Since that time, father figures have been presented in one of three ways.

Doddering fathers

These tend to be comical, fat and completely clueless: Belle's dad in *Beauty and the Beast*, Princess Jasmine's in

Aladdin, Jane's in *Tarzan,* Mulan's in *Mulan,* Princess Kida's in *Atlantis.*

Domineering fathers

These are generally strong but they are also impossible to please. Typically, they don't understand their children and impose great expectations on them (often dictating whom their children will or will not marry): King Triton in *The Little Mermaid,* Kerchak, Tarzan's bad-tempered surrogate father, Chief Powhatan in *Pocahontas,* Judge Claude Frollo, evil guardian of Quasimodo, in *The Hunchback of Notre Dame.*

Dead fathers

These are fathers who just don't appear, usually because they are dead and look on passively from heaven. Aladdin, Quasimodo and Tarzan have all lost their fathers; Hercules is separated from Zeus at birth – Zeus offers him little help thereafter (*Hercules*); and Simba's father Mufasa dies while Simba is a young cub (*The Lion King*).

So the three types of father we see in recent Disney cartoons have been doddering, domineering or quite simply dead – until, that is, *Finding Nemo,* where we have a fourth category: the dedicated father. Marlin is a truly committed father who overcomes his own weaknesses and fears to cross an ocean to save his helpless and lost son.

And what a great picture of God. The Bible reveals God to be the most dedicated father. Whatever kind of father figure you have been used to – doddering, domineering or distant – God is like Marlin. He has pursued us in love. As we read in the parable of the Prodigal Son (Lk. 15:20, NLT):

> 'And while he was still a long distance away, his father saw him coming. Filled with love and compassion, he ran to his son, embraced him, and kissed him.'

God is a father who is dedicated to coming after you in love and rescuing you from your captivity.

He is the Running Father.

He is the most dedicated of dads.

A love that will not let us go

I want to end by returning to the beginning of the film. After the terrible loss of his wife Coral, Marlin looks lovingly at the one remaining egg and says, 'It's OK, Daddy's here. Daddy's got you. I promise, I will never let anything happen to you ... Nemo.' This is a great picture. One reviewer wrote: 'The image that startled me above all came early in the film. We see Marlin, the proud father, assuring his son that everything will be all right while Nemo *is still in an embryonic state,* curled and quivering in his translucent egg. It's a beautiful image.'

Let me add that this is also a biblical image! God has been watching over your life before you were born. He loves you like no earthly father ever could. Everything that has happened to you is part of his plan. This doesn't mean that you live a life free from problems and difficulties. But it does mean that the Father turns to good what the devil intends for harm. As King David says in Ps. 139:13–16 (NLT):

> 'You made all the delicate, inner parts of my body
> and knit me together in my mother's womb.
> Thank you for making me so wonderfully complex!
> Your workmanship is marvellous – and how well I know it.
> You watched me as I was being formed in utter seclusion,

as I was woven together in the dark of the womb.
You saw me before I was born.
Every day of my life was recorded in your book.
Every moment was laid out
before a single day had passed.'

You may feel like a nobody – that you are too insignificant or too sinful to merit such love. Take heart: Nemo means 'nobody'. Nemo is small, he has a deformed fin, and above all, he is a clownfish! Yet he is loved by a passionate, pursuant father. And so are we. The Father is always there for us, even in the deepest ocean. Here is Ps. 139 (NLT) again, vs. 8–10:

'If I go up to heaven, you are there;
if I go down to the place of the dead, you are there.
If I ride the wings of the morning,
if I dwell by the farthest oceans,
even there your hand will guide me,
and your strength will support me.'

Isn't it time you came home to the most dedicated Father in the universe?

DISCUSSION STARTERS

(You'll need some olives.)

Personal reflection: Children's cartoons can sometimes hold a profound message for adults. But it's good to approach the message with childlike wonder and curiosity – especially when it's about being a son or daughter. For a few moments, pause to think about your own mother and father. (You may, like Nemo, have lost one of them.) What are your childhood memories of your parents? Try to thank God for them, even if yours hasn't been a happy relationship.

Discuss: How do you respond to a cartoon like this? What can it teach us? How can a child's film help us to approach the material in a less guarded way? How does it make you feel about your parents?

Read: Gen. 1. As you read this chapter, think about God, our heavenly parent – and imagine his pride and joy at creating the whole world.

Act: Write, and then share, a short paragraph about your favourite thing about God's creation – an animal you have seen, a view you have experienced, and so on. Try to write it poetically, or reflectively, so that as you each read out your paragraph in turn, you can do so in an attitude of worship or contemplation.

Discuss: Mark says that *Finding Nemo* helps to describe three 'biblical truths': first, that we live in a world spoiled by evil; second, that our rebellion separates us from the Father; third, that we are unable to save ourselves.

How does Marlin's dedication make you feel about our relationship with God, the Father? Have you ever stopped to put yourself in God's shoes before? Does this film help to teach you anything new about God?

Read: Lk. 15:20.

Act: The people listening to Jesus would have been shocked that the father chose to run towards his son – for it would have been humiliating and degrading. God was not too proud to run; but are we too proud, sometimes, to say sorry and head back home to God?

The olive branch symbolises peace and reconciliation. Each take an olive in turn, and eat it. As you do so, savour the taste of forgiveness and reconciliation. Think of God looking down the road to see if we are ready to return to him. If you feel able within your group, you might respond in a way that demonstrates your humility – by kneeling down, or even taking your shoes and socks off.

Pray: One of you could end with a short prayer, if appropriate: 'Heavenly Father, we've got so much more to learn about you. We're sorry for the way we've swum out into the ocean away from you. And we're so grateful that you've come looking for us. Please help us to admit that we need to come back home to you. Thank you that you're waiting for us with open arms of love. Amen.'

19

Sailing Through the Storms of Life
Seabiscuit

J. JOHN

UNIVERSAL PICTURES/DREAMWORKS SKG/ SPYGLASS ENTERTAINMENT, 2003

Directed by GARY ROSS
Book by LAURA HILLENBRAND
Screenplay by GARY ROSS

TOBEY MAGUIRE as *Red Pollard*
JEFF BRIDGES as *Charles Howard*

CLASSIFICATION: PG

Seabiscuit is a tale of triumph and perseverance. Set in America during the Great Depression of the 1930s, it is a true story (based on a book by Laura Hillenbrand) of one horse and three men: a jockey, a trainer and a businessman.

Seabiscuit was a horse that defied all the odds to become a champion. And in doing so, he captured the hearts of a struggling nation. In overcoming his difficulties, Seabiscuit became an icon of hope for the people of the Depression.

We all love a story about the lowly and broken being restored and claiming victory. We love it because we want it to be our story. Stephen Ives, the director of a documentary about the famous horse, has spoken of Seabiscuit's contagious appeal:

> 'We all love to root for the underdog. Seabiscuit makes us feel that we can do it. That it is possible to make something of yourself with hard work, commitment and a little luck. This message, both now and in the 1930s, was intoxicating for the Americans and seemed to embody their American Dream.'

The Seabiscuit story

Despite being a successful car manufacturer, Charles Howard (Jeff Bridges) loses his zest for life when his only son tragically dies in a car accident (which in turn leads to the break-up of his marriage). Charles gets a second chance through the love of Marcela (Elizabeth Banks), a woman who sees and understands his broken heart. She introduces him to horses – a great shift down in gear from cars and the pursuit of making money. Charles decides to buy a racehorse.

Tom Smith (Chris Cooper) is a horse trainer who has lost his world of wide-open space and ranges. Most people see him as a lunatic on the fringe of life. He is frequently awkward with people, yet finds horses far less complex – cultivating an almost mystic communication with them.

Charles and Marcela don't judge Tom by his external circumstances; instead, they see a man who will spend his last $5 to save a broken horse. When Charles hires him to find a horse and jockey, Tom picks two unlikely runners: Seabiscuit and Red Pollard are both at their lowest point.

They are broken, wounded, angry losers, and they seem incorrigible.

Pollard (Tobey Maguire) is a failed boxer who has spent much of his life on the streets and in bus shelters. He was abandoned as a teenager by his parents and has no family. He was left to fight for survival during an unforgiving time. His only inheritance is a bag of poetry books and the memory of the family and home he has lost. And he has changed his name from 'John' ('the beloved') to 'Red' ('the angry').

Despite Red not being a great jockey, being blind in his right eye and 5 foot 6 (which is tall for a jockey), Tom hires him.

Seabiscuit's early career is a disaster. He races 35 times as a two-year-old, and comes last nearly every time. When Tom finds Seabiscuit, he has a rugged appearance and frantic temperament; he is too small, and is considered worthless because he cannot be trained.

Clip 1: When like meets like

Tom Smith is sitting by a fire at night, when, through the bushes, Charles Howard appears and introduces himself. Standing near the fire is a horse, who has a bandage wrapped around his leg, with a piece of Hawthorn root inside it.

'Will he get better?' asks Howard.

'Already is, I reckon,' replies Smith.

'Will he race?' asks Howard.

'Not that one,' says Smith.

'So why are you fixing him?'

Smith thinks for a moment: 'Because I can. Every horse is good for something. You don't throw a whole life away just because it's banged up a little.'

Howard knows that this is the man he's looking for.

Three months on, Tom Smith is in Saratoga, looking for a horse and a jockey on behalf of Charles and Marcela. 'It ain't just the speed, it's the heart,' he tells them.

The first time he saw Seabiscuit, the film's commentator tells us, he didn't pay attention to his size, or to his wheeze. He looked him straight in the eye, instead, and saw something he liked.

Smith is having another look at the horse walking around the yard, when his attention is drawn to a fight that breaks out nearby. A man is challenging all comers. 'Come on, I'll take you all on!' he shouts. It's Red Pollard, the over-sized jockey with a spirit to match. Smith looks at Red, then turns to look at Seabiscuit. A connection is made.

Later, Smith introduces Red to Seabiscuit. The horse, who has been bought and sold by a number of trainers who failed to bring the best out in him, is now an impetuous animal who is pacing around his stable in a frightening manner. Red walks in, unafraid, and begins talking to him. He soothes him, and offers the horse an apple. 'I'm not afraid of you,' he says.

Outside, Tom talks to Red about Seabiscuit. How on earth is he going to become a champion? Smith has the answer: 'He just needs to learn how to be a horse, again.'

All four main characters are 'damaged goods': 'a horse too small, a jockey too big, a trainer too old and an owner too dumb to know the difference,' as Charles says.

The truth is, we all get beaten up and beaten down by life from time to time. But that fact doesn't define who we are or what we have to offer.

Clip 2: Sticking to the plan

Marcela shows Charles the jockey's new outfit, ready for the first race. It's red and white, but looks too big, she thinks. He reminds her that it's their jockey who is too big …

The runners and riders parade out in front of the main grandstand, and soon they're ready for the off. In the starting stalls, one jockey looks over to Red and taunts him: 'Kind of small, isn't he?'

Red looks back: 'He's gonna look a lot smaller in a minute, Georgie!'

Tom Smith has a game plan for the race. He's told Red to follow the grey horse, and only make a break for it when the grey does likewise. But in a mad moment, another jockey cuts Red up and almost causes him to come off the horse. Angered, Red makes Seabiscuit charge after the other horse, as Red seeks his revenge. The two horses storm into the lead; yet neither has the staying power. Red has gone too early, and the rest of the horses cruise past him on their way to the finishing line. He has blown it by losing his cool.

After the race, Smith rebukes Red. We had a plan, he says. Why didn't you stick to it? 'He fouled me, Tom. He fouled me. He fouled me.' There is deep anger in Red's voice. Charles Howard is listening to the conversation, and can sense this goes much deeper than simply a foul on a racetrack.

'Son, what are you so mad about?' he asks.

One of the things about problems is that a good many of them do not exist except in our imaginations. The best way to move on with our own problems is to help others to solve theirs. Seabiscuit is retrained while Red is reclaimed and finally both are reintroduced to racing.

Separately, the pair were weak; but a failing jockey and a broken-down horse, put together, prove to be great. They 'fit' and understand each other. And soon, they set about winning races and setting records; in particular, they enjoy an outstanding victory over the triple-crown winner, War Admiral, at Pimlico in 1938, where 'no horse ever covered the distance so fast'.

Seabiscuit is an American hero. He earns the nickname 'The Wonder Horse', and becomes a proxy for the nation. Millions of displaced, downtrodden Americans rooted for this pint-sized horse and his unbeatable spirit to win.

The underlying message is one of community and wholeness. In times of deepest tragedy, healing can be found and with perseverance, victory can be achieved.

What does the Bible say?

The problem with problems

In the New Testament, the book of James tells us to 'Consider it pure joy ... whenever you face trials of many kinds' (Jas. 1:2, NIV). But how on earth can we consider trials as pure joy? It feels like James is having a laugh with us. He doesn't know *our* problems. Why should we consider it pure joy when we are facing trials?

'Because,' he says, 'you know that the testing of your faith develops perseverance. Perseverance must finish its work so that you may be mature and complete, not lacking anything' (Jas. 1:3,4, NIV). How we handle problems depends on our attitude towards them and how we choose to respond to them. There are a number of things we can observe about life in terms of our problems.

First, *problems are inevitable.* Remember that James says, 'Whenever you face trials'. If you find a path with no obstacles, it probably doesn't lead anywhere.

Second, *problems vary*. James mentions 'trials of many kinds'. There are lots of different sorts of problems, some big, some small. We are guaranteed never to be bored!

Third, *problems are unpredictable*. An alternative translation of the book of James says, 'When all kinds of trials crowd into your lives, don't resent them as intruders.'

Do you ever have a problem and feel like saying, 'Not now!'? You might need to access something from your computer when it crashes. You might have a flat tyre when you're late. You might be getting ready to speak when you blow your nose and find you have a nose bleed …

The problem with problems is that they can catch us off guard. They are inevitable, variable and unpredictable.

But the good news, fourthly, is that *problems are purposeful*. They can develop something good in our lives. They have value. But how does that work, exactly?

Well, problems test our faith. James says, 'because you know that the testing of your faith …'. The word 'testing' carries the sense of refining. When silver or gold are heated to a very high temperature, they melt and are refined by the melting away of any impurities they contained.

I'm sure we've all been under the heat in some way. The classic example in the Bible of someone under intense pressure is Job. Everything went wrong for the man. He lost his family, wealth, friends and his health. He lost everything, except a nagging wife. And this was all a test, according to the Bible. We are like tea bags: we don't know what we are really like until we are dropped in hot water.

Problems come to test our faith. They also develop our perseverance. As James writes, '… the testing of your faith develops perseverance'. The result of the difficulties in our life can be perseverance, or 'staying power'. The ability, if you like, to keep on keeping on.

In Rom. 5:3–5 (NIV), Paul writes, '… we know that suffering produces perseverance; perseverance, character; and character, hope. And hope does not disappoint us …'. We learn perseverance by having to persevere. Our problems mature us and develop our character. As James writes, 'perseverance must finish its work so that you may be mature and complete, not lacking anything'. God wants to use the problems we have to build character in our life. And he uses all sorts of things to do this: circumstances, problems, difficulties and pressure.

How do we respond to problems?

It's a crucial question, for, as we have seen, we all face difficulties. It's how we deal with them that counts, along with what we can learn through them.

First, we are called to rejoice. 'Consider it pure joy when you face trials,' says James. He is not instructing us to pretend we don't have any problems. God is not asking us to deny reality. Sometimes it's irritating when people say, 'Cheer up, things could be worse!' I did cheer up once, and things did get worse.

We rejoice *in* the problem, we don't rejoice *for* the problem. But how can we be happy in the problem? The answer lies in the fact that God has a purpose – testing our faith, developing our endurance, maturing our character. If we are only happy when we never have any problems we will never be happy.

The 'consider' part of 'consider it pure joy' means to deliberately make up your mind. It's a choice. Problems in life are inevitable. Misery is optional. We don't *have* to be miserable over it.

'How are you?' someone might ask. And you might reply, 'I'm not great, under the circumstances.' The question is, what are you doing under the circumstances? Circumstances are like a mattress: if you lie on top, its comfortable; if you lie underneath, you suffocate.

First, we rejoice. Then, we *request*. We must pray about our problems. But what do we pray for? James also says (1:5, NIV): 'If any of you lacks wisdom, he should ask God, who gives generously to all without finding fault and it will be given to him.'

God's wisdom gives us perspective on things. We need to pray for strength as well, to endure what we go through. This doesn't mean that problems don't hurt, but it does mean that they don't have to devastate us.

In all things, we can find something to be excited about. A schoolboy who brought home his report had very poor grades. 'What have you to say about this?' asked his mother. 'One thing for sure,' the boy replied, 'you can be proud. You know I haven't been cheating!'

Then, we must *relax*. We can look ahead with positive purpose. A man called Wallace Johnson wrote this:

> 'When I was 40 years old, I worked in a sawmill. One morning the boss told me, "You're fired." Discouraged and depressed I felt the world had caved in on me. It was during the Depression and my wife and I greatly needed the small wages that I was earning at the sawmill.
>
> 'When I went home I told my wife what had happened and she said, "What are you going to do now?" I replied, "I'm going to re-mortgage our home and go into the building business."
>
> 'My first venture was the construction of a small building which developed into Holiday Inns. Today if I could locate the man who fired me I would sincerely thank him for what he did. At the time it happened, I didn't understand why I was fired. Later I saw that it was God's plan to get me into the ways of His choosing.'

Instead of letting circumstances make you bitter, allow them to make you better. It's our attitude that counts.

James goes on to write (1:12, NLT), 'God blesses the people who patiently endure testing. Afterwards, they will receive the crown of life that God has promised to those who love him.' We cannot control all the things that are going to happen. We cannot control the direction of the wind – but we can set out the sail.

One day, a farmer's donkey fell down into a well. The donkey cried piteously for hours as the farmer tried to figure out what to do. Finally, he decided the animal was old and the well needed to be covered up anyway. It just wasn't worth retrieving the donkey, so he invited all his neighbours to come over and help him. They all grabbed a shovel and began to shovel dirt into the well.

At first, the donkey realised what was happening and cried horribly. Then, to everyone's amazement, he quietened down. A few shovel loads later, the farmer finally looked down the well and was astonished at what he saw. With every shovel of dirt that hit his back, the donkey was doing something amazing. He would shake it off and take a step up. As the farmer's neighbours continued to shovel dirt on top of the animal, he would shake it off and take a step up. Pretty soon, everyone was amazed as the donkey stepped up over the edge of the well and trotted off!

The best way out of a problem is through it. We must be willing to shake ourselves off and continue upwards.

Triumph over adversity

In *Seabiscuit*, we see triumph over adversity. Red Pollard's and Seabiscuit's racing careers seem doomed when they both experience severe injuries. Pollard was thrown off another horse he was riding, badly damaging his leg; doctors told him that he would never ride again. Seabiscuit also had an accident – six weeks after his great victory over War Admiral, he stumbled and ruptured a ligament in his left foreleg. It seemed very likely that he would never run again.

Over the summer of 1939, both horse and jockey convalesced together. Tom Smith's motto, 'You don't throw a whole life away just because it's banged up a little' became the driving force that resulted in these three men, Tom, Charles and Red achieving amazing things, despite their setbacks.

Clip 3: The comeback race

It's the day of the comeback race, after both Seabiscuit and Red have been injured badly. The grandstands are packed, although Marcela is sitting by the stables, unsure of whether to watch. As the race starts, she walks around to where her car is parked, near the track, and climbs on top of the roof. She has to see what happens.

Seabiscuit is in the middle of the pack as the riders skirmish for position. Binoculars from the crowd focus on how the plucky horse will fare. And then, disappointment. Seabiscuit starts drifting from the pack, moving slower. It looks like this won't be the great comeback everyone was hoping for.

'Come on!' Red shouts and the horse begins to respond. He reels in one horse – and as he comes alongside, Red sees that Georgie is the rider. 'How are you doing, Red?' he asks. 'Have a nice ride!' And with that, Red and Seabiscuit find form. Runner and rider charge through the pack, and coming around the last bend, they are neck and neck with the leader. The crowd are cheering him on. The packed stands erupt. Seabiscuit takes the lead and wins the race. Red's commentary over the jubilation says it all: 'Everyone thinks we found this broken-down horse and fixed him. But we didn't. He fixed us. Every one of us. And I guess, in a way, we fixed each other, too.'

With great determination, Seabiscuit and Red Pollard won their race and clocked the second fastest time ever to be recorded at Santa Anita. Sports commentators called it 'the greatest comeback in the history of American sports'.

Healing in times of brokenness

The brokenness of the characters and the nation find a sense of healing in the story of this horse. As they work together for a common aim, they discover fulfilment and success: Red's voice-over at the end of the film comments that 'Seabiscuit healed the broken people'. He captured the hearts of the struggling nation because if *he* could overcome his difficulties, the people of the Depression had a chance to overcome theirs. Newspapers described him at the time as 'a horse that runs with perseverance'.

It seems that rather than the horse healing the situation, Seabiscuit helped to create a situation in which all of these broken characters were brought together. The community (the three broken individuals and the American people) was healed in the process of uniting in the celebration of the unpromising horse.

The film challenges society's belief in individualism. Often, we are persuaded to think that it is up to us – as individuals – to determine whether we succeed or fail. We sometimes try to face our troubles alone. *Seabiscuit* shatters this notion – it is instead a reminder that we only truly find healing when we come together. None of the individuals were able to overcome their tragedies on their own. They needed their community to bring healing to each other.

Whatever problem you are facing now, you can:

1. ask God for wisdom to understand that problem, because the more you understand what God is doing, the less you are overwhelmed;
2. ask God for the faith to remove it or endure it;
3. cast all your cares upon him, for he cares for you.

In other words: don't give up. If life gives us lemon, let's make lemonade. As Corrie Ten Boom, a holocaust survivor, once said, 'Never be afraid to trust an unknown future to a known God.'

The writer of Hebrews (12:1–3, NLT) says, '... let us run with endurance the race that God has set before us. We do this by keeping our eyes on Jesus, on whom our faith depends from start to finish. He was willing to die a shameful death on the cross because of the joy he knew would be his afterward. Now he is seated in the place of highest honour besides God's throne in heaven. Think about all he endured when sinful people did such terrible things to him, so that you don't become weary and give up.'

DISCUSSION STARTERS

(You'll need some paper and pens.)

Personal reflection: The film celebrates triumph in the face of adversity. Think about times when you have overcome difficulties, or when you have acted together with others in a team to achieve more than you'd expected. Perhaps you don't feel as if God could ever use you to do anything worthwhile. If you don't, offer those feelings to God before you start, and ask him to help you understand how you can work with *him* as a team.

Discuss: *Seabiscuit* is reassuring, because it's a historical film. This happened, it's not wishful thinking. If you were Charles, would you have taken on Tom, or Red or Seabiscuit? Have there been times when you have dismissed someone or something too quickly, only to be proved wrong? How willing are you to take a chance on people who don't seem up for the task? Are there ways to ensure you look for someone's potential, not their faults?

Act: J. John writes, 'All four main characters are "damaged goods": a horse too small, a jockey too big, a trainer too old and an owner too dumb to know the difference ... But that fact doesn't define who we are or what we have to offer.'

Sometimes, it's easier for others to see our potential than for us to see it. So, draw around your hand on a piece of paper, cut it out and write your name in the middle of it. Then, send round the hands, for everyone to write on, in a word or phrase, how they see you (positively).

Personal reflection: When you get your paper hand back, read it. Now, place your real hand against it, and think, for a few moments, about the things people have written. Try to remember that people see you in a very different light, sometimes, from how you see yourself. Try to accept those thoughts as you place your hand on your cut-out.

Read: Jas. 1:1–5 and Rom. 5:3–5.

Discuss: J. John writes that problems are inevitable, they vary, they're unpredictable but they are also purposeful. Discuss together how you might have turned out, if you had a problem-free life. How have you grown through your problems?

Act: Place all the hands together – on the floor, or on a wall. Although we might feel weak, personally, there is great strength in our teamwork. In your group, now place your (real) hand against the hand of the person sitting next to you, so that you form a circle.

Pray: One of you could pray the following short prayer: 'Dear God, thank you for the good you see in us. Thank you that you are our real strength and that we can do nothing without working as a team – together, here, and with you. Thank you that we are 'one, but not the same' – that we're all unique, but that our sum is greater than the parts. Amen.'

Personal reflection: The writer of Hebrews (12:1–3) says, 'Let us run with perseverance the race that God has set before us.' Any racer – whether it's Seabiscuit or Paula Radcliffe – needs to train. You can't just win a race without putting in the work. It's the same for the race of life and faith. We need stamina and strength to keep going. Write yourself a few thoughts about your 'training regime' for life. Do you try to pray every day? Do you try to encourage your fellow runners at least once a week? How could you work a little more discipline into your schedule, so that you become 'fitter' for the race?

Act: If you feel comfortable doing so, say a short prayer, thanking God for each member of the group, and asking that all of your talents and potential will be realised – together.

20

Winning Your 'Soul War'
The Lord of the Rings: The Two Towers

MARK STIBBE

NEW LINE CINEMA/WINGNUT FILMS, 2002

Directed by PETER JACKSON
Novel by J.R.R. TOLKIEN
Screenplay by FRANCES WALSH, PHILIPPA BOYENS, STEPHEN SINCLAIR, PETER JACKSON

ELIJAH WOOD as *Frodo Baggins*
IAN McKELLEN as *Gandalf the Grey/ Gandalf the White*
LIV TYLER as *Arwen Undómiel*
VIGGO MORTENSEN as *Aragorn*
SEAN ASTIN as *Samwise 'Sam' Gamgee*
CATE BLANCHETT as *Galadriel*
JOHN RHYS-DAVIES as *Gimli*
BERNARD HILL as *Théoden, King of Rohan*
CHRISTOPHER LEE as *Saruman the White*
BILLY BOYD as *Peregrin 'Pippin' Took*
DOMINIC MONAGHAN as *Meriadoc 'Merry' Brandybuck*
ORLANDO BLOOM as *Legolas Greenleaf*

MIRANDA OTTO as *Éowyn*
DAVID WENHAM as *Faramir*
BRAD DOURIF as *Gríma Wormtongue*
ANDY SERKIS as *Gollum/Sméagol*

CLASSIFICATION: 12A

The Lord of the Rings: The Two Towers takes up where the first movie ends. The fellowship of the nine – whose goal is to take the ring of power to Mordor to destroy it – has now been broken up. The two hobbits Merry and Pippin have been captured by the Uruk-Hai. Aragorn, Gimli and Legolas are in hot pursuit, trying to rescue the hobbits. Meanwhile, Frodo and Sam are on their way to Mount Doom where they intend to throw the ring into the lake of fire. The remaining member of the fellowship, Boromir, has been killed. Gandalf the Grey, who seems to have died at the end of the first film, has a resurrection experience, and reappears as Gandalf the White. He comes to the aid of Aragorn, Gimli and Legolas. *The Two Towers* tracks the journeys of these three groups as they seek to save Middle Earth from the wicked Sauron, whose mission is to capture the ring and to bring the whole world under his evil rule.

This second film in *The Lord of the Rings* trilogy comes to a dramatic finale in one of the most realistic and powerful battle scenes ever seen on film, the siege of Helm's Deep. Here King Théoden and Aragorn make a courageous but extremely costly last stand against Saruman's vast army. Though the forces of good triumph against all the odds, the words of Gandalf the White ring loud at the end of the film, 'The battle for Helm's Deep is over; the battle for Middle Earth has just begun.'

A war film at different levels

The Two Towers is really about war. Yet the most dramatic war in the film is not so much the battle at Helm's Deep. The real war in *The Two Towers* is a war of the soul. The most intense battlefield in this movie is that of the human heart. So potent is this internal warfare that one movie critic even called the film 'Soul Wars'!

In *The Two Towers*, we see people struggling with issues of right and wrong not just externally (with swords and shields) but internally (with their consciences). In fact, it is all somewhat reminiscent of what Paul wrote in the book of Romans 7:15–25 (NLT):

> 'I don't understand myself at all, for I really want to do what is right, but I don't do it. Instead, I do the very thing I hate. I know perfectly well that what I am doing is wrong, and my bad conscience shows that I agree that the law is good. But I can't help myself, because it is sin inside me that makes me do these evil things.
>
> I know I am rotten through and through so far as my old sinful nature is concerned. No matter which way I turn, I can't make myself do right. I want to, but I can't. When I want to do good, I don't. And when I try not to do wrong, I do it anyway. But if I am doing what I don't want to do, I am not really the one doing it; the sin within me is doing it.
>
> It seems to be a fact of life that when I want to do what is right, I inevitably do what is wrong. I love God's law with all my heart. But there is another law at work within me that is at war with my mind. This law wins the fight and makes me a slave to the sin that is still within me. Oh, what a miserable person I am! Who will free me from this life that is dominated by sin? Thank God! The answer is in Jesus Christ our Lord.'

These words help to explicate what we see in *The Two Towers*. Paul says he knows what's right and he knows what's wrong. This is called God's law, and it is implanted within every human heart in the form of our conscience. But there is also another law, the law of sin. Sin is our determination to live life in a self-centred rather than a God-centred way.

While God's law says 'I'll do it God's way', sin says, to misquote Frank Sinatra, 'I'll do it my way'. Put another way, one law says, 'Do it your way', the other, 'Do it Yahweh!'

The Two Towers brilliantly explores this war. Indeed, *The Two Towers* shows that the fiercest fights do not occur in the battlefields of Middle Earth but within the souls of its frail inhabitants. It is these 'soul wars' that I want to explore in this chapter by looking at four characters in *The Two Towers* who in one way or another fight a 'soul war'.

The first we're going to look at is Gollum. In my opinion, director Peter Jackson's greatest achievement is his portrayal of Gollum – made convincing by virtue of Andy Serkis' extraordinary voice, and the achievements of CGI. Gollum, the dark side of the creature also known as Sméagol, has been taken captive by Frodo and Sam to be their guide to Mordor. All along the way, Gollum has sought ways to turn on the hobbits, even kill them, in order to recover his 'precious', the one ring of power. However, countless acts of kindness from Frodo have allowed Sméagol to reassert himself, and face down his evil Gollum side. In the first clip, we see Gollum engaging in the following monologue.

Clip 1: Must have the Preciousss!

[Gollum is off by himself at night]

GOLLUM. We wants it, we needs it. Must have the Preciousss. They stole it from us. Sneaky little Hobbitses. Wicked, tricksy, falssse!

SMÉAGOL. No! No! Master!

GOLLUM. Yess. Preciousss first. They will cheat you, hurt you, lie!

SMÉAGOL. Master's my friend.

GOLLUM. You don't have any friends. Nobody likes you.

SMÉAGOL. Not listening. Not listening.

GOLLUM. You're a liar, and a thief.

SMÉAGOL. No.

GOLLUM. Murderer!

SMÉAGOL. Go away.

GOLLUM. Go away?! Ahahhaa!

SMÉAGOL. I hate you, I hate you.

GOLLUM. Where would you be without me? Gollum. Gollum. I saved us. It was me. We survived because of me.

SMÉAGOL. Not anymore.

GOLLUM. What did you say?

SMÉAGOL. Master looks after us now. We don't need you.

GOLLUM. What?

SMÉAGOL. Leave now and never come back.

GOLLUM. No!

SMÉAGOL. Leave now and never come back!

GOLLUM. Ahh!

SMÉAGOL. LEAVE NOW AND NEVER COME BACK!

[Silence]

SMÉAGOL. We told him to go away! And away he goes, preciousss. Gone, gone, gone, Sméagol is free!

Confronting the dark side

In this scene we are allowed to overhear Gollum's inward struggle. Sméagol wants to do good, but Gollum struggles against him to do evil. Sméagol has to confront Gollum, his dark side, and tell him to 'leave now and never come back'. This illustrates step 1 to winning your soul war: we must confront the dark side of our hearts.

Let's look again at the words of Paul in Romans 7:

> 'I don't understand myself at all, for I really want to do what is right, but I don't do it. Instead, I do the very thing I hate. I know perfectly well that what I am doing is wrong, and my bad conscience shows that I agree that the law is good. But I can't help myself, because it is sin inside me that makes me do these evil things.'

This could be Gollum speaking! The truth is we all need to face down the evil that makes us do what is wrong. 'Good and evil have not changed since yesteryear, nor are they one thing among Elves and Dwarves and another among Men.' So says Aragorn. In other words, in spite of our own society's rejection of moral absolutes, the fact is good and evil still exist, and deep down we all know that. There is a common and absolute standard of morality and it applies to everyone. As Paul says earlier on in the book of Romans, in chapter 2:15,16 (NLT):

> 'Even when Gentiles, who do not have God's written law, instinctively follow what the law says, they show that in their hearts they know right from wrong. They demonstrate that God's law is written within them, for their own consciences either accuse them or tell them they are doing what is right.'

We can't pretend that there isn't a dark side. We must face it honestly. There is a law of sin at work in our hearts. Hiding behind the idea of 'moral relativism' will not save us. We must confront the dark side – the Gollum-like aspects to our character. We may try to conceal our shortcomings, but one day they will surely find us out.

Consider the following story. A drunk husband snuck up the stairs quietly. He looked in the bathroom mirror and bandaged the bumps and bruises he'd received in a fight earlier that night. He then proceeded to climb into bed, smiling at the thought that he'd pulled one over on his wife. When morning came, he opened his eyes and there stood his wife.

'You were drunk last night weren't you!'

'No, honey.'

'Well, if you weren't, then who put all the band-aids on the bathroom mirror?'

Step 1 to winning your soul war is to confront the dark side! Step 2 can be illustrated by our second character, King Théoden. In the second clip, we witness one of the most remarkable exorcism scenes in the history of film. To set the scene, the wicked wizard Saruman has secretly sent his spy, Gríma Wormtongue, to poison the mind of Théoden, the King of Rohan. But Gandalf the White arrives to break Gríma's spell and cast the evil spirit of Saruman out of Théoden.

Clip 2: Drawn like poison from a wound

GANDALF. Théoden, Son of Thengel. Too long have you sat in the shadows.

[Gimli spots Gríma cowering on the floor, and holds him down]

GIMLI [*to Gríma*]. I would stay still if I were you!

GANDALF [*coming closer to Théoden and addressing him directly while extending his hand towards him. Behind him, the others, including the guard, watch closely*]. Hearken to me! I release you from the spell.

THÉODEN [*suddenly with a much stronger voice. Saruman has taken over completely*]. Hahahahahahahaha! You have no power here, Gandalf the Grey. Haha! Ah!!

GANDALF [*throws aside his grey cloak to reveal his now white appearance. Théoden draws back and exclaims in surprise*]. I shall draw you, Saruman, as poison is drawn from a wound.

[Éowyn rushes in, tries to go to Théoden, but Aragorn holds her back]

ARAGORN. Wait.

THÉODEN [*in Saruman's voice*]. If I go, Théoden dies.

GANDALF. You will not kill me, you will not kill him.

THÉODEN [*in Saruman's voice*]. Rohan is mine!

GANDALF. Be gone!

[Théoden lunges forwards, and Gandalf aims his staff at him, pushing him back in his seat]

[In Orthanc, Saruman falls to the ground. Then, now weary, Théoden folds forward on his seat, as though about to collapse. Éowyn rushes up to him, and Aragorn releases her from his grasp. Off to the side, Hama puts his hand on Gamling's shoulder, as they both watch in wonder. Éowyn supports Théoden by his shoulders, and sets him back in his seat. Panting, he looks around the hall in awe. And as he does so, he seems to shed many years. At last, his gaze falls onto Éowyn]

THÉODEN. I know your face.

[Éowyn smiles, and the king looks at her, as though trying to recall a distant memory. Then he remembers, and he smiles]

THÉODEN. Éowyn … Éowyn.

[She smiles, and puts her hand to the king's face, tears of joy in her eyes]

[Gandalf steps forward, and Théoden and Éowyn look up at him]

THÉODEN. Gandalf?

GANDALF. Breathe the free air again, my friend.

Admitting our powerlessness

Théoden has been completely enslaved by an evil power. The Bible also talks about slavery. Here is what Paul the Apostle says in Romans 7:23 (NLT): 'But there is another law at work within me that is at war with my mind. This law wins the fight and makes me a slave to the sin that is still within me.'

We are all of us slaves to something toxic called sin. We are powerless to defeat this enemy in our own strength. This is because sin is attractive and alluring. Sin enslaves us with pleasure not pain. How are we to win our soul war?

If step 1 is to confront the dark side, step 2 is to admit our powerlessness.

It is an amazing thing about us – young or old – that we cannot sometimes resist doing the thing that will be most destructive for us.

Not long ago, ABC Evening News reported on an unusual work of modern art – a chair attached to a shotgun. It was to be viewed by sitting in the chair and looking directly into the gun barrel. The gun was loaded and set on a timer to fire at an undetermined moment within the following hundred years. The extraordinary thing was that people waited in queues to sit and stare into the bullet's path! They all knew the gun could go off at any moment, but they were gambling that the fatal blast wouldn't happen during *their* minute in the chair.

The Bible teaches that we are all of us like this with sin. We find it irresistibly enticing and yet it has an inevitable power to destroy us. We need to admit that we are powerless to rescue ourselves from sin's addictive and enslaving potency. Like King Théoden, we need to recognise our utter helplessness and our critical need of someone utterly good, utterly pure and utterly powerful to do what we in our own strength can never achieve. In short, we need to admit our powerlessness.

This leads me to the third character from *The Two Towers*. Arwen, an elf princess, waits in Rivendell for the return of her mortal lover Aragorn, to whom she has pledged her life. Her father, Lord Elrond, comes to plead with her to change her mind, to come away with the other elves, who are leaving Middle Earth for their home in Valinor.

Clip 3: Choosing to give up everything

[At Rivendell]

ELROND. Arwen. Tollen i lû. I chair gwannar na Valannor. Si bado, no círar. [*Translation: 'Arwen. It is time. The ships are leaving for Valinor. Go now before it is too late.'*]

ARWEN. I have made my choice.

ELROND. He is not coming back. Why do you linger here when there is no hope?

ARWEN [*whispers*].There is still hope.

ELROND. If Aragorn survives this war, you will still be parted. If Sauron is defeated and Aragorn made king and all that you hope for comes true ... you will still have to taste the bitterness of mortality. Whether by the sword or the slow decay of time, Aragorn will die. And there will be no comfort for you, no comfort to ease the pain of his passing. He will come to death. An image of the splendour of the kings of men in glory, undimmed before the breaking of the world. But you, my daughter, you will linger on, in darkness and in doubt. As nightfall winter that comes without a star. Here you will dwell, bound to your grief, under the fading trees, until all the world has changed and the long years of your life are utterly spent. Arwen ... there is nothing for you here, only death.

A im ú-'erin veleth lîn? [*Translation: 'Do I not also have your love?'*]

ARWEN. Gerich meleth nîn, ada. [*Translation: 'You have my love father.'*]

[The Elves (including Arwen) depart Rivendell.]

Asking Jesus Christ to rescue you

It is important when analysing the plot of *The Lord of the Rings* to remember that Tolkien was a committed Christian and that his work is suffused with biblical themes. This does not mean that Christianity is visible in Middle Earth because Tolkien is describing a mythological world that exists before and indeed beyond Christianity. What it does mean is that the characters and events of Middle Earth often contain an implicit Christian commentary or subtext.

Arwen is an example of this. She is one of several 'Christ figures' in *The Lord of the Rings*. This comes out very strongly in the clip above. Arwen is essentially considering a momentous choice. 'Shall I give up living in the immortal world of the elves and choose, out of love for Aragorn, to live in the mortal world of men? Or shall I stay in the immortal world of the elves, and turn my back on Aragorn?'

Here we can detect some narrative resonances with the overarching story – the archetypal story – of the Bible. The truth is that the Bible is the greatest love story ever told. In the Scriptures, God is portrayed more as a Lover than a Lawgiver (though the church has often reversed this description in its theology and life). The New Testament drama shows how Jesus Christ left his Father in heaven to come and live and die in the world of men and women. And it reveals that he did this out of great self-sacrificial love. He who knew no sin came into our world and became sin for our sakes. On the cross he took all our sins upon his shoulders and rescued us from the destructive power of sin.

If we are to win our soul war, the Bible teaches not only that we must confront our dark side, not only that we must admit our powerlessness, but also that we must ask Jesus Christ to rescue us. His very name ('Jesus', 'Yeshua' in the original) means 'God is our Rescuer'. Jesus Christ came to save us from that which we had no power to rescue ourselves. The first words you see in the movie *The Passion of The Christ* tell us this. They are from Is. 53:5 (NIV):

> 'But he was pierced for our transgressions, he was crushed for our iniquities; the punishment that brought us peace was upon him, and by his wounds we are healed.'

Jesus Christ is the only one who can rescue us. He has conquered the power of sin. As the Apostle Paul wrote in Romans 7 (NLT):

> 'It seems to be a fact of life that when I want to do what is right, I inevitably do what is wrong. I love God's law with all my heart. But there is another law at work within me that is at war with my mind. This law wins the fight and makes me a slave to the sin that is still within me. Oh, what a miserable person I am! Who will free me from this life that is dominated by sin? Thank God! The answer is in Jesus Christ our Lord.'

The answer is Jesus Christ. So step 3 to winning our soul war is to ask Jesus Christ to rescue us. Everything necessary for our salvation has already been done on the cross. Our task is to repent – to turn from the self-rule of sin – and believe in the finished work of the cross. As we do this, sin's power over our lives is broken and we are at last set free from its potent grip on our hearts.

But there is one step more beyond this, and here we come to our fourth and final character, Frodo. In the last clip, Frodo makes his way up the steps to a landing, and suddenly the black rider appears, mounted on a fell beast. Frodo has the ring of power in his hand; he is struggling not to place it on his finger, but his ability to resist is waning. At the last possible moment, Sam grabs Frodo and pulls him to the ground, out of the reach of the black rider.

Clip 4: There's a good worth fighting for

[Back to Osgiliath, Frodo walks out into the open]

SAM. What are you doing? Where are you going?

[The ringwraith riding the fell beast approaches. Frodo is about to put on the ring when Sam runs up and tackles him. Faramir shoots the ringwraith's steed with his bow. The hobbits roll down the stairs, Sam landing on Frodo who rolls over and draws his sword preparing to kill Sam]

SAM. It's me. It's your Sam. Don't you know your Sam?

[Frodo comes to his senses and drops Sting]

FRODO. I can't do this, Sam.

SAM. I know. It's all wrong. By rights we shouldn't even be here. But we are. It's like in the great stories, Mr. Frodo. The ones that really mattered. Full of darkness and danger they were. And sometimes you didn't want to know the end. Because how could the end be happy? How could the world go back to the way it was when so much bad had happened?

[At Helm's Deep, Aragorn and Éowyn embrace as Rohan, with the help of the Rohirrim, is victorious]

SAM. But in the end, it's only a passing thing, this shadow. Even darkness must pass. A new day will come. And when the sun shines it will shine out the clearer.

[The sun shines on Isengard, as Merry, Pippin and the Ents celebrate victory]

SAM. Those were the stories that stayed with you. That meant something. Even if you were too small to understand why. But I think, Mr. Frodo, I do understand. I know now. Folk in those stories had lots of chances of turning back only they didn't. They kept going. Because they were holding on to something.

FRODO. What are we holding on to, Sam?

SAM [*he helps Frodo up*]. That there's some good in this world, Mr. Frodo. And it's worth fighting for.

[Frodo looks at Sam, a tear in his eye, and as the camera moves to Gollum, we see that even he is moved by Sam's words, for a confused sadness comes into his face.]

Don't fight the war alone

This is a great scene and one that never ceases to move me. Frodo here is the focus of the drama. He is about to put the ring on to hide himself from the black rider. But at the critical moment his closest friend Sam rescues him and brings him back to his senses.

In *The Lord of the Rings* it is fair to say that Frodo would never have succeeded in his quest without the encouragement of his closest friend, Sam. Sam is like one of the many World War I foot soldiers that Tolkien met in his experiences on the battlefields of France. Much of Sam's character resembles the down-to-earth wisdom and the relentless loyalty of these ordinary men who served King and country. Indeed, Tolkien was clearly inspired by the wisdom of such men. In 1944, he was to tell his son – who served in World War II – 'You are inside a great story.'

The great lesson of Frodo's reliance on Sam is this: don't fight your soul war alone. Sam is Frodo's greatest cheerleader. Sam takes Frodo out of his tiny world and places him within a bigger story. He reminds him of the larger purpose and the bigger picture.

We cannot fight our soul wars alone. Yes we have to confront our dark side, admit our powerlessness, and ask for Christ's rescue, and these steps are our individual responsibility. But once we have taken these steps, the battle doesn't end. In fact, the battle for our souls intensifies. It is for this reason that we need each other in the fight. No one person has got it altogether. But altogether we've got it.

The Bible teaches that we are all created for community. We are created for an eternal friendship with Jesus. We are created for earthly friendships with Christian brothers and sisters. We cannot fight this fight without Jesus. And we cannot fight this fight without each other. Every person who becomes a Christian needs at least two or three other Christians that will be like Sam to them.

The story of the Twelve Steps Programme is instructive on this point. Alcoholics Anonymous began on 10 June 1935, co-founded by Bill Wilson and Dr. Robert Holbrook Smith. Wilson dreamed up the idea of Alcoholics Anonymous while he was hospitalised for excessive drinking in December 1934. During his recovery, Wilson had a spiritual experience in which God totally set him free from the desire to drink. In the following months, Wilson helped Smith to catch the vision. Four years later, Wilson and Smith published the book *Alcoholics Anonymous* which contains the Twelve Steps Programme of recovery from alcoholism.

In his book, Wilson described the steps needed for recovery. The first three steps were:

1. We admitted that we were licked, that we were powerless over alcohol.

2. We made an inventory of our defects or sins.
3. We confessed or shared our shortcomings with another person in confidence.

Notice the third of these steps. In recovering from addiction, community is essential. A recovering alcoholic needs a 'recovery family'. No one is expected to conquer their problems on their own. They are encouraged to embrace community and to be accountable within the context of friendship.

This perfectly illustrates the point I am making here. If the first three steps to winning our soul war are steps we can take on our own, the fourth is emphatically not. The fourth step shows the importance of fighting the fight with a Samwise, with a Sam who is wise – a Sam who is available and ready to share wisdom and love with us on the journey. I am very blessed in that my closest friend – the co-author of this book – is someone I can look to for help in overcoming difficulties. But every one who wants to win their soul war needs such friendships.

A final day of deliverance

The Two Towers is full of battles and skirmishes but the fiercest struggles occur within the hearts of the characters in the film. In one way or another, Gollum, Théoden, Arwen and Frodo all illustrate aspects of this inner war between the law of sin and the law of God. We are in a fight between good and evil. The battlefield is the human heart. To experience freedom, we need to do the following.

Step 1: Confront the dark side
Step 2: Admit our powerlessness
Step 3: Ask Jesus to rescue us
Step 4: Don't fight the war alone.

The good news is that it will not always be like this. The Bible teaches that we live between two great events, the first and second comings of Jesus Christ. We live in a world between two advents or arrivals. We are part of a big story. There will be an end to the great war between good and evil. As at the battle of Helm's Deep, a trumpet will sound. When the world appears to have got as bad as it possibly can be there will be a day of deliverance. When the forces of evil and lawlessness have been unleashed with such overwhelming superiority that it seems that there is absolutely no hope left, then a new day will dawn. When it seems that all is lost, Jesus Christ will appear in great glory, like Gandalf the White as he appears on the mountain above Helm's Deep. Every eye shall look up and see him. And he will ride on a white horse, with the armies of heaven behind him, bringing light into our darkness.

On that great day of deliverance, evil will finally be eradicated and there will be heaven on earth. That day will mark the end of our soul wars. Until then, we struggle on, knowing that ultimately those who choose the light are on the winning side.

It is only a matter of time before the dawn breaks and the White Rider returns.

DISCUSSION STARTERS

(You'll need enough card, scissors and elastic to create face masks for everyone.)

Personal reflection: *The Two Towers* is a very powerful film. Take a few moments to reflect on its many scenes, messages, characters and conflicts. Which characters moved you the most? Which were the bravest? The most loyal? How did the film help to set the context in which we are all fighting 'soul wars'?

Discuss: Mark writes, '*The Two Towers* is really about war. Yet the most dramatic war in the film is not so much the battle at Helm's Deep. The real war in *The Two Towers* is a war of the soul. The most intense battlefield in this movie is the battlefield of the human heart.' Do you agree? Have you thought before that your heart might be a battlefield? Can you think of any other moments in film or literature that describes the battle of the divided soul?

Act: Robert Louis Stevenson wrote the famous short story *Dr Jekyll and Mr. Hyde,* in which a respectable doctor is tormented by his evil side. Jeckyl admits in the book that no side is less real; he is truly both characters.

Cut out a mask and attach elastic. Colour each side of the mask a different colour, to symbolise your good and bad side.

Now, go round the group, and (if they're happy to) each member in turn should wear their 'bad' mask first. Describe, briefly, the bad elements, influences and voices within you.

Read: Rom. 7:14–20.

Discuss: Mark says that the first step to 'recovery' in the battle of the soul is to confront the dark side, which we just did. Step two is to admit our powerlessness. Discuss with each other ways in which you feel powerless – even as Christians (if you are) – to stop the dark side pulling at us. Is there anything within the film that illustrates the sense of powerlessness? What forces might the ring help to symbolise in our own lives?

Act: Tolkien told his son, 'You are inside a great story', as he went off to fight in the Second World War. But as Mark suggests, we are all characters within the greatest story ever told – for Jesus came to rescue each one of us.

Turn your mask around to symbolise your good nature. Your good nature, like Gollum's Smeagol, is calling out for rescue. Allow yourself a few moments of quiet to reflect on the battle within your soul. If people are comfortable, it would be good to voice your desire to stand with Jesus. You might like to do this by affirming some of the good sides of your better nature, and end this short list aloud by saying, 'And this side of me chooses Christ for the whole of my life, and the whole of my self.'

Discuss: The band U2 had a number one hit in February 2005 with a song called 'Sometimes You Can't Make It On Your Own'. How many times do you try to do things by yourself – too proud, or too afraid, to ask for help? Try to remember when you last received help from a friend. How did it make you feel? What have you done for your friends recently? Discuss how your group can, in some way, become like the fellowship of the ring. What can we learn together about the relationship between Sam and Frodo?

Look Before You Leap

J. JOHN

We are constantly being told that marriage is a doomed institution. The prevailing attitude is that you can try marriage if you want – just don't expect it to last.

J. John has written *Look Before You Leap* and *Till Death Us Do Part* because he believes that marriage *does* work and he wants to help make it work for others too.

In *Look Before You Leap* J. John demonstrates the foundations required to build a healthy marriage that will work. Specifically he covers the following areas:

- What marriage and love are all about.
- Singleness.
- The delicate issues of dating.
- The alternatives to marriage.
- The awesome seriousness of making *that* decision.

Whether engaged or contemplating marriage this book, with its thoughtful and witty, down-to-earth wisdom, is for all those thinking about getting married.

Till Death Us Do Part

J. JOHN

In *Till Death Us Do Part* J. John discusses:

- Creating a marriage: the wedding, the early days, and the principles of making your marriage a success.
- Defending your marriage: resolving conflicts, affair-proofing, crisis management and marriage repair.

Whether you are just married or have been married for years, are happily married or struggling, this book, with its thoughtful and witty, down-to-earth wisdom, is for all those already married, or for those thinking about getting married.

The Father You've Been Waiting For

Portrait of a Perfect Dad

MARK STIBBE

It has been said that today's generation of young people – those in the 14–35 age bracket – are the generation of divorced parents, absent fathers and broken homes. More than any other in history, this generation is the 'fatherless generation'. Everywhere people are asking, 'where is the love?'

In this book, popular author and speaker Mark Stibbe answers that question by pointing to a story told 2,000 years ago by Jesus of Nazareth. The story tells of a father who demonstrates the qualities of a perfect dad. More than that, the story paints the clearest picture of what Jesus thought God is really like.

This book is a source of extraordinary hope for people of all ages and all beliefs (and indeed no beliefs). It provides a wonderfully accessible introduction to 'The Father You've Been Waiting For'. It also contains many new insights into a story loved by millions and known as 'the parable of parables'.

> *'If you are searching for answers, if you are yearning for wholeness, if you are interested in exploring the meaning of life and/or the relevance of the God of the Bible in the twenty-first century, then Mark's book is definitely worth a read. In fact, this is a must-read for anyone who wants a direct, honest explanation of how the remarkable God who created the universe, loves and is interested in an exclusive, intimate, life-transforming relationship with you. Who knows, it may well contribute to changing your life – forever!'* DIANE LOUISE JORDAN

Prophetic Evangelism

When God Speaks to those who Don't Know Him

MARK STIBBE

In this compelling book, Mark Stibbe argues that God wants to speak prophetically into the lives of unbelievers, waking them up to the fact that Jesus is alive and he knows their every thought, word and action.

There are many biblical examples of God's people using prophecy in their witness to unbelievers. Jesus used prophecy in his ministry to seekers. After Pentecost, God gave the gift of prophecy to believers as one resource among many in their witness to the world. Furthermore, Christians today receive prophecies for those who don't know Christ, often with immediate and life-changing effects. This book contains many such testimonies.

This is the first book to explore how the gift of prophecy can be used with potent effects in our outreach to non-Christians.

The Life

A Portrait of Jesus

J. JOHN and CHRIS WALLEY

There is no denying the importance of Jesus Christ in the history of humankind. He has walked through the last two thousand years of history, of empires, governments, political systems and philosophies and has remained as a dominant, challenging, yet mysterious presence.

In *The Life: A Portrait of Jesus* J. John and Chris Walley achieve an uncommon blend – a serious book for popular use and a popular book for serious reading.

If you want to know who Jesus is, then read *The Life* and be rewarded.